LECTURES ON MACROECONOMIC PLANNING

Part 1
GENERAL ASPECTS

LECTURES ON MACROECONOMIC PLANNING

Part 1

GENERAL ASPECTS

LEIF JOHANSEN

Institute of Economics, University of Oslo

1977

NORTH-HOLLAND PUBLISHING COMPANY

AMSTERDAM · NEW YORK · OXFORD

189010

HD 82

ISBN North-Holland for this volume: 0 7204 0565 3

Publishers:

NORTH-HOLLAND PUBLISHING COMPANY
AMSTERDAM · NEW YORK · OXFORD

Distributors for the U.S.A. and Canada:

ELSEVIER NORTH-HOLLAND INC.
52 VANDERBILT AVENUE
NEW YORK, N.Y. 10017

Library of Congress Cataloging in Publication Data

Johansen, Leif.
Lectures on macroeconomic planning.

Includes bibliographical references and indexes.
Contents: v. 1. General aspects.
I. Economic policy.   I. Title.

HD82. J57   339.5   76–45446
ISBN 0–7204–0565–3 (v. 1)

PRINTED IN THE NETHERLANDS

PREFACE

The exposition of macroeconomic planning which is given on the following pages is based on lectures which I have given for some years for students of economics at the University of Oslo.

The term macroeconomic planning is used here in a rather broad and flexible way. Although the main emphasis is perhaps on types and aspects of planning which are relevant for instance in a country like Norway, I include references to and treatment of planning problems also under other conditions and systems. Various definitions of economic planning are discussed in Section 1.4, and towards the end of the section, I present a rather eclectic definition of my own. The main point of the definition is that it includes both planning in the form of preparation of decisions which are to be taken directly by the Central Authority itself, and various types of activities which aim at influencing and coordinating decisions which are controlled by decision-makers outside the direct control of the Central Authority. This means that the lectures are intended to cover both planning as it is conceived in rather highly centralized socialist economies and planning in the "softer" form often referred to as indicative planning, as well as intermediate cases. Occasionally I have some doubts whether it is meaningful or useful to treat so widely different cases in the same exposition. However, the reason for trying to do so rather than concentrating on one pure and tidy type of system is that any planning system in practice employ a wide range of different methods and approaches in spite of the fact that one could in most cases point to one form or approach as the basic one. Systems are also undergoing changes through time. For these reasons I think it is useful for a student of economic planning, regardless of where he is going to apply his knowledge, to know about different approaches and problems occurring under different systems.

When I started thinking of writing this book I contemplated calling it a book on "Methods of Economic Planning" or "Theory of

Economic Planning". Although there is an emphasis on methods, I chose the simpler expression "Economic Planning" because I include some descriptive material on institutions and other facts, a little bit of history and at various places considerations of practical problems. The elements of description of history, institutions and facts should however not be taken too seriously. They are included not in order to give a systematic presentation of these aspects, but rather to illustrate ideas and approaches and check that the reasoning is not diverted into abstractions which are too remote from actual planning problems. There is a danger involved in this approach: A theoretician might find several parts of the book incomplete and unsatisfactory from a theoretical point of view, and a planner with practical experience and knowledge of history may find that my references to history and institutions are superficial and chosen somewhat at random. It might have been safer to concentrate on the one side or the other, but my feeling is that one might loose in usefulness and relevance by doing so.

It follows from what has been said above that I consider macro-economic planning as an "applied" field of economics. I assume therefore that the student has some training in economic theory before he starts on this book. The main part of the text does however not require any very much advanced theory. At many places I touch upon and refer to problems and methods which would require specialized and advanced studies for a full understanding, but the idea is then only to make the student aware of the existence of these problems and methods and give a clue as to how and where to start if one should be interested in pursuing a special subject beyond what is covered by the present exposition. When I utilize results from economic theory I deliberately avoid providing proofs. Instead I try to stimulate the intuitive understanding of what is involved, and otherwise refer to the specialized literature for strict proofs. If all assertions should be proved, it would be impossible to cover the topics which I consider necessary for a useful introduction to economic planning in a course of acceptable size. Furthermore, in an applied field like economic planning I think economists must get used to applying theoretical results of which they have not gone through the complete and strict proofs.

Some readers might find the list of references which I provide somewhat out of proportion with the rather modest level of exposition which I have chosen. The reason is partly given by the considerations just referred to. In addition comes the fact that economic planning as treated here is not a well-defined and settled field of teaching. I therefore think there is a need to pull together quite many useful threads which can be found in rather different quarters and different types of publications. I have not taken time and space to refer to the most central and well-known economic literature of relevance, but I have at least in some sections tried to refer to literature which may not be so well-known to general economists, but which may be of particular relevance to the study of economic planning.

Some readers may also find that I have inserted too many direct quotations from various authors. This is partly a matter of taste, but I think this approach can add something to the information contents of the exposition. If a viewpoint is presented as it is expressed by a living person in a special country in a special historical period or under special circumstances, then it often tells much more than when the viewpoint is presented impersonally and with no connection with time and place.

It will be clear from this preface that the following exposition will not be very narrow and specialized. The whole approach and way of exposition implies that I must deal with quite many aspects of economics where I can by no means claim to have expert knowledge. In fact I think it would be impossible to be an expert at the same time on all the fields which I shall deal with or at least touch upon in the following exposition. I must apologize to experts in special fields who will perhaps find my exposition deficient when I go into their fields of specialization; what I hope is that the structure taken as a whole shall be useful and interesting in spite of such partial deficiencies.

This volume is subtitled "General Aspects" and constitutes Part 1 of the complete set. The following volume, Part 2, which I hope to publish within one year after the publication of Part 1, will deal with some more specific subjects such as centralization versus decentralization and economic planning under uncertainty.

Oslo, June 1976   *LEIF JOHANSEN*

CONTENTS

Chapter 1

INTRODUCTION

1.1. Brief Historical Sketch

Macroeconomic planning is concerned with the development in the short and the long run of the entire economy of a country, more or less subdivided into sectors. Planning for individual enterprises, sectors or regions is not macroeconomic planning unless it is integrated into a system which takes into account the mutual interrelationships and comprises the entire economy.

For brevity we shall in these lectures in most cases omit the prefix "macro" and simply speak about economic planning apart from contexts where it is especially important to emphasize the distinction between macroeconomic planning and more partial or limited economic planning.

The first example of economic planning in this sense, at least in modern times, is the planning initiated in the USSR after the October Revolution. The idea of economic planning under socialism was (contrary to what some economists writing on economic planning have asserted) quite explicit and clear in the classical writings of *Karl Marx* and *Friedrich Engels*, although they did not work out in any detail the *methods* of such planning. *V.I. Lenin* saw clearly the dimensions of the task of planning the economy immediately after the revolution, and in March 1918 he wrote about "the transformation of the whole of the state economic mechanism into a single huge machine, into an economic organism that will work in such a way as to enable hundreds of millions of people to be guided by a single plan – such was the enormous organizational problem that rested on our shoulders." In was clear to him that such planning must rely heavily on scientific work, and in April 1918 he proposed that the *Academy of Sciences* should be instructed to "set up a number of expert commissions for the speediest possible compilation of a plan for the reorganization of industry and the economic progress of Russia." Many of the planning efforts in the first years of the USSR were of course very much marked by the special circumstances of that period, and did not set any pattern which could be of more general validity. The first plan which is of general methodological interest seems to be the so-called GOELRO plan, i.e., the state plan for the electrification of the Russian Soviet Republic, published in 1920. The basic aim of this document was to work out plans for the electrification of the Russian Soviet Republic through a period of 10 to 15 years, but since it should be concerned both with construction activities, production of electricity and consumption of electricity, and since electricity is of central importance to so many branches of the economy, the plan developed into a comprehensive plan covering the most important sectors of the economy. The plan was highly praised by Lenin who called it "a real scientific plan" and pointed out the need to tie this plan with short-term plans. The GOELRO commission was later merged in the broader State Planning Commission GOSPLAN, and evidently influenced planning methods there to a large extent.

Of great interest in connection with early attempts at comprehensive planning in the USSR was the "balance-sheet" of the USSR national economy for 1923–24 which was published in 1926. This balance-sheet can be considered as the first comprehensive national accounts including an input–output core for a break-down of the economy into agriculture, industry and mining, building and construction, transport and trade (and to some extent also further subdivisions of these sectors). The balance-sheet also contained figures for exports and imports, private and public consumption as well as stocks and changes in stocks. Furthermore, for some sectors figures for important individual commodities were also given. Although the way of presenting the tables was somewhat different, this balance-sheet clearly anticipates the later input–output tables which have been so important in economic research and planning since the Second World War.

Since 1928 the USSR has had a system of fairly regular five-year plans besides the more detailed annual plans. The earliest annual plans were guidelines or "control figures" which did not possess the power to commit the individual enterprises apart from certain key sectors. However, from 1931 the annual plans acquired the strict binding force which they have retained ever since. Basic tools in working out these plans have been the "material balances", to which we shall return in a later chapter. Highly centralized planning based on such material balances has continued in the USSR up to now, but the degree of centralization has been changing to some extent. Particularly since 1965 there has been a tendency towards more scope for decisions taken at lower levels than the Central Planning Commission and more use of market relations. Central planning does however retain its fundamental role in shaping the pattern of development of the economy.

Economic planning has of course also been predominant in the socialist countries in Eastern Europe after World War II. For some years the planning procedures were very much patterned according to the example of the USSR, with highly centralized systems. During the 1960s the systems changed to varying degrees from one country to another in this region so that planning methods and the way of combining central planning with market relations now show a somewhat diversified picture.

In the Western countries many ideas about economic planning have been developed in theoretical literature at a rather early stage, particularly related to the discussion on the economics of socialism by *Barone, Mises, Taylor, Lange* and others. Although it was a very interesting discussion which has stimulated further developments in recent years, it remained at that time at a rather academic level and did not influence economic policy and planning methods in any country. More concrete ideas about comprehensive planning first developed as a result of the economic depression in the 1930s. Already in the early 1930s rather detailed proposals for a reorganization of the Norwegian economy so as to create a basis for national economic planning were put forward by groups belonging to the Labour Party. These proposals influenced thinking in broader circles to some extent, but were not adopted as a basis for practical policy to anything approaching the scale originally conceived. In Germany an interesting initiative was taken by the so-called WTB Plan of 1932, so named after the economists *W.S. Woytinsky, F. Tarnow* and *F. Baade* who elaborated the plan and launched a campaign for it. This was a plan for counteracting mass unemployment through large-scale public works and other measures. It was supported by the Trade Union Federation. Similar but usually less elaborate plans and proposals were certainly put forward in other countries as well. However, the development of "Keynesian" ideas a few years later (by *J.M. Keynes* himself, but also by many others like *R. Frisch* in Norway, *J. Tinbergen* in the Netherlands, *M. Kalecki* in Poland and England, and by *"The Swedish School"*), which showed in a theoretically more general way how governments by a conscious use of fiscal and monetary policy could influence the course of development of national economic aggregates such as total investment, total income, total employment and so on, had more practical consequences and also a more lasting influence on economic-political thinking and actual policy. More or less parallel with, and related to this development came the first attempts at constructing national accounts. In Norway research projects which explicitly aimed at establishing national accounts were launched as early as in 1936 with *R. Frisch* as the initiator and driving force. Combining the ideas of national accounting with the recognition of the fact that the course of development of the economy could be influenced by monetary and fiscal policy, it was a natural step to start thinking of constructing national *budgets* which should comprise the generation and use of income for a country as a whole and not only for the State as in the traditional state budget. The idea of national budgetting seems to have developed in several quarters in the late 1930s and in the 1940s. *R. Frisch* used the very term "National Budget" in unpublished notes from January 1940, and the term was used already for the economic program presented by the Norwegian Government as a supplement to the State budget for 1945–46. In England *W.H. Beveridge* in his well-known report on *Full Employment in a Free Society* (1944) proposed the introduction of a "New Type of Annual Budget". According to his proposal the novelty of this new type of budget should lie in two things: first, that it should be concerned with the income and expenditure of the country as a whole and not only with the public finances; second, that it should take the available labour force of the country as a datum and "plan outlay to that datum rather than by consideration of financial resources." These two aspects are perhaps the most important ones characterizing national budgets as compared with previous thinking on economic policy, i.e., the emphasis on the *total* economy, and the priority of considerations concerning the *real* economy as opposed to monetary or financial aspects.

At the same time *Beveridge* acknowledged the need for more and stronger government actions in order to secure the goal of full employment: "Full employment cannot be won and held without a great extension of the responsibilities and powers of the State exercised through organs of the central Government. No power less than that of the State can ensure adequate total outlay at all times, or can control, in the general interest, the location of industry and the use of land. To ask for full employment while objecting to these extensions of State activity is to will the end and refuse the means."

In the Netherlands *J. Tinbergen* illustrated the use of a mathematical macroeconomic model for elucidating the possibilities of influencing the economic development by government instruments already in 1936, a fact which gave the Netherlands a flying start in the use of such models in connection with national budgetting or planning after World War II.

Ideas about economic planning also emerged in the United States. (See, e.g., the volume *Planned Society* from 1937, especially *W.C. Mitchell's* contribution.) The New Deal policy and the Tennessee Valley Authority project contained interesting *elements* of planning. Interestingly enough *C. Landauer* published a book with the title *Theory of National Economic Planning* already in 1944. It is here evident that the interest in planning sprang mainly from the desire to avoid depressions. The scheme of planning which was proposed by C. Landauer was very similar to what has later become known as "indicative planning" where the government influences the development more by coordination and by providing information than by direct decisions and commands. The main tool should be an exchange of plans and information between the Government and private entrepreneurs. As a result of this exchange there would emerge "a scheme of economic growth, comprising those expansion projects which in its (a Government agency's) opinion are mutually compatible and preferable to all alternatives. We are in accordance with general usage when we call this scheme a national economic plan, on the assumption that the agency – the planning board – is operating on behalf of a national, not a regional or international community."

Landauer points out that "if it had not been for the desire to avoid depressions, planning in the western countries might never have become the object of serious thought and widespread discussion." Once planning was instituted there was, however, according to Landauer, no reason why it should not serve other purposes as well, and he pointed out problems about the distribution of national income and problems related to economic growth as fields of concern for planning.

Although the title of Landauer's book is particularly striking, there were of course many other economists in the USA arguing in the same direction. This influenced the preparation of the "Full Employment Bill" to some extent, and in early versions of the bill the annual compilation of a "National Production and Employment Budget" was requested. When the bill was finally adopted as "The Employment Act" of 1946 the planning aspect was, however, considerably watered down (as was the commitment to full employment).

In Western Europe the development towards a more conscious macroeconomic policy and some sort of national budgetting which started in the late 1930s was considerably enhanced by the war experiences and the need for reconstruction after the war. The aim of the planning was not only to avoid depressions, but also to allocate important commodities which were in short supply, and the governments had at their hands many tools of direct control of physical allocation of commodities and foreign trade as well as of prices and financial flows. In some countries enterprises in some key sectors had also been nationalized.

Among the countries in Western Europe France is a particularly interesting case to which we shall return particularly in connection with the discussion of so-called "indicative planning".

In some countries the adoption of economic planning as a regular part of the activities of the Government was given formal expression by the establishment of special planning agencies, most famous among which are the *Centraal Planbureau* of the Netherlands and *Le Commissariat Général au Plan* in France. The fact that special planning institutions are established in some countries and not in others does however not necessarily imply that planning is more important in the former group. In Norway the plans have all the time been elaborated directly in ordinary government offices, in the Ministry of Finance. The Government is then more directly responsible for, and committed by the plans than when the plans are worked out in special and perhaps partly independent institutions. Thus the Dutch "plans" are nearer to being forecasts rather than plans in a stricter sense as compared with their Norwegian counterparts. An observer of French planning (*D. Liggins*) reports that in certain periods "the Government's attitude to the Plan was not friendly," and "two Ministers of Finance ignored the Plan and substituted it with their own personal economic programmes."

After the completion of the post-war reconstruction, direct government controls of the economy have been gradually weakened or abandoned in most countries in Western Europe, and foreign trade has also been liberalized to a very large extent. Economic planning or national budgetting in one form or another has, however, remained a central part of the formulation of economic policy. In many countries there have been important developments from the original national budget type of plans, in two directions: first, one has to an increasing extent used more sophisticated tools of analysis for working out the plans; second, the scope of planning has become richer partly by the increasing emphasis on medium-term and long-term planning besides the more traditional short-term plans, and by the integration of such planning with planning for sectors like education and health. Long-term concern for the development of environment has also added new dimensions to economic planning. However, policy instruments and power to influence the development have not always increased to a corresponding extent, and many "plans" are therefore nearer to being forecasts than real plans intended to be reasonably strictly implemented. In many countries conflicting interests, political tensions and frequent political changes have also impaired the possibility of adhering reasonably consistently to macroeconomic plans. This, however, does not necessarily prevent the methods and analytical work used in preparing the plans from being of great interest and potential practical fruitfulness under other conditions.

Besides the socialist countries and the economically advanced Western countries there are of course interesting cases of planning in some of the developing countries. A few initiatives are known from before World War II. Thus already in 1928 the President of Mexico proposed the formulation of a national economic plan for Mexico. In 1933 a plan was put forward for doubling the national income in India, and five years later a National Planning Committee was set up by the Indian National Congress. However, planning in the developing countries gained momentum only after World War II and decolonization. In many of the developing countries there have now emerged systems and methods of guiding the economy which have taken over elements both from the socialist countries and from the advanced capitalist countries and adapted them in various cases to specific national conditions.

References for Section 1.1

W.H. Beveridge, *Full employment in a free society* (Allen and Unwin, London, 1944).

P.J. Bjerve, *Planning in Norway 1947–1956* (North-Holland, Amsterdam, 1959).

P.J. Bjerve, "Trends in quantitative economic planning in Norway", in *Economic planning in Norway: Methods and models*, edited by L. Johansen and H. Hallaråker (Oslo University Press, Oslo, 1970).

G. Caire, *La planification* (Editions Cujas, Paris, 1972) Part 1.

G. Garvey, "Keynes and the economic activists of pre-Hitler Germany", *Journal of Political Economy* (1975).

R.A. Gordon, *The goal of full employment* (Wiley, New York and London, 1967).

Leif Johansen

L.R. Klein, "Economic planning – Western European style", *Statsøkonomisk Tidsskrift* (1948).

C. Landauer, *Theory of national economic planning* (University of California Press, Berkeley and Los Angeles, 1947). First edition in 1944.

O. Lange and F.M. Taylor, *On the economic theory of socialism* (McGraw-Hill, New York, 1964). First published in 1938.

V.I. Lenin, *On socialist economic organization: Articles and speeches* (Progress Publishers, Moscow, 1967).

D. Liggins, *National economic planning in France* (Saxon House/Lexington Books, Lexington, 1975).

V.S. Nemchinov, "Some aspects of the balance-sheet method applied in the statistics of interdependent dynamic economic systems", Paper presented at the 31st session of the *International Statistical Institute* (1958).

V.S. Nemchinov, "The use of mathematical methods in economics", in *The use of mathematics in economics*, edited by V.S. Nemchinov (Oliver and Boyd, Edinburgh and London, 1964). Translation from Russian.

Planned society, Yesterday, today, tomorrow, edited by F. MacKenzie (Prentice-Hall, New York, 1937). Especially W.C. Mitchell, "The social sciences and national planning".

Quantitative planning of economic policy, edited by B.G. Hickman (The Brookings Institution, Washington, DC, 1965).

T.V. Ryabushkin, "From the history of the balance-sheet of the USSR national economy", Paper presented at the 31st session of the *International Statistical Institute* (1958).

Soviet planning, principles and techniques (Progress Publishers, Moscow, 1972).

United Nations, Economic Commission for Europe, *Economic survey of Europe in 1962. Part 2: Economic planning in Europe* (Geneva, 1965).

1.2. The Background for the Development of Macroeconomic Planning

The brief sketch in the preceding section suggests that we may speak about a tendency of development in the direction of macroeconomic planning. In 1951 *G. Myrdal* published a paper under the title *The Trend towards Economic Planning* in which he asserted that economic planning was "gradually becoming the recognized frame of economic policies in Western democratic, industrialized countries." In the beginning of the 1960s a group of UN experts on planning could describe the development in the following terms: "In the course of the last few years, there has been a remarkable intensification of interest in national economic planning. Recent resolutions of the General Assembly and the Economic and Social Council, calling for international action to strengthen planning activity, attest to the almost universal character of this heightened interest. What is striking about this trend is not simply that the number of countries engaged in national planning has increased considerably; more important, planning has emerged as a tool of policy in countries differing widely, not only in their stages of economic development, but also in their economic and social systems."

Some elements of the background for this development in the direction of macroeconomic planning have already been touched upon in the preceding section. In the present section we shall review the factors somewhat more systematically.

The following discussion will perhaps be more relevant for economies which have been predominantly market-oriented and which have developed some sort of macroeconomic planning more or less gradually, than for the socialist countries. For a country which has been through a revolution or a radical change by which ownership of the main means of production has been taken over by the State, full-scale macroeconomic planning is immediately required so to speak by definition. State ownership means that the state has the power to take decisions directly affecting large spheres of the economy, and it is hard to imagine this being done without some sort of planning. The question in these countries is rather how detailed central planning should be and to what extent the power to take decisions should be delegated to lower levels or be regulated by market relations. These are questions to which we shall return later on.

Countries with mainly private ownership of enterprises and economic resources may exist, and have in fact existed without any central macroeconomic planning. Nevertheless there is, as briefly described in the preceding section, a tendency in the direction of such planning. The background for this development may be found in various factors which we can perhaps divide into factors pertaining to the *need* for planning and factors pertaining to the *possibility* of planning and steering the economy according to plans.

We first review factors relating to the need for planning.

(A) Experience tells that an unregulated market mechanism is unsatisfactory from the point of view of *macroeconomic stability*. There are cycles in production, total income and employment as well as in many other indicators. In the 1930s many countries experienced declines in industrial production by 20–30 percent or even more in the course of a few years, and there were millions of people unemployed. This situation also lasted for a longer time than previous troughs in cyclical movements, and a main element in the new macroeconomic theories towards the end of the 1930s was in fact the suspicion that the unregulated market mechanism not only generated cyclical movements, but might also gear the economy into an equilibrium position at a low level of production and employment with no endogenous tendencies for recovery. This problem of interpretation is still not settled in the theoretical debates on Keynesian versus neo-classical macroeconomic theory, and can perhaps also not be easily settled in operational terms since a long-lasting depression can always be seen as part of a sufficiently slow development which will in the sufficiently long run again turn into a recovery. But regardless of whether the depression is a low level equilibrium or part of a slowly moving cycle, the practical problem for economic policy which is concerned with the reasonably near future is very much the same. As pointed out in the preceding section the depression in the 1930s was the most influential factor persuading economists and politicians as well as large parts of the general public about the need for some sort of planning and government intervention for the purpose of macro-economic regulation.

In 1974–75 many Western countries experienced the most severe recession since the 1930s, with not only a slow-down of the expansion, but a considerable decline in production and hundreds of thousands or millions of unemployed. It is too soon to say whether this will give a new impetus to the development in the direction of planning, but it is interesting to observe an initiative recently taken by many leading economists and some politicians in the USA to establish a national planning institution for the USA, partly to adopt methods and elements of planning which have been used in several countries in Western Europe after the war. (See *The Initiative Committee for National Economic Planning.*) In a country like Norway the 1975 recession seemed to call forth claims for more direct and specific government actions, i.e., not only general demand management by means of fiscal and monetary policy, and some events accompanying the recession also resulted in the Government's taking over shares in private companies.

(B) There has been an *increasing proportion of collective or public consumption* in total consumption with increasing income level. If the consumption of such goods could be explained in terms of usual supply and demand relationships, then we could say that the income elasticities of demand for such goods and services are on average larger than one, and they will therefore make up an increasing share of the total consumption budget with increasing income. Furthermore there is a tendency for the cost of production of many of these goods and services to increase faster than the average cost of production because they are often labour intensive. This means that if we consider values rather than volumes, then there is an additional factor tending to make the share of these goods and services in the total consumption budget increase with income, but this effect will of course be modified by "price elasticities" so that the volume of public consumption will grow more slowly than it would have done in the absence of this bias in the development of relative costs. Now since the consumption of these goods and services is not regulated by the usual market mechanism, but have to be supplied through government agencies, these elements tend to enhance the share of the total resources in a country which are administered by the Government or government agencies according to non-market procedures, which

again increases the need for planning. (In Norway Government consumption takes some 16–17 percent of GNP, and Government consumption and investment together some 22 percent of GNP. If we
take into account also transfers of various sorts around 45 percent of
the total income of the country pass through Government accounts in
a wide sense. Although being in the higher brackets the figures for
Norway are by no means exceptional.)

The increase in the Government share of GNP makes it important
to extend planning models so as to elaborate the internal structure in
the education sector, the health sector and so on more than in
traditional models which elaborate on ordinary production sectors,
but take Government demand as exogenous factors represented by
broad aggregates.

(C) It is generally believed that there is an *increasing weight of
indirect or external effects in production and consumption*. Pollution
is the most obvious example. It is hard to say to what extent there is a
real increase in the weight of such effects and to what extent the
impression is due to an increase in the *awareness* of such effects
which have been there all the time. In any case there has been a
marked increase in the number and extension of spheres in which it is
felt that government intervention or regulation in some form is
necessary in order to protect against undesirable external effects or to
favour desirable effects as compared with what the market mechanism would produce if left to itself. Planning models for instance
of the input–output type have in recent years started to respond to
this need by including generation and absorption of pollutants in
addition to ordinary goods and services.

(D) Somewhat vaguely one may perhaps also point to *an increasing
degree of integration* of the various units and sectors of the economy,
resulting in more important and complicated forms of mutual dependencies. This means that difficulties at one point will easily be
transmitted to many other parts of the economy. If the chains of
dependencies are long and technologies are rigid and not easily
readjustable, then market forces may take too long to call forward the
necessary adjustments and may give rise to large losses so that there
is a need for conscious planning and actions which could take the
necessary precautions more speedily and accurately than price and
market adjustments. The *increasing size of individual investment*

projects in many branches generated by technological development works in the same direction since prices are less efficient in signalling the consequences of changes which are "more than marginal". More and more often initiatives to start large investment projects are followed by demands for investigations and evaluations of the consequences for existing enterprises, pressure on natural resources, labour market conditions, residential construction, service institutions, environment, health and so forth.

(E)   After it had become clear that the post-war economies did not return to pre-war conditions of economic depression, there appeared *a growing concern for long-term developments*. This concern has been enhanced by such factors as the economic competition between socialist and capitalist countries, concern for the problems of developing countries, and more recently increasing concern for the possibilities of depletion of exhaustible natural resources and also the gradual destruction of environment. These are problems with regard to which both theory and empirical evidence suggest that an unregulated market mechanism does not work in a satisfactory way.

(F)   To an increasing degree *groups and classes of people as well as firms have become organized* according to social and economic interests. This means that they put forward claims which are not automatically met by a free market mechanism, and accordingly there is a pressure for interventions of various sorts. The tendency towards organization often has a sort of cumulative effect since *one* organization by disrupting an existing equilibrium calls forth organization of other groups which are affected. This is one of the tendencies pointed out by *J.K. Galbraith's* concept of "countervailing power". In his explanation of the trend towards planning *G. Myrdal* assigned an important part to the increasing degree of organization: "Technological and organizational developments have been increasing the size of the units in relation to the market. At the same time the units have found the means to combine. . . . The market and the price have lost their character of being objective conditions outside the individual units to which they merely had to adjust. . . . I do not need to recall to what extent at the present time practically all markets are manipulated. Many markets are dominated by one or a few sellers or buyers. And apart from these cases, practically every single individual in our countries, who has something to sell or who earns an income or seeks a profit, is associating himself with his compeers with the intention of influencing the conditions under which he is acting."

(G) Finally there are *special situations which stimulate efforts in the direction of planning.* Most prominent among these have been war situations and needs for reconstruction after wars. But also experiences like the 1973–74 oil crisis stimulate demands for planning. As pointed out by Myrdal the role of such upheavals may however mainly be to "spur a development that in any case was under way."

The factors pointed out above are concerned with macroeconomic stabilization, resource allocation and income distribution, and some are relevant to special sectors of the economy rather than to the economy as a whole. Now each of the various needs pointed out here could of course be met by partial measures and ad hoc intervention. This is indeed what has happened in the Western countries. In the words of G. Myrdal: "The regular sequence has been that State intervention preceded planning. . . . State interventions have originally been introduced *ad hoc* to serve limited and temporary purposes, often to meet an immediate emergency of one sort or another." However, the more there are of such attempts at sporadic and partial intervention, the larger will often be the chance that each endeavour will fail to reach its goal and the greater will be the need for some overall planning framework within which the various endeavours can be coordinated. Again to quote Myrdal: "It was usually the growing mesh of uncoordinated State interventions which called for coordination. The demand for order and rationality has been an afterthought." The problem has also been put very well by *R. Stone* (1964). He describes, as one type of reaction to *laissez-faire,* scattered and uncoordinated government intervention in specific spheres of the economy, and points out the shortcomings of this reaction in the following way: "Its shortcomings, which derive partly from the partial abandonment of one coherent political philosophy without the acceptance of a new one, lie in an exaggerated notion of the usefulness of modifying some part of a system while ignoring the others: specific acts are justified in terms of the necessity to do something in the area concerned and of the immediate effects intended. The bad consequences of this kind of sporadic planning are becoming every day more obvious, but it is not yet realised that the more one tries to plan a system without studying it as a whole, the less one is likely to succeed." (The last words suggest, by the way, that the process from *ad hoc* interventions to more conscious overall planning and coordination described by Myrdal in 1951 had not yet come to fruition by 1964 when Stone published the book quoted.)

Many of the points surveyed above can be subsumed under the general Marxian proposition about the increasing social character of production (which eventually, according to the same theory, brings it into conflict with the system of private ownership and appropriation).

As already suggested the development of the need for economic planning is only one part of the full explanation of the increasing degree of economic planning actually observed. The other part is concerned with the possibilities of planning. Some of the elements mentioned above in relation to the need for planning do, however, reappear on the other side as influencing also the possibilities of planning.

(A') *The increasing share of the resources of a country which in one way or another are administered by the Government* or government agencies, as mentioned under point B above, should contribute positively also to the possibilities of planning and coordination. This obviously applies to the planning and coordination for resources directly under government control. But indirectly it also applies to resources in the private sphere of an economy since, as is well known from general macroeconomic theory and public finance, government revenues and expenses also influence the use of resources in the private sector, and these influences are more powerful in an economy with a large public sector.

(B') As mentioned under point F in the list above there has been an *increasing degree of organization of people and enterprises* according to social and economic interests. To some (and only some!) extent this is also favourable for the possibilities of planning and controlling the economy, since the Government is, in many cases, able to influence the economy and to promote coordination of the actions of the various agents by using such organizations as intermediaries between the Government and the individual agents. Examples are found in many countries in connection with foreign trade and banks and other credit institutions, and in some countries also in various branches of manufacturing industry and primary production. Organizations of employers and employees sometimes also help to integrate wage development with other aspects of economic policy.

(C′) *Practical experience from special situations* as mentioned under point G above, which may originally have been tackled in rather improvised fashions, have been useful for planning and controlling the economy also under more ordinary circumstances. They have sometimes led to the establishment of institutions which have continued to play a rôle after the immediate emergency is over.

(D′) Particularly since the 1930s there has taken place *a rapid development of economic theory and operations research* which has provided valuable general insights as well as many more specific techniques which are useful in economic planning. Some highlights of this development will be mentioned below, in Section 1.3.

(E′) More or less parallel with this *economic statistics* has been developed both with regard to coverage and quality. Most important is of course the development of national accounting and input–output statistics.

(F′) Finally, there is the tremendous development in *computational techniques and equipment*, making possible computations of scales and with speeds which would be judged as science fiction a few decades ago.

Starting out from the observed fact that there has been a historical tendency in the direction of more economic planning through some decades we have listed above a series of factors which indicate, on the one side, increasing needs for planning, and, on the other side, improving conditions and possibilities for planning and controlling the economy. Interaction between elements on both sides would seem to explain the observed tendency. One might perhaps say that the explanation is too good, since observed tendencies are by no means so monotonous and smooth as this explanation would suggest. In most countries there have been periods of retrogression or even break-down of national economic planning, and it would in my opinion be a very uncertain projection into the future to predict an ever more comprehensive and successful national economic planning. The lists which we have compiled above illustrate a rather dangerous method of historical explanation if they are not interpreted with care. We have started out from an observed fact and compiled lists of elements which seem to explain this fact without looking for possible counteracting tendencies. It is outside the scope of these lectures to go more deeply into this, but let me only suggest that important counteracting tendencies may be found in the sphere of international relations and the tendency for each country to become more and more dependent upon such relations. At the same time it seems easier to achieve international agreements about the dismantling of the use of certain instruments of influencing economic development than about positive measures and coordinated actions. In the internal sphere conflicts of interests may also rise to sharp confrontations. The development of organizations, which were mentioned as elements favourable to planning under points F and B' above, may also lead to struggle and a form of distribution of power which will impede overall planning. Frequent changes of political power may have the same effect. It must also be emphasized that ideas concerning the "needs" for planning and "possibilities" of planning give a very much simplified picture. The advantages and benefits to be reaped from planning are not universal or neutral. Planning often means to take explicit stands towards conflicting interests and to interfere with existing economic mechanisms and rules of conduct in non-neutral ways. Although everybody might agree that planning is good, conflicts concerning which one one should adopt from among many possible plans might be so sharp that no plan is adopted and implemented in any consistent way.

Other counteracting tendencies may be found in the growing concern in many countries for the right of smaller groups and communities within a country to decide about their local conditions without interference from more distant and higher ranking authorities. This is felt in several countries, for instance in the form of difficulties of reaching final decisions within a reasonable lapse of time concerning the location of power plants, airports and other projects which may be a nuisance to the local environment.

In spite of the factors adduced under A–G and A'–F' above it therefore remains a matter of political as well as economic development to what extent the tendencies towards macroeconomic planning – in deeds and not only in words – will continue. I am inclined to be less fatalistic about this issue than *G. Myrdal* was in 1951 when he concluded his discussion of the trend towards planning with, inter alia, the following words: "Popular controversy in our countries still turns around the old doctrinal question whether or not we should have a planned economy. In the light of the preceding discussion this is pretty much nonsense. There exists no alternative to economic planning. There is, therefore, no case to be made for or against economic planning, for or against free enterprise or free trade. Ever more State intervention and economic planning is part of the historical trends. These trends have deep causes which can be analysed as has been attempted above. In reality, it was never, and is certainly not now, a choice. It is a destiny. We will have to do the best with the world we have. We must do better and better even with our economic planning."

References for Section 1.2

H. Aujac, "On the relationships between the effectiveness of national planning and the state of technical, economic, social and political structures", *Technological Forecasting and Social Change* (1975).

The Initiative Committee for National Economic Planning, "For a national economic planning system", *Challenge Magazine* (March–April 1975).

W.C. Mitchell, "Social sciences and national planning", in *Planned society* – See reference under Section 1.1.

G. Myrdal, "The trend towards economic planning", *The Manchester School of Economic and Social Studies* (1951).

R. Stone, *A programme for growth*: *5. The model in its environment* (Chapman and Hall, London, 1964).

United Nations, Department of Economic and Social Affairs, *Planning for economic development*, Report of the Secretary-General transmitting the study of a group of experts (New York, 1963).

1.3. Highlights of Theoretical Developments

Under point D' in the preceding section I announced the mentioning of some highlights of the development of economic theory and operations research which are particularly relevant to macroeconomic planning. There will be no attempt here to trace carefully the history of the various theoretical ideas and methods, but some of the basic advances will be mentioned and dated on the historical time scale just to put in perspective some of the theoretical ideas and tools which we shall meet in the following chapters.

The development of *general macroeconomic theory*, with reference to *J.M. Keynes* and others, was mentioned already in Section 1.1, and related to this the development of national accounting. These developments are of course of direct and central importance to macroeconomic planning. However, Keynesian and related types of models developed for general theoretical and expository purposes are in their original form highly aggregated and contain only very few variables and equations. For more direct applications in connection with economic policy and planning they are therefore too crude. Econometric research has gradually developed and worked out quantitatively larger and more detailed models of this type, an important step in this direction being the well-known econometric model for the US economy presented by *L.R. Klein* and *R.S. Goldberger* in 1955. This model contained more than twenty equations. Recent models for the US economy which may be considered as extensions of the Klein–Goldberger type of model contain several hundreds of variables and equations. Although these models are potentially useful for planning and policy purposes, they have been designed and used mainly for purposes of forecasting and simulation. Generally they emphasize and elaborate the demand side of the economy more than supply factors and resource scarcity.

Models designed more explicitly for planning and policy purposes were constructed quite early by *J. Tinbergen* and *R. Frisch*. As mentioned already in Section 1.1, J. Tinbergen demonstrated the use of macroeconomic models for elucidating the possibilities of influen-

independently, developed and used rather similar models in connection with the elaboration of Five Year Plans in India, first a two-sector model distinguishing between the consumption goods sector and a capital goods sector and later a four-sector model.

Because of the assumptions of fixed production coefficients for capital and labour and because of the linearity of the models also in other respects, growth models of the Feldman–Domar–Mahalanobis family are easy to implement empirically, both with regard to estimation and computations (but Feldman himself was very much worried about the uncertainty with regard to the *future* values of the technological coefficients). So-called *neo-classical growth models* have had a less widespread impact upon planning methodology, although some countries have started using such types of models in recent years. Neo-classical growth models are usually thought of as originating in the second half of the 1950s, but a remarkable precursor is an article of the mathematician *F.P. Ramsey* from 1928 (partly stimulated by *J.M. Keynes*) on *A Mathematical Theory of Saving*, and particularly so in the context of planning since it raised the fundamental issue of trying to determine an optimal rate of saving or accumulation, i.e., to make an optimal choice among feasible growth paths for the economy. Similarly to the later neo-classical growth models Ramsey's model used a macroeconomic production function with labour and capital as substitutable factors, but instead of closing the model by a behavioural assumption concerning saving this was left as a degree of freedom to be disposed of in the optimization. The problem did not attract much interest at that time, but it has been an intensively cultivated field of theoretical research in recent years. Although it has yielded theoretically interesting results, it has hardly influenced actual growth policy in any country directly to any perceivable extent. It has perhaps had a greater impact indirectly through the light it sheds on the problem of determining a normative discount factor for the appraisal and selection of investment projects.

For completeness it should be mentioned that neo-classical growth models were not completely neglected between Ramsey's 1928 contribution and the new developments starting in the 1950s. *J. Tinbergen* constructed and implemented empirically a neo-classical growth model already in 1942. This model contained all the basic elements of the later generation of neo-classical growth models plus several other elements so that it is altogether quite an elaborate model, but because of the time and place of publication it remained an isolated effort overlooked by economists in other countries. An even more over-looked contribution was a paper by *Ragnar Frisch* from 1940 on optimum population. This paper studied the problem of optimum population development in a dynamic setting with a neo-classical macro production function with labour and capital stock as inputs. But jointly with this it also studied the optimum rate of capital accumulation and arrived at conclusions which can easily be com-pared with Ramsey's. (But Frisch was evidently not aware of Ram-sey's contribution.)

Before leaving the growth models I think it worth mentioning that a growth model developed by *M. Kalecki* in a series of papers begin-ning in 1956 and in the book *Introduction to the Theory of Growth in a Socialist Economy*, seems to have been actually applied in long-term planning and projection in some socialist countries, notably Poland. This growth model is not very explicit with regard to technological assumptions. In appearance it could be compared both with the Harrod–Domar type of model and with the neo-classical model. But the parameters are not treated as constants, and the model also contains some additional parameters referring to technical change and scrapping of old capital equipment. Very much of the intention and meaning of the model therefore lies in the interpretation and use of these parameters. As interpreted and used by Kalecki and others the model to some extent represents ideas akin to the so-called putty-clay models and models with embodied technological progress. Savings decisions are related to planning rather than determined by behaviour.

The tool of economic analysis which has perhaps become most widely used for planning purposes is *input–output analysis*. In almost all countries in which planning models have been constructed input–output analysis has been used, either in the form of a straight forward input–output model or as one element in a more complicated struc-ture. The basic work is *W. Leontief's* book on *The Structure of American Economy 1919–1929* published in 1941, but there is a paper by Leontief containing the basic ideas already in 1936.

In theoretical presentations input–output models are sometimes seen as a special case of the Walrasian general equilibrium model and sometimes as a natural extension of Karl Marx's schemes of re-production. Leontief was in a position to draw inspiration from both these sources. He had got his training in economics in Russia before he moved to Western countries. The early Russian mathematical economist *V.K. Dmitriev* took important steps towards a mathematical formulation of input–output relationships in his explorations in value theory (published in 1904) where he presented a system of equations for calculating the full amount of labour expended directly and indirectly for the production of the various commodities. The possible usefulness of Dmitriev's approach for planning purposes was understood by some economists in the USSR in the early 1920s, and may have influenced work on balances of various sorts which can be seen as forerunners of the modern input–output tables. Otherwise Soviet authors on the theory and practice of economic balances at that time usually referred to Quesnay's "Tableau Economique" and Marx's "Schemes of Reproduction" as the basic theoretical sources of inspiration. W. Leontief had studied particularly the balance-sheet for 1923–24 mentioned in Section 1.1 and also wrote a review of this balance-sheet in a Russian planning journal in 1925, applauding the general idea, but being critical against the execution on some specific points.

Soviet economists emphasized particularly the completeness of the balance-sheet. Thus *P.I. Popov*, in the introduction to the 1923/24 balance, characterized it as follows: "Portraying the relations of equilibrium in statistical magnitudes, the balance classifies the relations of the national economy by production and distribution from the standpoint of equilibrium, and *finds a niche for every phenomenon and every fact of the national economy in the system of equilibrium*." (Further on he also emphasized that balances could be used to study how "equilibrium" could be disturbed.) Some economists also studied statistically the development of some proportions within the balances which we now call input–output coefficients. However, they failed to arrange the full system as a mathematical model. P.I. Popov emphasized explicitly that "the balance of the national economy is not yet a theory." On the other hand: "The balance provides the material for a theory, for in analyzing statistical evidence it shows how the annual output of the Soviet economy, plus imports, plus reserves, is actually realized and distributed among the branches of the national economy and the classes of society in any given year, through a system of exchange and planned regulation." [For a Western discussion of these early balances, see *N. Spulber* (1975).]

Although such interesting roots can be found, it remained for Leontief to give to input–output analysis the clear and efficient mathematical formulation which has made it one of the most important tools in economic planning, and to show the variety of problems which could be analysed by means of this tool. It was also W. Leontief who later developed the *dynamic* input–output model.

The standard input–output model makes very simple assumptions about the technology of production: each production sector produces only one type of output, and there are no substitution possibilities. For many purposes this framework is too rigid. A more general framework under the designation *activity analysis* was developed by *T.C. Koopmans* and others around 1950. This type of model retains the linearity of the input–output analysis, but allows for joint output of several commodities in each production activity, and for choice between several technologies for producing each type of output. A production model of the activity analysis type will then typically involve many more degrees of freedom than a standard input–output model, and the system therefore lends itself naturally to an optimization approach. Activity analysis was for this reason developed in close contact with *linear programming* which is a method of solving optimization problems with a linear function to be maximized (or minimized) subject to constraints in the form of linear equations and/or inequalities. The linear programming model and an efficient method of solving such problems – *the simplex method* – were developed by *G.B. Dantzig* around 1947 as a planning technique for some of the activities of the US Air Force. Activity analysis and linear programming have proved to be very important tools of economic analysis and planning in practice as well as in theory.

In the USSR the linear programming problem was formulated by the mathematician *L.V. Kantorovich* in a publication as early as in 1939. Kantorovich illustrated the usefulness of this formulation by applying it to several problems of organizing production and transportation and also developed a method of solution of such problems. This algorithm was, however, not so efficient and so easy to mechanize as the simplex method mentioned above. Kantorovich's original contribution seems to have passed rather unnoticed, but in the 1950s Kantorovich resumed his research in this direction and broadened the scope of the analysis. In 1959 he published a very important book on *The Best Use of Economic Resources*. Here and in subsequent papers Kantorovich used his linear programming theory to elucidate a wide range of planning problems also at the level of national economic planning. Besides giving a framework for computable planning models this approach has had a great impact upon the understanding of the rôle of prices as implements in a system of partly decentralized decision-making in the USSR economy (via the dual variables, or "objectively determined valuations" as Kantorovich called them). The economist *V.V. Novozhilov* published works in the same vein in the 1940s, emphasizing economic interpretations and applications for price-fixing and rational investment decisions rather than mathematical and computational aspects. (In 1965 *L.V. Kantorovich* and *V.V. Novozhilov* together with *V.S. Nemchinov*, who has been instrumental in reviving the interest in, and use of mathematics in economic research and planning in the USSR, were awarded the Lenin prize in recognition of their scientific achievements. This symbolized the definitive break-through for mathematical methods in economic research and planning in the USSR.)

The links between concepts and methods of linear programming and more traditional economic theory were clearly exposed and very forcefully presented in an important book by *R. Dorfman, P.A. Samuelson* and *R.M. Solow* published in 1958.

From the middle of the 1950s the idea that the linear programming models could be constructed for purposes of macroeconomic planning seems to have come up in many quarters, with economists like *R. Frisch* (Norway), *O. Lange* (Poland), *J. Sandee* (The Netherlands) and others besides *L.V. Kantorovich* mentioned above. Within the class of optimization models this is by far the most widely used type of model.

I cannot leave this subject without calling attention to *R. Frisch's* article from 1934 on *Circulation Planning* which foreshadows many of the later developments in the field of input–output analysis and mathematical programming, but which has largely been neglected up to the present time. The problem treated by Frisch in this paper, was how to organize distribution of commodities so as to revive the economy from a depression. Later developments have shown that some of the methods and model elements proposed are more powerful in other directions than those towards which Frisch turned them. Furthermore Frisch burdened his paper with a rather elaborate description of an organizational set-up which was hardly very practical. These are probably some reasons why the very interesting novel ideas in the paper were not discovered and absorbed in wider circles.

Also *J. von Neumann's* now well-known growth model from 1938 must of course be mentioned. The brief paper presenting this model contained several important ideas which have inspired later developments particularly in the combination of activity analysis, optimization and growth.

After the first development of linear programming there has taken place a rapid development of programming theory in several directions. There are now efficient methods of solving reasonably large problems for some classes of *non-linear programming problems*, with non-linearities either in the function to be maximized or in the constraints (or both places). This is obviously important for many economic applications. An early example of the application of non-linear programming to economic planning – in fact originating from before the real spurt in the development of computational methods for such problems – is *H.B. Chenery's* and *K.S. Kretschmer's* development planning model from 1956, illustrated by an application to Southern Italy. The non-linearity in this case stems from the external trade part of the model where volumes are multiplied by prices which depend on volumes. There have also been developed methods of at least approximate solution of quite large linear programming problems involving some variables which are restricted to take on *integer values* (perhaps only the values zero or one), a technique which is important for economic planning for instance in cases where the problem of choosing among investment projects is integrated into a larger model. [For early examples of this type of computations for planning purposes, see *D. Kendrick* (1967).] A field of special significance is the solution of programming problems with special structures which permit *decomposition* of the full problem into a series of partly interconnected smaller problems. The most well-known method of this type has been developed by *G.B. Dantzig* and *P. Wolfe* in 1960. An alternative approach, especially designed in a planning context, has been developed by *J. Kornai* and *Th. Liptak*, and the most interesting application of such ideas in the context of economic planning is a Hungarian project directed by J. Kornai. This development may prove to be of particular significance since there are many reasons why the application of mathematical models to economic planning will probably take the course of integration of several models at various levels rather than the construction of an ever bigger overall model.

An important book which illustrates the use of both techniques mentioned here, i.e., programming with integer variables (besides "ordinary" continuous variables) to represent acceptance or rejection of investment projects and decomposition of a large problem into

partly interconnected smaller problems, is *Multi-Level Planning:
Case Studies in Mexico* from 1973, with contributions by *A. Manne, J.
Kornai* and others. Besides illustrating the analytical techniques the
book also discusses the prospects for further progress and practical
use of this type of planning models in the future.

Recent years have witnessed interesting developments also of
many other new theories and techniques which may prove to be of
great value to economic planning, such as the theory of *rational
behaviour under uncertainty, information and communication theory,
general systems theory, team theory* and *game theory*. Elements from
these fields have found some more specific applications in economic
planning, but have not yet become parts of the standard methodology
of planning in practice. Nevertheless, viewpoints from these branches
are valuable as parts of the general background even if the more
specific techniques and models are not explicitly used.

In Section 1.1, I mentioned the theoretical discussion on the
economics of socialism by *Barone, Mises, Taylor, Lange* and others
(which is very well summarized by *A. Bergson*). This branch of
theory, which is closely related to market theory and economic
welfare theory, has been enriched since around 1960 by several new
ideas by *K.J. Arrow* and *L. Hurwicz, A. Malinvaud* and others, as
surveyed in a recent book by *G.M. Heal, The Theory of Economic
Planning*. The emphasis here is on constructing efficient schemes of
exchange of information between a central planning agency and
subordinate units so as to arrive, by iteration, at an optimal plan for
the whole system. The purpose is sometimes to simulate actual
planning procedures so as to learn about their properties, but in most
cases to suggest new and improved procedures. The feedback from
this research to actual planning in the form of explicit applications
has so far been rather meagre, but again insight into the results is very
valuable as part of the background for organizing planning processes.

Under point F' in Section 1.2, I mentioned the development in
computational techniques and equipment as one of the factors preparing the ground for improved methods of planning. This development has of course been closely related to the development of
operations research mentioned above. For applications in economic
planning we may distinguish between two branches: solution of
systems of equations, and problems of optimization.

For the solution of systems of equations linear equations are of course most easily handled. Here there are no difficult problems of principle, only a question of effort, capacity and accuracy. Fairly large systems could be solved on pre-electronic desk calculators. For instance, in the early 1950s the coefficient matrix of an input–output model with 30 sectors was inverted by means of desk calculators at the Institute of Economics at the University of Oslo and at the Central Bureau of Statistics of Norway. (Such an inversion is comparable in order of magnitude to solving a system of 30 linear equations 30 times.) Such matrices are, however, particularly suitable for simple iteration procedures. When I, in 1957/58, worked on a multi-sectoral long-term model for the Norwegian economy (the "MSG-model") I needed the inversion of an 86×86 matrix with a less convenient structure than the Leontief matrix of an ordinary input–output model. There was at that time no computer available in Norway which could solve this task, but simultaneously with the preparation of the matrix it happened that a computer was being installed which proved to be able to do it. This was probably the largest matrix which had been inverted in Norway by that time. Since then the capacity of computers has increased very much so that with regard to the solution of systems of linear equations there is now hardly any limit of practical importance, particularly since very large systems always have many zero coefficients and special patterns of distribution of the non-zero coefficients which can be exploited in the computations.

The 86×86 matrix mentioned here was constructed by linearization of a model which was, in its basic form, non-linear and dynamic. In recent years this model (with some more sectors so that the number of equations is somewhat larger) has been used in practice and solved in its non-linear form for the time paths of all the variables over 20–30 years. The large American econometric models mentioned earlier in this section are non-linear and highly dynamic and contain several hundreds of variables. When such models were first constructed before and around the middle of the 1960s there were great difficulties in solving them, but in recent years they have been solved efficiently and used for extensive simulation experiments.

Among optimization techniques linear programming has been most successfully programmed for large-scale computations. Linear programming problems with thousands of variables can now be solved. For efficient computations it is important also here to exploit special patterns of distribution of zero and non-zero coefficients in the coefficient matrices. For non-linear optimization it is very hard to give any general statements since there are so many different cases, but also in this field there is a fast progress which often makes it possible in practice to solve numerically quite large optimization problems (also in cases where it is difficult to characterize the optimum analytically). Many sorts of rather fanciful search techniques are used.

It is difficult to give good illustrations of the size of modern computations, but one example is given by *R. Stone* in connection with the solution of a growth model for the British economy with many production sectors (the project *A Programme for Growth*). Here it is explained that "in our model the British economy is represented by the entries in a set of 253 accounts, each of which contains the incomings and outgoings of some branch or sector of the economy. The numerical inputs, that is the coefficients and quantitative assumptions, needed for a computer-run number between five and six thousand. A run involves about thirty million multiplications: on a desk calculator this is equivalent to some sixty man-years of work: on the Atlas computer it takes twenty-two seconds." Compared with the largest computations now being performed this example would probably be characterized as rather modest.

In Section 1.2, I referred to the development of certain branches of economic theory and the development of computational techniques and equipment as factors tending to prepare the ground for expanded and improved planning. By comparing the account given in the present section with the brief historical sketch of the development of planning given in Section 1.1, we see that relevant aspects of economic theory and computational techniques have indeed developed very much parallel with the trend towards macroeconomic planning, and there have of course been several instances of contact and influence between the two spheres. One should, however, be careful not to overate the effects. Many theoretical models where some sort of "Central Planning Board" appears as a decision-maker are not very much in touch with actual economic planning problems and procedures, and in some countries which are very advanced with regard to economic theory and computational equipment actual economic policy is far from being characterized by conscious and systematic macroeconomic planning. It is not too long since it was considered a victory for economic thought that budgetary policy in the United States was to some extent influenced by quite elementary

Keynesian ideas, and even this victory sometimes seems to rest on a shaky ground. On the other hand, when concrete circumstances make the need for planning clear to the decisive political authorities, then planning is initiated without waiting for a stock-taking to find out whether adequate theories and techniques are available. After all, the government administration of a country is used to solving problems, taking decisions and coordinating actions as best it can without feeling too much inhibited by the fact that deeper analysis might show that the decisions are not optimal or perfectly coordinated. Writing on planning problems in the USSR in 1928, the economist *S.G. Strumilin* (member of the State Planning Commission from 1921, one of the leaders of the elaboration of the First Five Year Plan, and the grand old man of Soviet economics for decades until he died in 1974 at the age of 97) remarked that although it is impossible by classical tools of geometry to divide an angle into three equal parts, the problem is overcome in practice every day with a sufficient degree of accuracy. Turning more directly to the economic problem he saw the practical solution to the theoretically almost insuperable problem of establishing a fully balanced plan in "the method of successive approximations", or what may be called some sort of administrative iteration: "The fact is that when we get down to drafting the perspective economic plan for any period ahead, the difficulty we always run up against first is this: it is impossible to lay down rational perspective plans for development in any branch of the economy taken separately unless we know beforehand what the rates of development are going to be in allied areas and what over-all rate of development has been scheduled for the national economy as a whole. On the other hand, projecting over-all rates of development for the national economy as a whole is impossible unless we have a basis for it in estimates of possible rates of development in the economy's individual branches. Only the method of successive approximations can extricate us from this vicious circle."

In this connection it is interesting to observe that several economists working in planning in the USSR in the early period were well aware of the potential usefulness of mathematical methods in the future, but found it impossible to use them in practice at that time. In an article "On the Methodology for Drafting Perspective Plans", published in 1926, an economist by the name of *V.A. Bazarov* presented considerations which it is interesting to quote at some length. Bazarov posed the problem of finding an optimal path of development. He mentioned initial conditions and the requirements of smoothness of development and fulfillment of certain proportions as constraints, and from the "family of curves" satisfying these conditions he sought the "shortest path" to certain goals for development. He continued: "It must be pointed out in advance, however, that we are not in a position to plot the optimum curve of perspective development with complete accuracy and rigor, not only because we do not have sufficient factual data at our disposal but also because of the very nature of the problem. To compute the shortest or optimum paths given definite, previously stipulated conditions is, as we know, one of the most difficult problems of the art of calculation. Modern mathematics offers methods of solving problems of this nature for only a few very simple cases, and even here the methods to be employed are highly sophisticated (the methods of the so-called "calculus of variations"). In our cases, meanwhile, not only is the problem itself infinitely complex, but the factual data are of necessity most incomplete and not always reliable. It is therefore understandable that no sufficiently detailed and accurate methodology of perspective planning should exist at the present time, and that evolving one at short notice should be impossible; it can only develop gradually, step by step, in the process of prolonged and intensive collective work. For the time being, however, in our search for the optimum we must fall back on rather rough estimates and feel our way to the sought-for goal using variant approximations."

It is interesting to observe that the "calculus of variation" approach here suggested for the optimum path problem was the approach actually used by *F.P. Ramsey* in his 1928 paper on optimal growth mentioned above, but the way Bazarov posed the problem (by seeking the "shortest path" to some goals) is in fact nearer to an exploratory planning model for optimal growth constructed for Algeria by the French economist *L. Stoleru* in 1965. Under realistic assumptions various types of constraints which cannot be tackled by classical calculus of variations will be involved, and the more general *optimal control theory* as developed particularly by *L.S. Pontryagin* and his associates may be required. Stoleru's paper was perhaps the first to use this mathematical tool in connection with an economic planning model. The field still appears to be rather complicated and most "applications" to be found in modern literature are tentative and experimental.

In other fields theory and computational techniques have, however, made possible the solving of very large and complicated problems as described above so that the scope for practical applications of mathematical methods is of course now much wider than when Bazarov put down his considerations. Yet mathematically formulated models and large-scale computations cannot replace economic insight and experience and good administration in connection with economic planning. Mathematical models can only form *one* of the components in a planning system, and even now results of model calculations are never taken at face value for planning purposes, but almost always compared with results and ideas formed by other approaches (often by "traditional" or "administrative" planning methods parallel with model calculations) and more or less adjusted according to experience, intuition and information not taken into account by the formal models.

References for Section 1.3

A. Bergson, "Socialist economics", in *A survey of contemporary economics*, edited by H.S. Ellis (Blakiston Company, Philadelphia, 1948).

H.B. Chenery and K.S. Kretschmer, "Resource allocation for economic development", *Econometrica* (1956). See also H.B. Chenery and H. Uzawa, "Non-linear programming in economic development", in *Studies in linear and non-linear programming*, edited by K.J. Arrow, L. Hurwicz and H. Uzawa (Stanford University Press, Stanford, 1958).

V.S. Dadajan, *Ökonomische Gesetze des Sozialismus und Optimale Entscheidungen* (Akademie-Verlag, Berlin (GDR), 1973). Translation from Russian. Especially pp. 228–229.

G.B. Dantzig and P. Wolfe, "Decomposition principle for linear programs", *Operations Research* (1960); and "The decomposition algorithm for linear programs", *Econometrica* (1961).

V.K. Dmitriev, *Economic essays on value, competition and utility* (Cambridge University Press, London, 1974). Original Russian edition in 1904. English translation published with an introduction by D.M. Nuti.

E.D. Domar, *Essays in the theory of economic growth* (Oxford University Press, New York, 1957). Besides Domar's original essays this book contains, as essay IX, a review of G.A. Feldman's Soviet growth model from 1928–29.

R. Dorfman, P.A. Samuelson and R.M. Solow, *Linear programming and economic theory* (McGraw-Hill, New York, 1958).

G.A. Feldman, *Zur Wachstumstheorie des Nationaleinkommens* (Europäische Verlagsanstalt, Frankfurt, 1969). Translation from the original 1928–29 works in Russian. English translation of some parts of Feldman's works are found in *Foundations of Soviet strategy for economic growth* – See reference below.

Foundations of Soviet strategy for economic growth: Selected Soviet essays, 1924–30, edited by N. Spulber (Indiana University Press, Bloomington, 1964). Contains translations of several of the works from the USSR in the 1920s referred to in the text, including V. Bazarov, G.A. Feldman, W. Leontief, P.I. Popov and S.G. Strumilin.

R. Frisch, "Circulation planning", *Econometrica* (1934) No. 3, July and No. 4, October.

R. Frisch, "Befolkningsoptimum", *Statsøkonomisk Tidsskrift* (1940).

R. Frisch, "Price–wage–tax policies as instruments in maintaining optimal employment", UN Document E/CN.1/Sub.2/13 (18 April 1949). Also published as a
Memorandum from the Institute of Economics at the University of Oslo (28 March
1949). *A Mathematical Appendix* to this report is published as a *Memorandum* from the
Institute of Economics at the University of Oslo (23 September 1949).

R. Frisch, "L'emploi des modèles pour l'élaboration d'une politique économique
rationelle", *Revue d'Économie Politique* (1950).

R. Frisch, "Principles of linear programming", *Memorandum* from the Institute of
Economics at the University of Oslo (18 October 1954).

R. Frisch, "From national accounts to macroeconomic decision models", in *Income
and wealth*, Series 4, edited by M. Gilbert and R. Stone (Bowes and Bowes, London,
1955).

R. Frisch, "Macroeconomics and linear programming", in *25 economic essays in
honour of Erik Lindahl*, Ekonomisk Tidskrift (Stockholm, 1956). Especially the
introductory part.

G.M. Heal, *The theory of economic planning* (North-Holland, Amsterdam, 1973).

M. Kalecki, *Introduction to the theory of growth in a socialist economy* (Basil
Blackwell, Oxford, 1969). Translation from Polish, first Polish edition in 1960.

L.V. Kantorovich, "Mathematical methods of organizing and planning production",
Management Science (1960). Originally published in Russian, Leningrad, 1939. With
minor changes published in English also in *The use of mathematics in economics*,
edited by V.S. Nemchinov (Oliver and Boyd, Edinburgh and London, 1964).

L.V. Kantorovich, *The best use of economic resources* (Pergamon Press, London,
1965). Original Russian edition published in 1959.

D.F. Kendrick, *Programming investment in the process industries: An approach to
sectoral planning*, M.I.T. Monographs in Economics 8 (M.I.T., Cambridge, 1967). See
also "Investment planning and economic integration", *Economics of Planning* (1967).

G. Khanin, "Methodological problems in the development of the state national
economic plan", in *Contemporary Soviet economics, Vol. I* (International Arts and
Sciences Press, White Plains, 1969). Translation from Russian. Contains an assessment of G.A. Feldman's contributions.

L.R. Klein and A.S. Goldberger, *An econometric model of the United States 1929–52*
(North-Holland, Amsterdam, 1955).

T.C. Koopmans, ed., *Activity analysis of production and allocation* (Wiley, New York,
1951). This volume contains G.B. Dantzig's fundamental paper on linear programming written in 1947.

J. Kornai and Th. Liptak, "Two-level planning", *Econometrica* (1965). Earlier Hungarian version appeared in 1962.

J. Kornai, *Mathematical planning of structural decisions* (North-Holland, Amsterdam,
1967). Originally published in Hungarian, Budapest, 1965.

O. Lange, "The output–investment ratio and input–output analysis", *Econometrica*
(1960).

W. Leontief, "Quantitative input and output relations in the economic system of the
United States", *Review of Economic Statistics* (1936).

W. Leontief, *The structure of American economy 1919–29* (Harvard University Press,
Cambridge, 1941).

P. C. Mahalanobis, "Some observations on the process of growth of national income",
Sankhya (1953). Also "The approach of operational research to planning in India",
Sankhya (1955).

Multi-level planning: Case studies in Mexico, edited by L.M. Goreux and A.S. Manne
(North-Holland, Amsterdam, 1973).

L.S. Pontryagin et al., *The mathematical theory of optimal processes* (Interscience Wiley, New York, 1962). Translation from Russian.

F. P. Ramsey, "A mathematical theory of saving", *The Economic Journal* (1928).

J. Sandee, *A demonstration planning model for India* (Indian Statistical Institute, Calcutta, 1960).

N. Spulber, "The pioneering stage in input–output economics: The Soviet national economic balance 1923–24, after fifty years", *The Review of Economics and Statistics* (1975).

L.G. Stoleru, "An optimal policy for economic growth", *Econometrica* (1965).

R. Stone, "A framework for economic decisions", *Moorgate and Wall Street* (1964). Reprint No. 222 from The Department of Applied Economics, University of Cambridge.

J. Tinbergen, "Zur Theorie der langfristigen Wirtschaftsentwicklung", *Weltwirtschaftliches Archiv* (1942). Available in English as "On the theory of trend movements" in his *Selected papers* (North-Holland, Amsterdam, 1959).

J. Tinbergen, *On the theory of economic policy* (North-Holland, Amsterdam, 1952).

J. Tinbergen, "An economic policy for 1936". Paper originally read before the Dutch Economic Association, published in English in his *Selected papers* (North-Holland, Amsterdam, 1959).

A.L. Wainschtein and G.I. Chanin, "Dem sowjetischen Ökonomen und Mathematiker G.A. Feldman zum Gedenken", *Sowjetwissenschaft, Gesellschaftswissenschaftliche Beiträge* (August 1968). Translation from Russian.

1.4. A Sample of Definitions of the Concept of Planning

We have not yet tried to give a definition of the concept of planning. Perhaps this is not necessary. In very much of the literature on economic planning the term is obviously taken to be self-explanatory, not in need of any further definition and elaboration. This applies to much of the Marxian literature, both classical and more recent literature from the socialist countries as well as Western countries. Also writers like R. Frisch and J. Tinbergen, who have contributed very much to the theory of economic planning and to whom I often refer in these lectures, do not seem to feel the need for discussing the definition of the concept at any length.

It seems that attempts at defining the concept are most often found in connection with discussions of less clear-cut systems, such as in connection with the introduction of some sort of "planning" in otherwise predominantly market-oriented economies or in connection with economic reforms in the socialist countries in Eastern Europe where there is great concern for not letting reforms introduce changes in the system which mean abandoning "planning". We shall consider a somewhat variegated sample of such definitions in this section, not because it is very important to settle for a very specific definition, but because these attempts at defining the concept draw attention to important problems and aspects of planning systems and methods. No doubt one could easily find many other authors than those mentioned below with more or less interesting definitions. All the considerations brought forward by this survey of definitions could also have been presented more briefly without being attributed to authors, countries and time periods. However, to bring the viewpoints in the form of quotations from named authors helps to illustrate how they are conditioned by history, political systems and attitudes as well as specific problems of various countries.

In the Western discussion on the economics of socialism perhaps the British economist *H.D. Dickinson*, in a book from 1938, has given the most careful definition. According to this definition planning is "the making of major economic decisions – what and how much is to be produced, and to whom it is to be allocated – by the conscious decisions of a determinate authority, on the basis of a comprehensive survey of the economic system as a whole." This is a very demanding definition in the sense that planning should be concerned with many spheres: with what, how, how much, when, where and to whom. This is perhaps a necessary consequence of the emphasis on *decisions* in this definition. In order for a decision to be operational in practice, it must in the end be particularized so as to be meaningful for the practical actions to be taken. It is much more meaningful to decide on production of particular goods than to take a decision about the magnitude of the national product. A command about the magnitude of the national product has no specific addressee. What one can do in this case is rather to put up a *target value* for the national product and *decide about the means to be used* in order to reach this target (more or less accurately).

The last part of Dickinson's definition is meant to make planning realistic by taking into account limitations and interconnections in the economy as a whole, i.e., to make it something more than a statement of desires.

In *C. Landauer's* book from 1944 on national economic planning (already referred to in Section 1.1) we find the following description of planning: "Planning means coordination through a conscious effort, instead of the automatic coordination which takes place in the market, and that conscious effort is to be made by an organ of society. Therefore, planning is an activity of a collectivistic character and is regulation of the activities of individuals by the community. This is true whether or not the plan is enforced by compulsion. Even if the plan is carried out through councel voluntarily accepted, the weight is shifted from individual decisions to the deliberations of communal bodies." Further on we find the following statement which is meant as an explicit definition: "Planning can be defined as guidance of economic activities by a communal organ through a scheme which describes, in quantitative as well as qualitative terms, the productive processes that ought to be undertaken during a designated future period. To achieve the main purpose of planning, these processes must be so chosen and designed that they secure the full use of available resources and avoid contradictory requirements, making a stable rate of progress possible." This definition is not meant for a socialist economy. Accordingly there is less emphasis on decisions and more on guidance than in Dickinson's definition. From the first quotation it is interesting to observe that Landauer distinguishes between a plan which is "enforced by compulsion" and a plan which is "carried out through councel voluntarily accepted". This is similar to the distinction between "imperative planning" and "indicative planning" which has been common in more recent literature.

Some definitions of planning given in Western countries naturally consider the market mechanism as the main method of allocation of resources, and planning as a supplementary activity. The American economist *G. Sirkin* (1968) considers "planning" to be "a word in search of meaning", and considers the failure to give a precise meaning to the word to have caused confusion with costly results. The definition which Sirkin arrives at runs as follows: "Planning is the attempt, by centralizing the management of the allocation of resources sufficiently, to take into account social costs and social benefits which would be irrelevant to the calculations of the decentralized decision-maker." Evidently, a centralized management which fails to take into account and compare social costs and benefits generated by the various dispositions might be a very costly affair, which is what Sirkin wants to emphasize. Such centralized management will, in his view, miss the whole purpose of planning, and should therefore not be identified with planning.

In Sirkin's definition it is important to observe the word "sufficiently". The starting point is a system of decentralized decisions, and planning means centralizing management to a "sufficient" degree. Presumably the intention is not to go beyond this degree, so that one might more precisely say centralizing the management of the economy to the smallest degree which is sufficient for the purpose. When this degree is reached the costs and benefits which are "external" to the individual decision-maker are "internal" to the centralized authorities.

At a first glance Sirkin's definition might seem to be very narrow in that it refers only to the need for planning which was mentioned under point C in Section 1.2, the "increasing weight of indirect or external effects in production and consumption". However, it is possible to give this definition a somewhat broader scope, for instance by observing that, in a situation of unemployment wages give false or distorted "signals" concerning the cost of employing labour so that decentralized calculations of the ordinary type will yield misleading conclusions with regard to social costs and benefits of production activities. Also some of the other points listed in Section 1.2 can, perhaps by stretching the terms to some extent, be subsumed under Sirkin's definition.

The title of Sirkin's book, *The Visible Hand: The Fundamentals of Economic Planning,* is in the same spirit as his definition. The counter-part of "The Visible Hand" is of course "The Invisible Hand" which is the famous metaphor used by *Adam Smith* to visualize the ability of the market mechanism to generate an optimal allocation of resources. Where The Invisible Hand fails, The Visible Hand must be used to guide the economic processes.

In France, where there is a rather extensive literature on planning, several definitions are given in a similar vein. In discussing such definitions, *G. Caire* (1967) in fact distinguishes between approaches to planning which consider planning as a *supplement* to the market mechanism, and definitions which consider planning as something which should *replace* the market mechanism. In France activities and arrangements which are intended to improve the functioning of the market mechanism are often considered as the most essential elements of planning. For instance, the influential French economist *F. Perroux* (1965) emphasizes the absence of competitive conditions in the various markets as the main reason for economic planning. The reduction of uncertainty created by the market mechanisms is also often considered as a main aspect of planning as suggested by *P. Massé's* book (1965) with the title *Le plan ou l'anti-hasard.*

The definitions given above are ranked from a definition which emphasizes centralized control over a wide range of activities to definitions which consider planning as a supplement to the market mechanism or as a means of improving the working of the market mechanism. It is possible to go even further, as is in a way done by the British economist and econometrician *R. Stone* (1964). He explains that "a plan tells us how to set about achieving our policies given the operating characteristics of the system. It can be identified with administration or control. These words can in turn be identified either with coercion, exemplified by the policeman, or with means of self-regulation, exemplified by the Watts governor or the thermostat. The opposite of plan is no-plan, or anarchy." To make the point clear he adds: "In theory, *laissez-faire* is not an example of no-plan; it is a perfectly coherent plan for operating an economic system." This of course refers to well-known propositions in economic welfare theory about the optimality properties of the perfectly competitive system.

However, to this it may be objected that *laissez-faire* is not necessarily the same as perfect competition. It may be necessary to interfere with the markets in order to make competition work, as suggested by the French references above. Furthermore, both theory and empirical facts make it clear that *laissez-faire*, or even perfect competition, leads to many failures, both with regard to stability, allocation and income distribution. Although a world in which *laissez-faire* is an example of "a perfectly coherent plan" is logically conceivable, if economic theory should be more than logical analysis of hypothetical economies, then it is hardly very bold to venture the proposition that *laissez-faire* is not an example of planning.

The definitions quoted above aim at rather broad and general characterizations of economic planning. Many other definitions emphasize more specific aspects.

A Soviet definition from the period of discussions about economic reforms, by *V.S. Nemchinov* in a book published in 1962 (here quoted in English translation from *R. Bícanić* – see the list of references), runs as follows: "Practical planning consists in harmonious coordination of the economic principle of conscious control of the social production (in accordance with the known objective laws of economic development) with the cybernetic principle of the automatic, autoregulatory and autoorganizing flow of the economic process.... This solution is possible only under certain decentralization of the planning decision making, reserving the most important functions, and decisions regarding the principles of planning, to the directive-issuing centers, and transferring a considerable mass of problems connected with economic planning to the leadership of local organs, which will make decisions about them following the principle of democratic centralism." The "cybernetic principle" involved will in practice take the form of some sort of market mechanism. This definition thus emphasizes the coordination of central decision-making with some use of market mechanisms, but retains the latter confined within the planning system by letting the scope of the market mechanism and the principles according to which it operates be determined by central authorities. This definition has of course something in common with other definitions which allow for the joint use of centralized management and market mechanism. But whereas definitions like Sirkin's start from a decentralized system and call for sufficient centralization as the active step, Nemchinov's definition starts from a system of centralized management and points out the necessity of some degree of decentralization. This of course reflects the difference in the economic systems from which the definitions originate.

V.S. Nemchinov was a leading person in the great progress which took place in Soviet economics from the late 1950s, partly by taking into use mathematical methods and modern computational techniques, and his views can be taken as representative of the period.

The Yugoslav economist *R. Bícanić*, in a broad discussion of the definition of planning (1967), emphasizes especially the institutionalized nature of planning. According to him planning is institutionalized in the sense that it must be well defined "who is planning with whom and for whom", and he especially points out that the following four types of institutions or authorities are necessary for planning: (i) institutions for the *preparation* of plans, (ii) institutions for *decision-making* concerning the plans, (iii) authorities for the *execution* of the plans, and finally (iv) institutions for *controlling* the fulfilment of the plans. It is interesting to notice that a definition which especially emphasizes the necessity of a well-defined institutional structure comes from Yugoslavia where exactly this aspect of planning has been in flux for a long period.

In Czechoslovakia an interesting discussion about the purpose and methods of planning took place in the reform period in the 1960s. One aspect of this discussion, which appeared also in other socialist countries, was the confrontation between those who see planning in very deterministic terms, searching for the one objectively determined, correct plan, and those who emphasize the possibility of conscious choice, where preference elements which are not objectively determined must be brought to bear on the plan. In a contribution to this discussion *L. Rychetnik* and *O. Kyn*, who belonged to the second group, assigned two different functions to "central management". The first was the coordination of economic activities which in some form is included in all definitions of planning. However, what they considered to be the basic task was indicated as follows: "The basic task of central management should therefore be to humanize the course of the economy, to adapt it to social and extra-economic ends of society . . . ." From this point of view they criticized the deterministic conception of planning as harmful. The quotation given here is of course not intended to give a complete definition of the concept of planning, but it emphasizes an aspect which is an important supplement to elements laid down in other definitions, and which helps to put economic planning in its proper place in a broader view of society.

Also *J. Kornai* (1970) criticizes the deterministic, or "fatalistic philosophy" of planning. If this philosophy were true, then "planning would be practically equivalent with forecasting." We would have to discover "objectively given trends, describe them and accept them as plans of our future activity." This way of looking at the planning problem is characterized by Kornai as a "one-sided misinterpretation of Marxian historical materialism, the overrating of the deterministic side, and the underrating of the freedom in human action." In another paper (with *L. Ujlaki*, 1967) Kornai mentions that "occasionally, when working out their proposals and giving them a definite form, the planners would even make themselves believe that they succeeded in finding this only 'true and inevitable' plan."

Kornai also criticizes approaches to planning which are based on simple applications of decision theory, pretending that there is a single decision-maker with well-defined aims or preferences. Such approaches tend to disregard conflicts and are based on an "over-optimistic hope in the power of strict rationality."

Kornai then launches his own characterization of planning: "*Planning: a process of cognition and compromise.* Planning is an instrument of cognition. The main purposes of planning are the *collection and careful evaluation of information* about the future. It helps in understanding our own desires, wishes, goals; and helps to confront them with the realities. It is a framework for the *exchange of information* and the co-ordination of otherwise independent activities. Since the activities of all participants of the economic system are mutually interdependent planning is a device to understand the interdependencies and to *reconcile the conflicting interests*."

This description is based on Kornai's practical experiences with planning, as well as theoretical considerations. It does not necessarily contradict other definitions. Definitions which are more one-sidedly based on theory may appear to conceive planning as a very rational, orderly, and tidy process, whereas definitions which are to a larger extent based on practice will reflect many sorts of imperfections. The orderly process according to theoretical definitions may stand as a sort of ideal towards which practical planning should try to move. It may therefore be useful to have both "ideal models", and definitions which reflect more of current practice. This may give rise to a sort of dialogue which may help to improve planning performance. However, if the gap is too large, then the "ideal models" may fail to give guidance and stimulus to practical planning and thus remain as academic exercises. It is apparently Kornai's view that this has happened to part of the literature and theory on methods of economic planning.

The problem about "conflicting interests" mentioned in Kornai's description is deeper and may throw doubt upon very much of the decision-theoretic approach to planning. We shall return to this issue in the discussion about planning versus a game approach to economic policy in a following chapter.

In these lectures we are concerned with *macro*economic planning, and the definitions surveyed above refer to this kind of planning. From a broader point of view there is of course economic planning at many levels, and there are correspondingly more general definitions of planning to be found in the literature. For instance, the British economist *L. Robbins*, whose discussion of the scope of economic science is well known, also discussed the concept of planning. He related the discussion to his definition of economic activity as activity involving the disposal of scarce goods. According to his definition (from 1937), "to plan is to act with purpose, to choose; and choice is the essence of economic activity." On the basis of such a general definition one naturally arrives at the conclusion that "strictly speaking, all economic life involves planning." In early debates on planning such viewpoints tended to confuse matters to some extent. Proposals for establishing a system of economic planning were met with arguments to the effect that economic activities are always and everywhere planned. It was then often not easy to see what the issue was about. Robbins, however, clarified this in his further discussion. He made it clear that "as soon as there is more than one individual planning, the different plans may not harmonize." This meant that "in the absence of coordination and authority, the one plan may be frustrated by the other ... The result of our separate planning may be disorder and chaos. To avoid this, to secure that social relations involve a greater realization of individual plans rather than their mutual frustration, a coordinating apparatus, a social order, a social plan is necessary. It is in this sense that the term plan figures in contemporary discussions of policy." (Robbins proceeded to distinguish between a liberal policy which aimed at creating a framework within which private plans might be harmonized, and "modern" proposals for planning which aimed at superseding private plans by public, "or at any rate to relegate them to a very subordinate position." This is a distinction which is pertinent to the distinction between what is in more recent literature called indicative versus imperative planning.)

An interesting aspect of Robbins' definition is his pointing out that "a coordinating apparatus, a social order, a social plan" is necessary in order to achieve "a greater realization of individual plans rather than their mutual frustration." Planning does accordingly not necessarily mean to subordinate individual desires and plans to those of a central authority, but it may in fact be a precondition for the fulfilment of the individual desires and plans. The "savings paradox" discussed in connection with Keynesian theory illustrates this clearly. In a depressive economy individual desires and plans to increase savings may easily prove to be mutually frustrating, but well-designed fiscal and monetary actions by a central authority may prevent this frustration and accordingly make the individual desires and plans come true.

An early and most remarkable general discussion of economic planning was given in a book by the Swedish economist *I. Svennilson* in 1938. On the background of the ideas developed by "the Swedish School of Economics", which emphasized dynamic economics by studying the interactions between expectations, plans and realizations, it was natural for him to elaborate the time dimension of the planning concept. Svennilson saw planning as being concerned with coordination into one plan of actions under different future periods. Having thus introduced the time dimension, he raised the question about new information which accrues during plan execution, and the possibilities of revising the plans. The actually realized development will be a sequence of pieces of successively initiated new plans, none of which are implemented in full. According to Svennilson this raises a planning problem of a higher order, namely the problem of designing a plan for how the lower-order plans should be revised in the light of information and experiences which are gained as time passes and which may contradict previously held expectations. This is in fact a general formulation of the *strategy* problem which is of paramount importance in modern theory of rational behaviour under uncertainty. Svennilson worked out the idea in more details for enterprise planning, but the general idea is equally important for macroeconomic planning. It helps, inter alia, to overcome the simplicist idea that a plan is something which should be unconditionally adhered to, and that revisions of plans are indications of deficient planning. We shall return to the strategy concept in the following chapter and in a chapter especially devoted to planning under uncertainty.

At the most general level the concept of planning is defined and elucidated in the branch of philosophy called *praxiology*. This is sometimes defined very broadly as the general theory of human action, sometimes more narrowly as the general theory of rational behaviour or rational use of means to achieve goals. (An outstanding praxiologist is the Polish philosopher *T. Kotarbinski*. Formal economic theory was considered as a branch of praxiology by the Russian mathematician, statistician and economist *E. Slutsky* in an interesting contribution from 1926. More recently the relationship between economics and praxiology has been discussed particularly by *O. Lange*.) In praxiology "plan" is part of the "preparations for later actions". Another element of the preparations consists of "tests", which means investigations of the possibilities of alternative actions. A third element is "cognitive substantiation" which means to gain knowledge about objective relationships relevant to the actions and goals. The general definition of a plan is then, as given by Kotarbinski: "description of a future possible choice and composition of actions united by a common goal." All elements mentioned here can be easily identified in the planning scheme which we shall develop in the following chapter.

New dimensions are added when actions have to be executed by more than one actor or agent. Then, in the terminology of praxiology, the "synchronization" of actions by the various agents becomes an essential consideration which necessitates flows of information and some sort of leadership. The organization of these aspects is then also considered as parts of "planning". We shall take up these aspects particularly in a chapter on centralized versus decentralized plan elaboration.

It is clear from these definitions and considerations that macro-economic planning as conceived by most authors referred to above could be seen as an application of praxiological principles to planning, decision-making and organization for the national economy.

None of the aspects brought forward by the definitions quoted above will be considered as lying completely outside the scope of these lectures, although not all aspects will be emphasized to the same degree. We could leave it at that, but as a sort of summary we may perhaps put down an eclectic definition drawing on those quoted above:

> Macroeconomic planning is an institutionalized activity by, or on behalf of a Central Authority for (a) the preparation of decisions and actions to be taken by the Central Authority, and (b) the coordination of decisions and actions by lower-order units of the economy, as between themselves and vis-à-vis the Central Authority, for the purpose of governing the development of the whole economy and its constituent parts so as to achieve certain (more or less detailed and more or less explicitly specified) goals for the economy and harmonize the development of the economy with broader non-economic goals.

It should be observed that this is a definition of macroeconomic planning as such; it is not an attempt at saying what is *good* planning. It would be to go beyond the purpose of a definition to include assertions which could be doubted or even falsified by reference to observed facts, although some of the definitions quoted above might be said to border on this. For instance, points (a) and (b) are included in the definition above only to make clear that both these aspects will be considered to belong to macroeconomic planning as conceived here; the definition does not say anything about how to strike the best balance between these two spheres of planning activity. Different economic systems will clearly differ with regard to the emphasis on (a) and (b), with socialist planned economies putting more weight on (a) and market-oriented economies with "indicative planning" emphasizing (b). But generally both elements will be present, cf. the definitions quoted above from *C. Landauer, G. Sirkin, V.S. Nemchinov* and *J. Kornai*. The insertion of the word "institutionalized" at the beginning of the definition refers to such considerations as were emphasized particularly by *R. Bícanić* so as to distinguish macroeconomic planning from various sorts of more incidental orientations about future economic development. The last element of the definition corresponds to considerations emphasized by *L. Rychetnik* and *O. Kyn.*

References for Section 1.4

R. Bícanić, *Problems of planning: East and west* (Mouton, The Hague, 1967).

G. Caire, *La planification* – See reference under Section 1.1.

H. D. Dickinson, *Economics of socialism* (London, 1938).

J. Kornai and L. Ujlaki, "Application of an aggregate programming model in five-year planning", *Acta Oeconomica* (1967).

J. Kornai, "The place of mathematical planning in the control of the economic system", Report prepared for the *United Nations Economic Commission for Europe, First Seminar on Mathematical Methods and Computer Techniques* (Varna, 1970).

T. Kotarbinski, *Praxiology: An introduction to the science of efficient action* (Pergamon Press, London, 1965).

K. Kouba, "The plan and market in a socialist economy", *Czechoslovak Economic Papers*, No. 11 (Academia, Prague, 1969).

C. Landauer, *Theory of national economic planning* – See reference under Section 1.1.

O. Lange, *Political economy: Vol. I, General problems* (Pergamon Press, London, 1963).

P. Massé, *Le plan ou l'anti-hasard* (Gallimard, Collection Idées, Paris, 1965).

F. Perroux, *Les techniques quantitatives de la planification* (Presses Universitaires de France, Paris, 1965).

H.C. Rieger, *Begriff und Logik der Planung* (Otto Harrassowitz, Wiesbaden, 1967).

L. Robbins, *Economic planning and international order* (MacMillan, London, 1937).

L. Rychetnik and O. Kyn, "Remarks on long-term prognosis of economic development of CSSR", *Mathematical studies in economics and statistics in the USSR and Eastern Europe* (IASP, 1966). Translation from Czechoslovakian.

G. Sirkin, *The visible hand: The fundamentals of economic planning* (McGraw-Hill, New York, 1968).

E. Slutsky, "Ein Beitrag zur formalpraxeologischen Grundlegung der Oekonomik", Supplement to *Annals of the social and economic branch of the Ukrainian Academy of Sciences*, Vol. IV (Kiev, 1926).

R. Stone, *A programme for growth, 5. The model in its environment* – See reference under Section 1.2.

I. Svennilson, *Ekonomisk planering* (Almquist & Wiksell, Uppsala, 1938).

1.5. Some Remarks on the Scope of the Lectures

The survey of definitions of macroeconomic planning given in the preceding section suggests the scope of these lectures. In particular, the lectures will treat problems pertaining to both the spheres (a) and (b) in the definition given towards the end of the preceding section, i.e., problems related both to the preparation of decisions and actions to be taken by the Central Authority and problems related to the coordination of decisions and actions by lower-order agents in the economy.

We shall mainly be concerned with *methods* of economic planning. We shall not go much more into the history of planning than we have already done, and we shall not attempt to give a systematic description of the systems of planning in various countries. However, we shall refer to factual evidence and concrete circumstances at various places in order to illustrate the use of various methods and to satisfy ourselves about the relevance of the problems treated.

As already pointed out, economic planning does not take place in a political vacuum. It is always conditioned by political circumstances, power relations and group or class interests. It may be planning for fulfilling goals of a central power complex, planning in the interest of one particular class of society or planning which, as a genuine aim or out of "political necessity", aims at striking a sort of balance between the different interest groups or classes. Many of the concepts, methods and techniques which we shall treat are relevant more or less independently of this broader setting. To characterize the planning in various countries according to such criteria as are suggested here, and to discuss the probable development of the nature of planning in various countries on such a background would be to go beyond the scope of these lectures. It would require much more of *political* economy and theory of economic systems. Some elements which we have already touched upon and also some of the themes which we shall treat in the following chapters would however be relevant, though not sufficient, for such a broader discussion of economic planning.

Not too much should be read into the statement that many of the methods and techniques to be treated in these lectures are relevant regardless of the broader purpose and political setting in which the planning takes place. Some methods are, for instance, particularly relevant in highly centralized economies, and others more relevant for decentralized, market-oriented economies. This will be discussed explicitly. Some assumptions will however remain more implicit. Many of the methods would, for instance, be irrelevant if we are not at all concerned with efficient utilization of resources. Some would be less interesting if we do not allow for some measure of consumer sovereignty, i.e., if we do not attempt to satisfy the needs of consumers as they themselves see the needs. If, for instance, concerns for the income distribution, or for problems of urbanization versus preservation of rural settlements, should be given absolute priority over total efficiency and the development of consumption, then the methods and models which we shall discuss would be, if not wrong or irrelevant, then at least not the most efficient, direct and suitable tools of analysis and planning.

Although we emphasize *macro*economic planning it is clear that many of the themes will be of relevance also to planning for smaller regions than a country and also for planning in spacial sectors – traditional production sectors as well as health, education, etc. We shall not go much into such applications since they would in any case require elements which are more specific in addition to the general ideas and methods to be presented in these lectures. A similar consideration applies to planning for developing countries. The methods and techniques to be treated here are important for planning also in such countries, but in addition many more special aspects need to be taken into account.

Technically we shall assume some prior knowledge of basic economic theory, including macroeconomic theory and basic elements of welfare theory. We also assume some knowledge of input–output analysis and linear programming, but not beyond the basic ideas and formulations. To the extent that we shall use analytical tools beyond these levels we shall state results and try to explain them intuitively rather than give mathematical proofs. When precise statements tend to be too complicated we shall make do with statements and arguments which are roughly correct for practical purposes though not mathematically complete, and instead refer to the more specialized literature for more rigorous treatment. I think this is the only possible way to proceed if a rather broad survey of problems and methods shall be within reach, since theory and methods from so many different fields are involved. It would give a wrong impression to pretend that macroeconomic planning is so well-defined and narrow a field that the relevant theories and methods could be given a rigorous treatment and all analytical results proved within a lecture series of reasonable extension.

The overall strategy of the lectures is to start with rather broad and general themes – the start having already been made in this chapter – and then from chapter to chapter to take up themes of a more specialized nature.

Although we emphasize methods and techniques, this is not meant to imply that these are *sufficient* for successful planning. As a terse statement as well as an inspiration and challenge, I think one can do no better than quoting from *Barbara Wootton's* (1934) description of the conditions for successful planning: "Successful planning is dependent before everything upon knowledge and the ability to use that knowledge. It demands the most detailed information about the scale of existing production and trade, the distribution of income between different classes in the community, the organization and the limiting technical conditions in every industry, the age-composition and geographical grouping of the population – to mention only a few of the larger and more obvious matters. And it requires moreover an extremely high standard of administrative competence and integrity. Planning even for a fairly small and homogeneous community, much more for one like our own, is an extremely big job; and it cannot be effectively carried out by people who are stupid, careless or inaccurate, or whose minds are cluttered with vague generalities or with undigested detail, or who are ready to alter their course to suit the highest bidder."

Reference for Section 1.5

Barbara Wootton, *Plan or no plan* (Victor Gollancz, London, 1934).

Chapter 2

A DECISION-THEORETIC SCHEME OF PLANNING AND RELATED CONCEPTS

2.1. The Basic Scheme

The most orderly scheme of planning is obtained if we think of a central decision-maker as one central authority with a well-defined preference scale and a well-defined set of instruments at its disposal for governing the economy according to this preference scale. This scheme is too much simplified to reflect actual planning problems and practices (recall for instance the references to J. *Kornai's* discussion of the concept of planning in Section 1.4), but it is useful as a starting point and as a background for the more realistic schemes. With suitable interpretations of the elements involved and with appropriate constraints added such a scheme may also be useful in practice. In this chapter we shall first consider the simple scheme, then the more realistic and complicated schemes, and finally, return to the simple scheme and discuss its usefulness on the background thus obtained.

The basic elements of the simple decision-theoretic scheme are the following:

(1) a: This symbol represents *a possible policy* for the Central Authority, described in terms of what the Central Authority can directly decide upon, i.e., not in terms of what it intends, desires or hopes to achieve. The Authority will have at its disposal a set of policy *instruments* which can be used in various ways, such as tax rates, government expenditures, instruments of monetary and credit policy, some direct decisions about production and so on. If the various policies differ only quantitatively from each other, then we could think of a as a (very large) vector indicating the values assigned to all these instruments. If not all differences between possible policies can be characterized quantitatively, then a must be interpreted more generally as a complete description of a set of policy actions which can be taken in qualitative as well as quantitative terms.

(2) A: This is the set of all possible policies, i.e., a set such that any policy $a \in A$ (element a belongs to the set A) is a possible

policy, whereas any $a \notin A$ (element a not belonging to the set A) is ruled out by one or more conditions constraining the range of possible policies. The constraints delimiting the set A may be institutional, political, physical, or may have other origins.

(3) z: This represents factors which influence the development of the economy, but which are beyond direct or indirect control of the Central Authority. We shall call them non-controlled exogenous factors (or often only exogenous factors). Obvious examples are weather conditions of importance for agriculture and fishery, but for a relatively small country many elements of the development on "world markets" may also be taken as non-controlled and exogenous. In most practical cases we may think of z as a vector of variables.

(4) Z: This is the set of all possible states of the non-controlled exogenous factors, i.e., we have $z \in Z$. For the moment we do not go more deeply into this, but we shall give other formulations in connection with the treatment of planning under uncertainty in a later chapter.

(5) x: This represents a description of the state of the economy. In particular x includes a description of all those aspects of the state of the economy which are relevant to the preferences of the Central Authority. In aggregated terms it would be a list of figures for national product, comsumption, perhaps indicators of income distribution and so on. In principle, the description has to be as detailed as required by the Central Authority in order to judge about the desirability of the state. If only quantitatively different situations are under consideration we may think of x as a vector.

(6) X: This is the set of possible states of the economy, i.e., we must have $x \in X$. The set X is constrained by the set of possible policies A and the set of possible states of the exogenous factors Z in conjunction with the relationships described below under (7).

(7) $x = f(a, z)$:   This represents the working of the economic system or mechanism for which one is planning. The meaning is

the following: The state of the economy x is a function of the policy pursued by the Central Authority a and the exogenous factors z, i.e., to every pair (a, z) consisting of a possible policy a and a possible constellation of the exogenous elements z there corresponds a state or result x, and the form of this dependency is symbolized by f. This is a highly condensed, symbolic representation. In the most simple quantitative case x, a and z are all vectors. The actual functioning of the economy might be simulated or modelled by a set of equations. These would usually not directly give the state of the economy x as a function of a and z, but assuming that there corresponds a unique state of the economy to every policy and constellation of exogenous factors, the equations must implicitly define x as a function of a and z. in the terminology of model building $x = f(a, z)$ represents the *reduced form* of the model. In a similar way the "original" relationships in the general case with qualitative aspects involved will also define $x = f(a, z)$ implicitly. The fact that we symbolize the functioning of the economy by $x = f(a, z)$ does not mean that an explicit mathematical or numerical reduced form can actually be written down, but only that there corresponds a unique x to every a, z.

(8) $W(x)$: This represents the preference scale of the Central Authority. We might in general think of this as an ordering of the elements x of the set of possible states X. This ordering may not necessarily be representable by a function. However, for simplicity, and because this is likely to be sufficient for practical purposes, we shall assume that the preferences are representable by a function $W(x)$ which to every x in X assigns a value in such a way that if two elements x' and x'', both belonging to X, are equally desirable according to the preferences of the Central Authority, then $W(x') = W(x'')$, and if x' is preferable to x'', then $W(x') > W(x'')$.

(9) X_z: In addition to the elements introduced above it will sometimes be useful to have a special symbol for the set of states x which are possible when the exogenous elements z are given. Such a set will be symbolized by X_z. The full set of possible states X is then the union of all X_z for $z \in Z$.

Leif Johansen

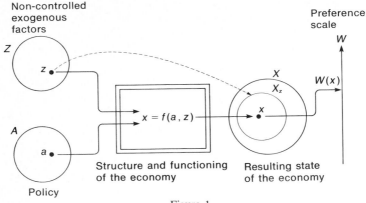

Figure 1

The relationships between these elements are indicated in Figure 1. The figure illustrates that the policy a is an element of the set of possible policies A, and the constellation of exogenous factors z is an element of the set Z of possible constellations of these factors. These two elements together act as inputs into the "model" or "structure of the economy" and produce a state of the economy x which is an element of the set X of possible states, or more specifically an element of the set X_z determined by the exogenous elements z as suggested by the dashed line.

The set X of possible states of the economy is generated by varying the policy a and the exogenous factors z over their possible sets A and Z. This means that any state x belonging to X can be produced by $x = f(a, z)$ for some a belonging to A and some z belonging to Z, whereas any x not belonging to X cannot be so produced. Similarly any x belonging to X_z for some specified z can be produced by some $a \in A$ while z is kept fixed, whereas any x not belonging to X_z cannot be so produced. Accordingly the sets X and X_z are not independent of, but determined by the sets A and Z (or by z in the case of X_z) via the function f.

In this description we have let the preference function W depend only upon the state of the economy, not upon the policy as represented by a. Sometimes there are clearly preferences attached also to policy instruments directly under the control of the Government, i.e., to components of a. This may apply for instance to some government expenditures which express desirable things in themselves besides being instruments which influence other parts of the economy. In such cases we may let the components of a reappear as part of the description of the state of the economy x, and the identity between some components of a and some components of x are counted as part of the structure $x = f(a, z)$. By this convention we may use the simplified scheme outlined above without restricting its generality. However, if it is found convenient and useful for clarification one may of course introduce $W(a, x)$ instead of simply $W(x)$, and correspondingly avoid repeating the instruments in question in the description of x. Whether we use the form $W(x)$ or $W(a, x)$ the function W will in practice only depend on *some* of the elements in x or a, x. We could then introduce special symbols for those parts of x, or a, x which actually count in the preference function. For the moment this is however not necessary.

For the elaboration of economic policy the presence of the exogenous factors z is of course a disturbing fact. As we shall argue in a later chapter, the best way of treating this element may be to consider it as stochastic. Then the random variation in z will be transformed to the state x so that this should also be considered as stochastic. To each policy a would then correspond a probability distribution for the state of the economy, and we must formulate preferences concerning choice between probability distributions for the state of the economy. In the meantime we shall however make the simple assumption that the planners predict the exogenous factors z and that they proceed on the basis of these predictions as if they are absolutely reliable.

The elaboration of the best plan would then consist of the following steps:

1. Delimit the set of possible policies A.
2. Find out about the structure of the economy and its mode of functioning, i.e., construct the model represented symbolically above by $x = f(a, z)$. This step includes the establishing of the list of exogenous factors influencing x.
3. Establish the preference function $W(x)$.
4. Predict the exogenous elements z.
5. For the values of the exogenous factors predicted in step 4, search through the possible policies a in the set A so as to find the one (or one of those) which gives the highest value of the preference function $W(x)$.

Symbolically the best policy, determined by step 5, is a policy a^* which satisfies the following relation:

$$(10) \qquad W(f(a^*, z)) = \underset{a \in A}{\text{Max}} \; W(f(a, z)) \quad \text{for given (forecasted) } z.$$

The corresponding state of the economy x^*, which we may call the *target* since it is the state aimed at by specifying the instruments at a^*, is given by

$$(11) \qquad x^* = f(a^*, z) \quad \text{for given (forecasted) } z.$$

This target could evidently also be indicated by

$$(12) \qquad W(x^*) = \underset{x \in X_z}{\text{Max}} \; W(x) \quad \text{for given (forecasted) } z.$$

In practice the various steps in the procedure cannot be carried out in a unidirected sequence like 1–5 above, each step being completed without considerations for the following steps. Some sort of initial overall orientation will in any case be necessary. In order to make a meaningful beginning by step 1 – the determination of the set of possible policies A – one must first have some idea about which variables will enter the preference function, so as not to overburden A by including instruments of no relevance for those aspects of the state of the economy to which there are attached preferences. Under point 3 the preference function $W(x)$ should be established over the full set X, but anticipating the results of step 4 one might do with establishing $W(x)$ over a smaller set deemed realistic in view of the neighbourhood in Z where the forecast of z is expected to lie. The steps preceding the final step must result in a structure which is not too complicated for the final optimization. However, for the time being we are concerned with a stylized picture, assuming away many practical difficulties. We shall return to practical problems and ways to overcome them, by simplifications and compromises, in Chapter 3.

A further observation should be made concerning step 1. It is of no use to enlarge A by including irrelevant instruments, i.e., "instruments" which do not affect x. But expansions of A by including additional relevant instruments and by widening the ranges of variation for the instruments will increase the set of possible states X and may accordingly raise the attainable maximum for $W(x)$ in (10).

Establishing A is not only a question of exploring facts, i.e., finding out what *is*, but also a question of inventiveness.

A very simple illustration of the scheme outlined above would be the following. Let the Government of a country be concerned with the development of national product and the balance of trade. The description x of the state of the economy must then include these variables (alongside with other variables which may be necessary for constructing the model represented by f), and the preference function W would be a function of the same two variables. The Government has at its disposal various elements of government expenditure and taxation, whereas exports and private investment are considered as non-controlled and exogenously determined. The set A would consist of possible constellations of government expenditures and tax parameters, whereas the set Z would consist of possible constellations of exports and private investment. An ordinary macro-economic multiplier model would give national product and imports as functions of the instrument variables and the non-controlled exogenous variables. For given (forecasted) values of exports and private investment, variations in the policy parameters within A would generate the set of possible states of the economy, including possible values of national product and the trade balance. In addition to the multiplier equations there may be capacity constraints further restricting the set of possible states of the economy. The resulting set corresponds to X_2 in the general notations. This set of possible states will for plausible values of the various multipliers have a frontier indicating a trade-off between national product and export surplus so that a higher national product can be "bought" at the cost of a smaller export surplus (because instrument variations which tend to increase national product also cause increases in imports while exports are exogenously determined). The preference function W will pick out the best state x^* among the possible constellations of national product and trade balance, and through the multiplier model we can trace the policy a^* (or one of the policies) which will generate this best result.

The case described here is suggested in Figure 2, which is analogous to Figure 1. In the figure G and t represent government expenditure and an income tax rate. A is a rectangular region in the G, t-plane. Exports and private investment are the exogenous elements, and one particular constellation is picked as the forecast of these elements. Through a multiplier model these inputs produce a

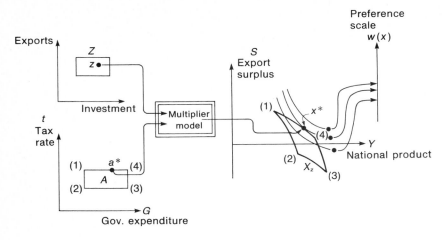

Figure 2

result in terms of national product Y and export surplus S. Thus x is now a Y, S-point. The set X_z is a region in the Y, S-plane. It may be as suggested in the figure. We assume that there are some non-linear effects involved (otherwise X_z would be a parallelogram in the Y, S-space). We assume that we can trace the boundary of X_z by moving around the boundary of A in the G, t-plane. (This is not always true; with sufficiently strong non-linearities involved a boundary point of X_z might be generated by an interior point in A.) We start from the most contractive policy represented by point (1) in the G, t-plane, which produces (for the given export and private investment) the point (1) in the Y, S-plane. Reduce taxes towards (2) in the G, t-plane. Then national income increases and the export surplus deteriorates so that the result approaches (2) in the Y, S-plane. Then expand government expenditures towards (3) in the G, t-plane. Then Y expands and S deteriorates further. There is a kink at point (2) in the Y, S-plane which may be due to the fact that government expenditures imply less imports in proportion to domestic goods and services than released private purchasing power. From (3), increase the tax rate towards (4), and further decrease government expenditures towards (1) again. A move from (4) to (3) is similar to the move from (1) to (2) already considered, but it takes place at a higher degree of capacity utilization and is therefore likely to involve more of changes in S in proportion to Y. In the same way a move (1) to (4) is similar to, but not identical in its effect with a move from (2) to (3). With regard to further details the curved shape of the boundaries of X_z may be due to differences in the marginal propensity to consume and the composition of demand with regard to imports versus domestic products at low and high income levels, as well as price effects as one approaches full capacity utilization. The most expansive policy (3) may for instance represent practically full capacity utilization.

In the Y, S-plane we have introduced indifference curves corresponding to a preference function $W(Y, S)$ and indicated the corresponding levels for W. We see that x^* is the best attainable point. This corresponds to a point situated at a^* in the set A, i.e., a point with a maximal tax rate and an intermediate level for government expenditure. With preferences more one-sidely concerned with national product one might get a solution nearer to (3), and with preferences representing a stronger concern for the balance of trade one might get a solution nearer to (1).

In the present case it is clear that (1)–(4)–(3) represents the "efficiency frontier". If government expenditures were taken into account in the preference function and preferences were attached to the division of total expenditure between private and public expenditure (as is realistic), then the possibility set X should be a set (in this case a surface) in the Y, S, G-space. Then a solution in the *interior* of the set A in the G, t-plane might be optimal.

We do not write out the formulas for the example discussed above and do not try to justify the shapes of the various sets and boundaries precisely since the main point is to illustrate the concepts, not to discuss a particularly realistic or theoretically interesting case.

If we now compare the simple scheme set out above with the definitions of planning discussed in Section 1.4, it soon appears to be too simple. With certain amendments and interpretations it can, however, be useful also in contexts where it does not immediately appear to be the appropriate formalization.

As it stands the scheme corresponds rather closely to the praxiological scheme for the case of one authority. It is easy to associate steps in the planning procedure leading to (10) with elements in the description of planning given for instance by *T. Kotarbinski* as quoted in Section 1.4.

The scheme in the form used above appears to be timeless or static.

However, by suitable interpretations the scheme can be used to cover also the time dimension of planning. We shall return to this in Section 2.6 of this chapter.

As soon as one admits the fact that there are more than one agent which is big enough so as not to have a behaviour appropriately represented as part of the "passive" structure symbolized by $x = f(a, z)$, and also conflicting interests, then the situation gets much more complicated. We shall take this up in Sections 2.2–2.4 below. In the same context we will then also give a more precise meaning to the concept of "coordination" which enters several of the definitions of planning, including the summarizing definition given at the end of Section 1.4.

In the remainder of this chapter we shall discuss interpretations and elaborations of the simple scheme given above and introduce some other useful concepts which can be defined in relation to this scheme.

The scheme presented in this section underlies planning methods advocated by *R. Frisch*, *J. Tinbergen* and others although the formulation is not quite the same on all points. For practical reasons they have proposed various types of simplifications of the scheme, to be discussed in Chapter 3. The works cited below use decision-theory schemes somewhat related to the one introduced here and elaborate special aspects further.

References for Section 2.1

J.L. Cochrane, "Optimal macroeconomic policies", *The Economic Journal* (1975).

M. Deleau and P. Malgrange, "Information et politiques dynamiques contraléatoires", *Annales de l'INSEE* 9 (1972).

R. Radner, "Mathematical specification of goals for decision problems", in *Human judgements and optimality*, edited by M.W. Shelly and G.L. Bryan (New York and London, 1964).

2.2. Team Theory and Game Theory Approaches

The simple decision-theoretic scheme of planning outlined in the preceding section assumed on one side a single central authority with a well-defined preference scale and on the other side the rest of the economy, the structure and behaviour of which could be described by a model symbolically represented by $x = f(a, z)$. A more realistic scheme will be obtained if we single out some of the larger decision-makers outside the Central Authority and let them be explicitly represented by their preference scales and ranges of possible actions. They may be institutions not directly governed by the Central Authority, various sorts of organizations, and big enterprises. Let there be N such non-central decision-makers. In addition to the concepts and symbols introduced in the preceding section, we then need the following:

(13) d_i: In the same way as a by (1) describes a possible policy for the Central Authority, d_i describes a possible decision by non-central decision-maker no. i. What is here represented by d_i will in practice consist of a number of components. If only quantitatively different alternatives are open, then d_i may be thought of as a vector.

(14) D_i: Similarly to A for the Central Authority, D_i is the set of all possible decisions which can be taken by non-central decision-maker no. i.

(15) $x = f(a, d_1, d_2, \ldots, d_N, z)$: This now replaces the expression (7) in Section 2.1, since the resulting state of the economy will now in general depend upon the actions taken by the non-central decision-makers as well as the policy decided by the Central Authority.

(16) $U_i(x)$: In the same way as the previously introduced $W(x)$ represents the preferences of the Central Authority, $U_i(x)$ re-

Leif Johansen

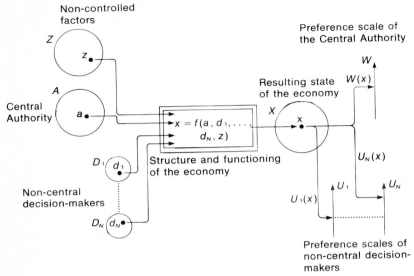

Figure 3

presents the preference scale of non-central decision-maker no. *i*.

The expanded scheme obtained when these concepts are introduced, is illustrated in Figure 3.

In Section 2.1 we assumed that the description x of the state of the economy was sufficiently detailed to give all information necessary for the Central Authority to evaluate the desirability of the state. In the present case x must contain sufficient information not only for the preferences of the Central Authority, but also for the preferences of all other specified decision-makers. In principle we let W, as well as all $U_1, \ldots, U_N$ depend upon the complete specification contained in x. In practice U_i will depend effectively upon only a limited number of components of x. If decision-maker no. *i* is an organization of enterprises in a certain branch of the economy, then the corresponding preference function will depend primarily upon those components of x which describe the development of the economic indicators for this branch. But the general scheme admits the possibility that some components of x enter all preference functions, i.e., that there are some aspects of the state of the economy which concern all the decision-makers.

The set X of possible resulting states is now generated by letting a vary over all A, d_1 over all $D_1, \ldots, d_N$ over all D_N, and z over all Z. As in the preceding case we could also introduce X_z as the set of all possibilities corresponding to a given constellation of the non-controlled exogenous factors z.

We may now give two different interpretations of this general scheme (but a combination of these two interpretations is also possible).

We first consider the *team interpretation*. A team is a group of people collaborating in solving a common problem, performing a common task or working for the same purpose, but in such a way that each member of the team has some scope for independent actions and some information not necessarily available to the other members. The running of a big and complicated economy is too big a task for it to be manageable by one authority deciding on everything and giving unambiguous commands to all lower echelons. Even if the Central Authority in principle has all power (an extremely unrealistic idea), it must therefore delegate power to take decisions within some ranges to other agents who are considered as members of a team, and at the same time instruct them with regard to the goals they shall pursue. These goals may be simpler and more partial than the overall goal of the Central Authority. This will then be done in such a way that the pursuit of these more partial goals helps to reach the overall goal. In this case we may interpret $W(x)$ as representing the overall goal whereas the preference functions $U_1(x), \ldots, U_N(x)$ are somehow derived from $W(x)$, the intention being that when decision-maker no. i pursues the maximization of $U_i(x)$ by means of his decision d_i, he helps to reach a high value of the overall preference function $W(x)$.

Besides the problem of stipulating the preference functions for the various decision-makers or members of the team, a decisive question for the success of the operations of the team is the dilimitation of the sets of possible decisions $D_1, \ldots, D_N$. (The stipulation of the preference function and the delimitation of the sets of possible decisions can of course not be seen as separate problems.) A main concern should here be the problem of information. The purpose of the delegation of power to take decisions is partly to circumvent the need to collect and process all relevant information in one central planning agency. The operations of the team should therefore be designed in

such a way that the decisions of the various units could be taken on
the basis of different pieces and amounts of information, none of the
units holding and using all information which is available somewhere
in the system. There would be a network of information exchanges,
some information being given as general information to all decision-
makers, and some having specific contents and specific addressees.
Very much of team theory is concerned exactly with the problem of
designing efficient systems of exchange of information for decision-
making, taking into account the costs of collecting, transmitting and
processing the information.

Recalling the discussion of definitions of economic planning in
Section 1.4, the idea that *laissez-faire* might be "a perfectly coherent
plan for operating an economic system" refers to the fact that, under
some ideal conditions, the individual pursuit of profits and utility
maximum can be interpreted as a well-designed team solution for the
purpose of reaching efficient use of resources with a limited amount
of exchange of information. As shown in economic welfare theory
prices are indeed very efficient carriers of relevant information to
individual decision-makers.

The elements of *V.S. Nemchinov's* description of planning, also
quoted in Section 1.4, can be associated with the elements of the
scheme above interpreted as a team. In his description there is a
Central Authority which reserves for itself the most important functions, and issues directives to the other decision-makers, but at the
same time transfers "a considerable mass of problems connected with
economic planning to the leadership of local organs." In other words,
many important decisions should belong to the sphere represented by
A in our scheme, and the Central Authority should also decide on the
"principles of planning", which inter alia means deciding about the
sets of possible decisions D_i of the other decision-makers. The
allusion to the "principle of democratic centralism" in Nemchinov's
description may be taken to refer to the requirement that the non-
central decision-makers should not pursue goals which do not comply
with the overall goal as defined by the Central Authority.

Also the theory of decomposition in connection with programming
for overall optimization, which was mentioned in Section 1.3 and to
which we shall return in a later chapter, can be seen as a theory of
how to design efficient teams for solving large problems. The same
applies to some of the ideas put forward in discussions on the
economics of socialism mentioned on some occasions previously, in

particular the so-called "competitive socialism" where enterprises under socialist ownership simulate competitive behaviour. In this system price-setting by a central agency and supply and demand responses to the prices constitute the system of information exchange.

The team interpretation of the scheme given above admits, and aims at overcoming, difficulties of coordination, but it assumes harmony of interests. The individual preference functions $U_1(x), \ldots, U_N(x)$ are in a team setting structured so as to support the reaching of the maximum value of the overall preference function $W(x)$. This is different in the *game interpretation* of the scheme. In this case we admit that the various non-central decision-makers have their own preferences which may be in conflict as between themselves, and also opposed to the preferences of the Central Authority. The attempt of decision-maker no. i to maximize $U_i(x)$ by choosing his decision d_i in his set of possible decisions D_i will then not necessarily help to reach the maximal value of the preference function of the Central Authority $W(x)$. For the Central Authority the level reached for the preference function W now depends on all decisions by

$$(17) \qquad W = W(f(a, d_1, \ldots, d_N, z)),$$

and similarly the level reached for the preference function of non-central decision-maker no. i is

$$(18) \qquad U_i = U_i(f(a, d_1, \ldots, d_i, \ldots, d_N, z)), \qquad i = 1, \ldots, N.$$

In the introduction to this section we remarked that "a more realistic scheme will be obtained if we single out some of the *larger* decision-makers outside the Central Authority ...". The point suggested by describing the decision-makers represented by $i = 1, \ldots, N$ as being "larger" is that all these decision-makers, in contrast to the "smaller" ones, have a perceptible influence in (17)–(18) through their decisions d_i, and secondly that all of them (as well as the Central Authority) understand the situation as described by (17)–(18) and make their decisions on the basis of this understanding. (This is the assumption in the most common classes of games which have been studied theoretically, but one may of course easily conceive of games where some or all players have wrong or incomplete information or misunderstand the situation.)

If now the situation were such that every change in a decision by decision-maker no. i, say from d'_i to d''_i, which raises the value of U_i, also raises, or at least leaves unaffected, the values of all other $U_1, \ldots, U_N$ and W, and this holds good regardless of a and all other $d_1, \ldots, d_N$, then there would be a perfect harmony of interest. In general, however, this will not be the case, i.e., we will have a game involving at least some degree of conflict.

Classical theory of maximization of functions is not sufficient to solve the problem for the decision-makers, including the Central Authority, when the situation is as described by (17)–(18) with inherent conflicts. *J. von Neumann* and *O. Morgenstern*, the founders of the theory of games as applied to economic problems, describe such a situation in the following terms: "Thus each participant attempts to maximize a function of which he does not control all variables. This is certainly no maximum problem, but a peculiar and disconcerting mixture of several conflicting maximum problems. Every participant is guided by another principle and neither determines all variables which affect his interest." The fact that every participant is a conscious player, understanding the implications of (17)–(18), corresponds to the following statement by von Neumann and Morgenstern: "Every participant can determine the variables which describe his own actions but not those of the others. Nevertheless those 'alien' variables cannot, from his point of view, be described by statistical assumptions. This is because the others are guided, just as he himself, by rational principles – whatever that may mean – and no *modus procedendi* can be correct which does not attempt to understand those principles and interactions of the conflicting interests of all participants."

Just to make clear that such a situation creates a difficult problem, consider Figure 4. We here let element a, the decision chosen by the Central Authority, represent one single variable; on the other hand, we let there be only one non-central decision-maker who controls a variable denoted by d. We neglect the influence of exogenous variables z. In this case the preference function of the Central Authority W will, through $f(a, d)$, depend on a and d, and similarly the preference function of the non-central decision-maker, now denoted by U, will also depend on the same variables. The contour lines of the functions in the a, d-plane may be as shown in the figure. If the Central Authority could control both variables, then it would choose a', d', and similarly the non-central decision-maker would

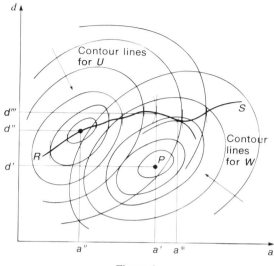

Figure 4.

prefer a'', d''. However, none of them is in control of both variables; the Central Authority controls only a and the other decision-maker controls only d. If nevertheless the Central Authority should choose a', then it would be frustrated in the hope of reaching the point P in the diagram (which maximizes W) since, if the other decision-maker knew about the choice of a', it would itself choose d''' which maximizes U given that a takes the value a'. On the other hand, the Central Authority cannot take for granted that the other decision-maker will choose d'' and adapt a to this so as to maximize W; if the other decision-maker anticipated such an adaptation of a, then he would himself find a better alternative than d''.

We shall not pursue these ideas further at this stage. The point now is simply to make clear that a game situation cannot be resolved simply by using classical methods of maximization. The combination of the facts that each participant is in control of only some of the relevant variables and that there are conflicting preferences, and furthermore that each participant is a rational player who understands the conflicts and mutual interdependencies and realizes that the other players are equally knowledgeable and intelligent, creates a problem to which it is difficult to find a unique solution. In particular, it is difficult to find out what would be a rational decision by the Central Authority in its efforts to reach a maximal value of *W*.

In the theory of games one distinguishes between many types of games and many types of solution concepts. Exact solutions are worked out only for very stylized and simple games. The simplest type of games are so-called constant sum games in which the result for each player is measurable in such a way that it is meaningful to speak about the total gain for all players, and furthermore, this total gain is restricted to a constant value regardless of the actions taken by the players. That means that we have a situation of pure conflict since an improvement in the result for one player must always take place at the cost of some other player. Furthermore, this type of game is most completely and convincingly solved for the case of only two players. As soon as the total gain is not restricted to be a constant, the game gets more complicated because there will then be a mixture of common and conflicting interests: Common interests, since all players are in a way interested in a large total gain, but on the other hand, conflicts about the distribution of the gain. Even for a constant sum game the case of more than two players causes complications because of the possibility of forming coalitions. In a game corresponding to situations of economic planning and policy we will typically have more than two players and also variable sum games, i.e., mixtures of common and conflicting interests. Game theory is not able to devise general rules of rational behaviour in such games, and we shall therefore not go into the formalities of such game theory. It is nevertheless useful to have the problem described as a game problem as a background for the further discussion.

The literature on game theory is by now enormous, but there is not much which relates game considerations explicitly to economic planning. The Swedish economist *K.O. Faxén* rather early (1957) recognized the need for studying monetary and fiscal policy in a sort of game setting, and developed some ideas along these lines. In the preface to his book he made the following statement: "One of the characteristic features of a society containing big firms engaged in long-term planning is that the Government's economic policy and the firms' actions are interdependent. The relations between the Government and the firms become in important respects analogous to game situations." In some recent works *F. Kydland* and *E.C. Prescott* have studied stabilization policy as a sort of game between the Government and other decision-makers in the economy, resolving the indeterminacy of the general game description by making the specific assumption that the Government always makes the decisions before the other players. In the simple situation in Figure 4 this means that the Central Authority would choose a first, and next the other decision-maker would choose d. The Central Authority would then know that for every possible choice of a which it might make, the other player would choose the decision d corresponding to the point on the line RS in the figure which connects points of vertical tangents to the contour lines for the preference function U since these maximize U with respect to d for given values of a. The Central Authority would then choose the policy a^* which produces the situation on RS which yields the highest value of W, that means the point of tangency between RS and a contour line of W.

In the field of international relations there are many potential applications of game approaches. Any country with foreign trade or other international economic relations is in principle in a game situation, since each country controls only its own instruments of policy, whereas the final outcome for each country depends upon the decisions taken by all countries with respect to their instruments. Some attempts have been made to study stabilization problems in a system of economically interrelated countries on the basis of game theory. (See for instance *H. Myoken.*) For the socialist countries some tentative studies on the basis of game theory have been made concerning the coordination of economic plans through CMEA (COMECON). A special problem which has been formulated rather naturally as a game problem is related to decisions about speci-alization of production. Such decisions are taken on the basis of forecasts of productivity or cost developement some years ahead in the various countries. These forecasts are also decisive for the prices stipulated for these commodities in the trade between the countries. The forecasts are supplied – simultaneously and independently – by the individual countries. The countries have preferences with regard to the final outcome of the decision process concerning the assign-ment of production tasks. Because of many uncertainties the pre-paration of the forecasts is not a task which can be solved on a purely objective basis, and within reasonable bounds the forecasts can be chosen with a view to the effects they may have on the final decision. The more favourable forecasts a country supplies with regard to the development of productivity in the production of a certain com-modity, the more likely will it be that this country will be assigned the task of specializing on this commodity. This may be desirable for the country. However, a favourable forecast also tends to bring the price down. Hence if a member country submits too optimistic a forecast and captures the production task on such a basis, then it may run into trouble because of unprofitable production. The whole mechanism is a typical game situation with the forecasts submitted representing the decisions of the individual players and the decision process of the CMEA with regard to prices and production assignments (together with actual production and cost developments) representing the function which transforms the collection of individual decisions into results for all players.

In spite of some such tentative applications to special and limited or partial problems, game theory is not – or rather not yet – sufficiently well-developed so as to form a good methodological basis for economic planning more in general. However, as already suggested, concepts and viewpoints from game theory are useful as a background even if we end up in practice with using a formalization more like the decision-theoretic approach. This will be further developed in the following sections.

References for Section 2.2

K.O. Faxén, *Monetary and fiscal policy under uncertainty*, Stockholm Economic Studies, New Series 1 (Stockholm, 1957).

L. Johansen, "Planlegging og spill", in *Økonomi og politikk*, 15 artikler tilegnet Ole Myrvoll (H. Aschehoug & Co., Oslo, 1971).

F. Kydland, "Noncooperative and dominant player solutions in discrete dynamic stochastic games", *Discussion Paper* (Norwegian School of Economics and Business Administration, Bergen, 1973).

F. Kydland and E.C. Prescott, "Optimal stabilization policy: A new formulation", *Discussion Paper* (Norwegian School of Economics and Business Administration, Bergen, 1973).

R.D. Luce and H. Raiffa, *Games and decisions* (Wiley, New York, 1957).

J. Marschak and R. Radner, *Economic theory of teams*, Cowles Commission Monograph No. 22 (Yale University Press, New Haven, 1972).

H. Myoken, "Non-zero-sum differential games for the balance-of-payments adjustments in an open economy", *International Journal of Systems Science* (1975).

J. von Neumann and O. Morgenstern, *Theory of games and economic behaviour* (Princeton University Press, Princeton, 1953). First edition in 1944.

G. Owen, *Game theory* (Saunders, Philadelphia, 1968).

H. Schleicher, *Staatshaushalt und Strategie* (Duncker & Humblot, Berlin, 1971).

W. Sledzinski, "A game-theoretic model of forecasting phenomena which partly depend on the will of a forecaster", Paper presented at *The Econometric Society Winter Seminar* (1974).

2.3. Non-cooperative and Cooperative Games – The Coordination Aspect of Economic Planning

In the definition of economic planning which concluded Section 1.4, we distinguished between two aspects of planning: in the first place, the preparation of decisions and actions to be taken by the Central Authority, and in the second place, the coordination of decisions and actions by lower-order units of the economy. If the planning situation corresponds to the simple decision-theoretic scheme presented in Section 2.1, then there is room only for the first one of these aspects, the preparation of decisions and actions by the Central Authority which then means carrying out the steps which lead to the plan defined by (10). (We neglect, in this discussion, the fact that the Central Authority is in itself a complex organization with a need for internal coordination.) If the realities are more correctly described by the scheme presented in Section 2.2, where there are other decision-makers in a game position vis-à-vis the Central Authority, then there is scope for both the aspects of planning comprised by the definition in Section 1.4. Coordination would then mean influencing in one way or other the decisions taken by other decision-makers so that they, jointly with the decisions regarding the instruments of the Central Authority, produce a good result as measured by the preference scale $W(x)$.

At this point one might raise the question as to whether the Central Authority should not also take into account the preferences of the other decision-makers. Although it may be problematic in practice, I think we may distinguish conceptually between two ways in which the preferences of the other decision-makers can or should be taken into account by the Central Authority. In the first place, so to speak before the game starts, the preference function of the Central Authority may reflect the preferences of the other decision-makers by being a function of these preference levels. The preference function $W(x)$ may for instance be of the following form:

(19) $W(x) = F(U_1(x), \ldots, U_N(x), V(x))$,

where $V(x)$ now represents some sort of welfare function for other agents in the economy than those who belong to the class of specified decision-makers nos. $1, \ldots, N$. Then the preference function $W(x)$ already performs the task of comparing and weighting against each other the interests of the various decision-makers, both those especially so designated and the "anonymous" ones. In pursuing the maximization of W the Central Authority then takes into account the preferences of the other decision-makers, but does in general not follow any one of them completely when there are conflicts between the evaluations expressed by $U_1, \ldots, U_N$ and V. This is one way in which the Central Authority may take into account the preferences of the non-central decision-makers; we may perhaps say that this is a free or voluntary consideration by the Central Authority. (As a result of the political processes the Central Authority may of course be compelled to, or feel committed to pay special attention to the interests of special groups, i.e., to give especially high weights to some of the kernels $U_1, \ldots, U_N, V$ in F in (19). The words "free and voluntary" should accordingly not be taken in an absolute sense.) Now in the set of decisions constituting the game, each one of the other decision-makers will pursue the maximization of his individual preference function $U_i(x)$. In deciding its own strategy, the choice of a, the Central Authority must take into account also what strategies the other decision-maker may choose, i.e., which collection of decisions $d_1, \ldots, d_N$ may be realized. In this overall view of the game the Central Authority must take into account the preference functions of the other players so to speak as conditions of the problem, in determining the most reasonable strategy for itself.

To elaborate on these points and make it clear that they are conceptually different: Even if the game should degenerate into a simple case where all other decision-makers in fact have no choice (each set D_i contains only one possible d_i) the Central Authority would, in taking its own decision, take into account the preference functions of the other players through (19). When the other players have some scope for choice of strategy (the set D_i contains more than one possible decision), then the Central Authority must think of how the other preference functions $U_1(x), \ldots, U_N(x)$ play a part in determining the strategies chosen by the other players and accordingly also influence what is the most rational action by the Central Authority. This latter consideration would count even if $U_1(x), \ldots, U_N(x)$ did *not* enter the function (19).

Now the need for coordination stems from the fact that the game under consideration is a mixture of joint and conflicting interests. It is not always the case that an improvement in the situation for one decision-maker implies a deterioration of the situation for another; thus the game is not a constant-sum-game or a game of pure conflict. On the other hand, the set of decisions $a, d_1, \ldots, d_N$ which leads to the best result for one decision-maker (the Central Authority or some non-central decision-maker) is generally not the same as the one which would lead to the best result for another decision-maker.

In discussing further the need for, and nature of coordination, it is useful to distinguish between two types of games: non-cooperative games and cooperative games. In doing so, we first assume that all parties have perfect knowledge and understanding of the situation, i.e., each of them knows the functioning of the economy, the sets of possible decisions, and the preference structure of all other players (as well as his own).

A *non-cooperative game* now is a game in which each player decides on his action in isolation, i.e., without communication, negotiations, agreements or formation of coalitions with other players. In such a situation many outcomes are possible, but one type of outcome suggests itself as a particularly interesting one. This is the *non-cooperative equilibrium*. This is the set of decisions by all players which are such that if any one of them knew about the decisions of the others, then this information would not make him change his own decision. On the basis of the formulations given in (17)–(18) of the preceding section, a set of decisions $\hat{a}, \hat{d}_1, \ldots, \hat{d}_N$ represents a non-cooperative equilibrium if the following conditions hold:

$$(20) \qquad W(f(\hat{a}, \hat{d}_1, \ldots, \hat{d}_N, z)) = \underset{a \in A}{\text{Max }} W(a, \hat{d}_1, \ldots, \hat{d}_N, z),$$

$$(21) \qquad U_i(f(\hat{a}, \hat{d}_1, \ldots, \hat{d}_i, \ldots, \hat{d}_N, z))$$
$$= \underset{d_i \in D_i}{\text{Max }} U_i(f(\hat{a}, \hat{d}_1, \ldots, d_i, \ldots, \hat{d}_N, z)),$$
$$i = 1, \ldots, N.$$

Formula (20) says that $\hat{a}$ is such that, corresponding to the decisions $\hat{d}_1, \ldots, \hat{d}_N$ by the non-central decision-makers, $\hat{a}$ maximizes W among all permissible policies for the Central Authority, i.e., for all $a \in A$. In the same way $\hat{d}_i$ maximizes the preference function U_i for decision-maker no. i when he predicts the decision $\hat{a}$ of the Central Authority and the decisions $\hat{d}_j$ of all other non-central decision-makers $(i = 1, \ldots, N, j \neq i)$. [In (20)–(21) we have assumed, as a consequence of perfect knowledge, that all parties have predicted correctly the exogenous factors z.]

For a similarly simple case as in Figure 4, we have in Figure 5 illustrated the non-cooperative equilibrium. Point P in the figure is

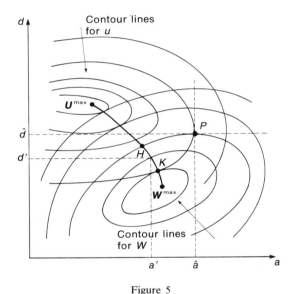

Figure 5

such an equilibrium point because for given decision $\hat{d}$ the Central Authority can do no better than choosing $\hat{a}$, and for given $\hat{a}$ the non-central decision-maker can do no better than choosing $\hat{d}$.

There are reasons to predict that a game of isolated decisions will tend to result in such a non-cooperative equilibrium. Such a solution is the only one which has the following property: After having taken the decisions and observed the results, each player sees his assumptions about the other players confirmed, and he will not regret his own decision. This is a convincing argument supporting the conclusion mentioned, when we have rational players with full information. For, if a player should forecast the decisions of other players and determine his own strategy in such a way that he afterwards gets surprised at the decisions taken by others and regrets his own decision, then he cannot have exploited all information and acted rationally.

In some presentations of the concept of non-cooperative equilibrium it is argued as if each player considers the decisions to be taken by other players as given and fixed. This is not correct. Each player knows the full range of possible decisions which can be taken by the other players and sees the problem also from their points of view in order to predict their decisions. This thought process goes on until each player has found predictions which will not be frustrated and an own decision which will not be regretted, and then we have arrived at the non-cooperative equilibrium. (Experience tells that this argument is somewhat difficult to grasp. In order to make the students see the problem and the argument clearly I performed the following experiment during the lectures. A figure like Figure 5, but containing nothing but the contour lines of the preference functions, was distributed to the students – 43 in number – *before the concept of non-cooperative equilibrium had been explained.* Some students should have *a* as their decision and others have *d*. The full situation was carefully explained. Each student should then, in isolation and after having given some minutes' thought to it, mark off his decision on the *a* or *d* axis, and also mark off the point in the *a, d*-plane which he expected to be realized. Out of the 43 students 26 selected decisions in conformity with the non-cooperative equilibrium, and almost all of them indicated correctly the expected *a, d*-point. In the discussion after the experiment it became clear that some of the students who did not behave according to the theory of the non-cooperative equilibrium had in fact not thought of the counter-player as fully rational or had given up predicting his decision; accordingly they had tried to find an own decision which would be reasonably safe in the sense that it would yield a result which would not be too bad regardless of what decision the other player would take. Others seemed to have sought a decision which could help to reach a result which would be reasonably good for *both* players, thus deviating from the basic premise of the game that each player should only aim at maximizing his own preference function. It was accordingly possible to convince most of the $43 - 26 = 17$ that they ought to have chosen a decision in accordance with the non-cooperative equilibrium as defined above.)

An important question for the application of this solution concept is whether we can be sure that a non-cooperative equilibrium really exists. This question was first investigated with mathematical rigour in a rather general setting by *J.F. Nash.* (A non-cooperative equilibrium is therefore often called a *Nash equilibrium.*) In wide classes of game situations encountered in economics a non-cooperative equilibrium will exist, but there are important and interesting exceptions. (The crucial points refer to such things as convexity or non-convexity of the sets of possible decisions and continuity or non-continuity of the functions giving the results as functions of all decisions.)

We next consider *cooperative games.* These are games in which the various players are allowed to get in contact with each other and, if they find it to their advantage, make agreements about the actions to be taken. In this case there is no solution concept as natural and convincing as the equilibrium concept in the case of non-cooperative games. However, one would expect a cooperative game to arrive at decisions which satisfy a requirement analogous to the Pareto optimum in general welfare theory. Consider again as an illustration Figure 5. We have here marked off the points which represent the maximal value of the preference function of the Central Authority, W^{max}, and the point which represents the maximum value of the preference function of the non-central decision-maker, U^{max}. Between these we have drawn a line which represents the points of tangency between the contour lines of the two preference functions. In a cooperative game we would expect the two players to arrive, by negotiations, at a set of decisions corresponding to a point on this line, such as a', d', since from all other sets of decisions it would be possible to make changes which improve the situation for both players or at least improve the situation for one player without making it worse for the other. In the game represented by Figure 5 it is hard to say anything more about what the outcome would be. Persuasiveness, bargaining ability, threats, and perseverance would play their parts. One might, however, expect the final settlement to be such that both parties gain from the cooperation. If both parties deem it likely that the outcome in case of no cooperation would be the non-cooperative equilibrium P, then the cooperative solution would be somewhere between points H and K in the diagram, i.e., points where both players are better off than at the non-cooperative equilibrium P.

In the case of more players, something more definite may sometimes be said. In this case we should consider the possibility of all sorts of coalitions between the players. Let us assume that players nos. $\alpha, \beta, \ldots, \gamma$ can reach at least preference levels $\bar{U}_\alpha, \bar{U}_\beta, \ldots, \bar{U}_\gamma$

by acting in cooperation, i.e., by jointly deciding on $d_\alpha, d_\beta, \ldots, d_\gamma$, regardless of what the other players do. Then it is unlikely that the final outcome of the complete game will be a situation in which these players get less than $\bar{U}_\alpha, \bar{U}_\beta, \ldots, \bar{U}_\gamma$ since in that case they would break off from the others, form their own coalition and implement the decisions which secure for them at least the levels $\bar{U}_\alpha, \bar{U}_\beta, \ldots, \bar{U}_\gamma$. The final outcome of the full cooperative game must be expected to satisfy such requirements for all possible coalitions, both among the non-central decision-makers themselves and between the Central Authority and one or more of the non-central decision-makers. In some games such considerations are sufficient to predict one particular outcome as the unique solution of the game. However, in most games this is not so. Sometimes the taking into account of all possible coalitions only narrows down the range of possible solutions very little, and in other cases it may happen that *no* outcome satisfies all these requirements. This is one reason why many different solution concepts are proposed in the theory of cooperative games. The one which we have discussed above is called the *core* of a game. When this gives a fairly sharp prediction of the outcome of a game, then it is a rather natural and acceptable concept. However, when it fails to do so, either because it gets too wide or because it fails to exist, then other solution concepts may be invoked. We shall, however, not go into this here. On intuitive grounds one might perhaps suggest that the core gives a very wide set of possible outcomes, i.e., no sharp prediction, if all individual players or all coalitions which are smaller than the total set of players are very far from being self-sufficient, i.e., if individual players and coalitions including fewer than all players are unable to provide a good situation for themselves independently of what the other players do. On the other hand, when coalitions are powerful or efficient in providing for themselves regardless of what the others do, then the restrictions mentioned in connection with $\bar{U}_\alpha, \bar{U}_\beta, \ldots, \bar{U}_\gamma$ are strong conditions and help to narrow down the prediction of the outcome of the game very much (and may even do so to an excessive extent so that no outcome satisfies all conditions). If there is one particular player who is important to all coalitions, i.e., if any coalition not including this player would not be able to provide a good result for the members of the coalition, then this player would be in a strong position and the set of likely outcomes of the game would include some possibilities which would be very favourable to this particular player.

It should be observed that a solution in the core always satisfies the

Pareto optimality criterion, since otherwise the coalition of *all* players would be able to improve on the situation. In this limited sense the outcome is "good". But the further delimitation of the core depends on the strength of the position of the various players, as just illustrated, and nothing can be said in general about its fairness or equitability.

At this point I think it is important to call attention to two points which go somewhat beyond the description of the game situation given above and which are often not stressed in expositions of game theory.

The first point is concerned with the sets of possible decisions. Above we have introduced sets A and $D_1, \ldots, D_N$ for all players. In the case of a cooperative game we have assumed that cooperation consists in coordinating the decisions from these sets for the players belonging to a coalition. However, a coalition will often be able to take actions which are not merely combinations of individually possible actions. In general we could introduce actions d_S taken by coalition S, where S is any coalition formed by some of the non-central decision-makers, with or without the Central Authority as a member. For instance, if the coalition S consists of players α and β, then the coalition will always be able to take actions d_α and d_β where $d_\alpha \in D_\alpha$ and $d_\beta \in D_\beta$, but it may also be able to take other actions not available to any of them individually. (This point is taken care of implicitly in the theory of cooperative games through the so-called "characteristic function" which indicates what each coalition is able to secure for itself regardless of what the other players do, but it is often not emphasized to the degree it deserves by comparisons between cooperative and non-cooperative games.)

The second point refers to the definition of cooperative games. Usually a game is called cooperative if the players are free to communicate and form coalitions for the coordination of actions by the members of the coalition. Now assume that some players $\alpha, \beta, \ldots, \gamma$ have formed a coalition and agreed that actions $d_\alpha^*, d_\beta^*, \ldots, d_\gamma^*$ should be implemented. There may then be a temptation for each player to violate the agreement. For instance, if player α now believes that the other players $\beta, \ldots, \gamma$ will observe the agreement and implement $d_\beta^*, \ldots, d_\gamma^*$, then some action d_α different from d_α^* may appear most profitable for player α, and similarly for the other members. If we adhere strictly to the assumption that each player tries to maximize his own preference function, and that the game is not to be repeated so that possible consequences for actions in some next round are not considered, then it seems that the actions "agreed upon" would not necessarily be undertaken. Some sort of arrangement for the enforcement of actions agreed upon seems to be necessary. This could take various forms. In the case of such joint actions as were mentioned under the previous points (by the definition of d_S and D_S for coalitions), control is automatic to the extent that participation of all members are required for the implementation of the agreement. In other cases possibilities of some sorts of sanctions against offenders "after the game" may be available. In many cases moral commitments and general rules of conduct will of course also be sufficient. But the point is that some sort of control and enforceability of agreements are required for the game to take a cooperative character. This is of course assumed by most writers on cooperative games even if it is not stressed explicitly. (At least one author, *J.C. Harsanyi*, does however include reference to the fully binding character and enforceability of agreements in the very definition of cooperative games.) In our context it is however particularly important to stress this point since it is important, in connection with economic planning and policy, to predict, or possibly influence, the character of the games taking place.

Up to now we have considered the game situation in rather general terms. The purpose of our consideration of game concepts is, however, to see if we can gain some insight into the nature of the coordination aspect of the planning activity of the Central Authority. We should then not only consider the Central Authority as one player among others in a symmetrical fashion as is largely done above. It may be possible for the Central Authority to influence the nature of the game in various ways. (There is a conceptual problem involved in this statement: every step the Central Authority takes in order to influence the nature of the game, can be seen as a move in a game of a higher order. In this way everything becomes part of an all-embracing game, a "super-game". However, this does not render it illegitimate to talk about games which are "sub-games" in relation to the overall game, and to discuss actions which change the nature of the sub-games, without setting out an overall game in a formalized way.)

First of all game theory usually makes an a priori assumption as to whether the game under consideration is a cooperative or a non-cooperative game. (Some elements towards an explanation of whether a game takes a cooperative or a non-cooperative form are however given, in a context somewhat different from ours, in a paper by *W. Buckley, T. Burns* and *L.D. Meeker.*) In formal games it is decided by the rules of the game. In the games created by individuals, enterprises and institutions in an economic system the nature of a game is only partly determined by strict formal rules. Other factors which enter the picture and influence the nature of the game are the number of players, problems of information and joint decision-making, problems of controlling or enforcing the implementation of agreements as pointed out above and so on. One will very rarely have a pure and clean case of either a completely cooperative or a completely non-cooperative game. There is here a large scope for actions by the Central Authority in order to influence the nature of the game. Most of the activities included under the coordination aspect of economic planning can be subsumed under this description.

Considering the case illustrated in Figure 5, we see that the non-cooperative equilibrium P represents a situation which is worse to both parties than situations which can be obtained by playing the game cooperatively (situations on the curve between H and K). Similar cases do of course arise when there are more than two players. The point may be even more striking if the coalition of both players can take actions which are not merely combinations of individually possible actions (a case which would require a more complicated figure). In such cases the Central Authority may try to change an otherwise non-cooperative game into a cooperative one. If it succeeds in this, it achieves a rise in the resulting level of the preference function W, and it may succeed in converting the other player into a cooperative player if it does not insist on settlements which are worse for the other player than the non-cooperative solution, i.e., settlements to the right of point K on the curve between U^{max} and W^{max}. Many of the activities subsumed under the term "coordination" or similar expressions in the definitions of economic planning surveyed in Section 1.4 can undoubtedly be described in the terminology of the present section as attempts to convert non-cooperative games into cooperative games (and consequently finding a good solution to the ensuing cooperative game).

But it would clearly be beyond realistic possibilities to turn the whole economy with all its agents into a fully cooperative game. It is furthermore a fact that some "sub-games" played as non-cooperative

games produce results which cannot be improved upon by cooperation. It may then be best, from the viewpoint of the Central Authority, to try to make the game fully non-cooperative for some
groups of decision-makers and with regard to some types of decisions.

The fact that a non-cooperative game may produce a result which is
not inferior to the outcome of a corresponding cooperative game is
best illustrated by the theory of perfect competition.

The competitive equilibrium of an economy can be interpreted as a
non-cooperative equilibrium, and under suitable conditions it will at
the same time belong to the set of cooperative solutions of the
core-type defined above. The two games mentioned here are two
different games concerning the same things, the production and
distribution of commodities. The non-cooperative game is played
within the framework of institutional arrangements implying the use
of prices and markets. The cooperative game is more "basic" in that
it does not a priori assume anything about prices and markets, but
assumes complete and perfect possibilities of communication, formation of coalitions and agreements on physical exchange of commodities. The statement just mentioned means that the outcome of
the perfectly competitive, non-cooperative market game is such that
no possible coalition could ensure for its members a better result by
production and distribution on the basis of its own resources only.
The relation between the allocations under the two types of game is
particularly interesting when the number of players is large. In the
limit when the number of players increases the set of cooperative
solutions – the core – collapses into a unique solution which then
implies the same distribution of goods as the non-cooperative market
solution. This is a very rough statement. Its full meaning and contents
can of course not be appreciated on the basis of this summary. The
idea is however so important that it cannot be by-passed in the
present context. The statement is true only on some further assumptions which are not specified here. There is in modern literature
precise analyses of the contents and range of validity of the assertion
quoted. For expositions and further references see for instance *E.
Malinvaud's Lectures on Micro-economic Theory* and *K. Arrow's*
and *F. Hahn's General Competitive Analysis*.

A fully non-cooperative solution concerning some elements of the
total set of decisions about the allocation of resources, choice of
techniques and distribution of goods to consumers, may accordingly

under suitable conditions be a good solution to these problems, at least in the Pareto sense. On the other hand, a set of decisions based on the formation of some coalitions without being fully cooperative, may correspond to monopolistic behaviour or collusion solutions in certain markets which are known to create non-optimal allocation of resources. If there are indirect or external effects (as defined in the general welfare theory) which may make the competitive solution non-optimal, then the Central Authority may in some cases use elements of the policy *a*, such as excise taxes and subsidies, to correct the solution so that the non-cooperative, competitive solution, conditioned by the policy represented by *a* including the corrective elements, results in a state of efficient allocation of resources.

According to these considerations the full range of efforts of the Central Authority to influence the nature of the game will consist of efforts to push the situation in the direction of cooperative decisions regarding some components, and in the direction of fully non-cooperative decisions regarding other components. Practical considerations regarding such things as costs of information, bargaining and administration as well as broader political and social considerations and power distribution will determine the relative weight on the two aspects.

In actual policy in most countries it is easy to find examples of both tendencies. Many countries have anti-trust laws or other regulations which aim at making market games non-cooperative and create competitive market conditions. On the other hand, in many countries the Central Authority has aided producers of export goods or export trade firms to establish cooperative solutions, i.e., to collude in order to exploit foreign markets so as to achieve a larger total gain than what would be obtained under competition. The same applies to some branches where the concern for natural resources is important, and also to some branches where competitive behaviour may imply particularly large costs or losses in efficiency. Obligatory membership in branch organizations or unions, laws and regulations, information systems and commissions of various sorts are instruments in attempts to make the game in such cases cooperative.

In many fields of policy there is a wavering between cooperative and non-cooperative solutions. This is perhaps most clearly seen in the efforts to cope with inflations. Such a wavering may be due to the fact that it is often difficult to control and secure that *all* elements of a cooperative solution are in the final instance implemented. In contrast to the non-cooperative equilibrium, the realization of a cooperative solution requires (as pointed out above) some means of seeing to it that all parties implement the decisions which are parts of the "package" agreed upon (not necessarily for all components of decisions by all parties, but at least for some of them unless the cooperative solution coincides with a non-cooperative solution). The state of confidence or distrust may therefore be important realities determining whether a cooperative or non-cooperative solution will result in such complicated games as take place in an economic system.

The best of all worlds is of course a world in which cooperative and non-cooperative solutions coincide. The fact that a solution is a non-cooperative solution implies that there are no incentives for the individual players to disturb the solution by isolated actions. The construction of systems of decentralized decisions will to a large extent aim at constructing rules of the game, including rewards and sanctions, in such a way that the players by playing non-coopera- tively, implement a solution which coincide with a cooperative solu- tion. The problematic fields of economic policy may, as a rough generalization, be described as fields in which it is difficult to secure such a situation, i.e., fields where any non-cooperative solution is considerably inferior to a cooperative solution while on the other hand problems of control and enforcement or lack of confidence prevent the playing of the game as a cooperative game. Problems of inflation, excessive pollution and destruction of environment and many other examples can be interpreted in this way.

In the preceding discussion we have for the most part assumed that all parties know the full structure of the problem, including the various sets of possible decisions, the mode of functioning of the economy and all preference scales. As a description of an actual economy this is of course unrealistic. As soon as we admit that there is imperfect knowledge, and then also incongruent beliefs held by the various players, then there is a much larger scope for the Central Authority to influence the nature of the game.

A field where different beliefs and assessments of the situation often prevail, relates to the question of whether a game is near to being a constant sum game or contains large potential benefits to all parties by cooperation. False beliefs that "somebody has to pay the cost" may block the realization of potential gains by cooperation. A central authority, presumably knowing more of the structure of the

game than most other players, might then try to push the game in the
direction of a cooperative game by trying to make the other players
perceive the situation correctly. Informative, educative and pro-
pagandistic efforts by the Central Authority would accordingly be an
important aspect of its coordinative activity.

Taking a look at Figure 3 it appears that the most obvious objects
for such activities are the structure and functioning of the economy
represented by $x = f(a, d_1, \ldots, d_N, z)$ and the set of possible states of
the economy X, since each player will generally know his set of
possible decisions and his own preference scale. Both wrong beliefs
on the part of the various players which overestimate the extension of
the set of possible states X and wrong beliefs which underestimate
the extension of X may prevent the realization of a cooperative
solution. Exaggerated beliefs about X may stimulate the players not
to acquiesce with solutions which give them less than they think fair
on the basis of their unrealistic beliefs about the possibilities.
Underestimation of the extension of X may prevent the realization of
good cooperative solutions at least when the underestimation is due
to the failure of the players to see the benefits which can be reaped by
joint decisions and accordingly hold mistaken views of the game as
being near to a constant sum game. If the Central Authority is in
possession of a reliable model of the working of the economy, and the
players accept as a fact that the model is a good representation of
realities, then a direct way of educating the players about the possibilities is to let them use the model. This actually happens to some
extent in Norway where the model underlying the national budgetting
work (MODIS) can be used also by political parties which are not in
the Government, and by other institutions and organizations. In this
way other players than the Central Authority may explore parts of X
which they find particularly interesting or find out about the consequences of combinations of decisions which they expect to be of
particular interest to them. This kind of activity would of course not
be interesting if the set of possible states of the economy could be
easily exhibited as is done symbolically in Figure 3; in actual fact the
set of possible states is a large and complicated set in a space of very
many dimensions which cannot be exhibited in full in a transparent
form.

Considering a large number of players, it would be in vain to try to
engage all of them in such educative experiments and exercises. In
practice a model of the economy would also be too simple and too

highly aggregated from the viewpoint of many players and would accordingly fail to show some aspects of particular interest to them. However, simpler approaches than large-scale educative experiments and exercises may often work. The fact that the Central Authority makes a plan and announces a certain element x of X as the state of the economy which it will strive to achieve may already in itself have important consequences. This is perhaps most clearly seen if a generally pessimistic attitude prevails among the players and each one of them adapts to this situation in such a way that the sum of all decisions tend to confirm the pessimistic expectations (as further elaborated in *J. Schwartz's* analysis of trade cycles in the terminology of non-cooperative games). Then the announcement of a more "optimistic" plan by the Central Authority may break through this circle of pessimism and call forth decisions $d_1, \ldots, d_N$ by the various players which help to realize the more optimistic target set by the Central Authority. The Central Authority may furthermore influence the situation not only by announcing its own targets, but also by influencing the expectations each non-central player holds about the decisions to be taken by other non-central decision-makers.

Looking again at Figure 3, important factors for the assessment of the possibilities are the exogenous elements z. In a state of imperfect knowledge, the various players might act on the basis of different assumptions about z. Different assumptions on this point may prevent agreement on what is a good set of decisions $a, d_1, \ldots, d_N$. The various players may be in possession of different bits of information concerning z, but the Central Authority would be the obvious candidate for pooling the most important information and making a more authoritative forecast of z. If this is acknowledged to be the best forecast available, then this may help to harmonize the assumptions on the basis of which the various players take their decisions, and then also make it easier to reach cooperation. (This is not meant to be an unconditionally true statement; I think one may rather easily find examples where different – and accordingly not all correct – assumptions about the exogenous factors might help to call forth agreement about decisions to be taken.)

An important and interesting question which is sometimes raised in this connection, is whether it is advantageous to have such an authoritative forecast of exogenous elements when even this forecast is inflicted with uncertainty. If all decision-makers make their decisions on the basis of the *same* wrong forecast, then the outcome may be more disastrous than when the various decisions are taken on the basis of *different* forecasts which may deviate in different directions from the true values of the exogenous factors. (This assumes absence of strong positive correlation between individual decentralized forecasts.) I think this points to a real danger. However, the mistake lies in the way in which the Central Authority according to the present assumptions transmits information to the other decision-makers. If there is uncertainty, then the appropriate information from the Central Authority would not be represented by a "point forecast" of the exogenous factors, presented as if it could be trusted firmly, but by a more complete description of the beliefs and uncertainties, for instance represented by probability distributions. It would then be up to the other decision-makers to decide on their actions on the basis of this description taking the uncertainty into account. This would tend to diminish the danger just mentioned. It remains, however, a little explored field to find out to what extent rational decisions in the face of uncertainty can be reached by independent actions. For instance, there may be uncertainty regarding future development of prices on export markets, which may make it advantageous not to concentrate on one or a few goods with expectationally favourable prices, but rather to diversify to some extent in order to reduce the relative uncertainty concerning the total gain from foreign trade. Whether the information, including the description of the uncertainties concerning the development of the exogenous factors, will be able to call forth a reasonable degree of diversification if the non-central decision-makers act independently is a very difficult question. Without being able to give definite answers we shall return to some aspects of such questions in a special chapter on planning under uncertainty.

The problem just discussed is part of a broader issue concerning the favourable or unfavourable effects of central planning. The broader issue is touched upon for instance by *J. Tinbergen* in response to arguments put forward by *J. Jewkes* against central planning. Tinbergen summarizes one of Jewkes' arguments in the following words: "Central decisions may imply bigger mistakes than decentralized decisions, since the latter are taken by a larger number of individuals whose decisions, when wrong, may partly neutralize each other." Tinbergen goes some way towards admitting the point, and sees it as one of the reasons why "there indeed seems to be an optimum degree of interference with production; beyond this level the advantages turn into disadvantages. On the other hand the draw-backs discussed seem to be of only secondary importance in many cases of a more global type of policy." As already suggested in connection with the more special issue about forecasts of z this line of thought cannot be rejected off-hand. In particular, there would be quite much to it if central authorities were so simple-minded that they considered their information and forecasts as perfectly certain and acted upon them in blind belief in own infallibility. But the argument loses some force if the central authorities recognize the uncertainties involved and take due account of them in preparing the decisions. Then the central authorities may themselves take decisions which "partly neutralize each other." (We shall not pursue the argument further here. One may easily get into an infinite regression by asking whether the central authorities can evaluate correctly the degree of uncertainty and so on.)

Concerning the remaining elements of Figure 3 – the sets of pos-sible decisions by non-central decision-makers and the preference scales – we have already remarked that a decision-maker is of course usually in no need of information from any other authority on these aspects of his own situation. There may, however, perhaps be cases where the Central Authority may help to generate a good solution of the game by informing each non-central decision-maker about the sets of possible actions and the preference scales of the *other* non-central decision-makers (to the extent that the Central Authority itself has such information). It is easy to conceive of cases where each player's misconceptions about the possible actions and the preferences of other players may generate results of the game which are very bad for all parties. Furthermore, there is a point about sets of possible actions which is not displayed in Figure 3. This refers to possible joint actions by a coalition which are more than mere combinations of individually possible actions. These possibilities were symbolized above by D_S where S stands for a coalition of players. It requires more of information, insight, inventiveness and organization to perceive clearly and correctly the full extension of these sets than for each player to find out about his own set of possible actions. At this point there may therefore be an important educative and organizational task for the Central Authority which may be considered as a part of the coordination aspect of planning.

Although better information and understanding on the part of the various players may often help to reach a good outcome of a game, it should not be concluded that this is always so. In many countries governments have hesitated in announcing expected rates of inflation, evidently in the belief that a better outcome of the game, perhaps for all parties, will be generated if the players act on the basis of a lower rather than a higher *expected* rate of inflation, and then to some extent also generate a somewhat lower *actual* rate of inflation – though not quite as low as expected. In Norway forecasts of the increase in nominal prices and wages were given in the National Budget for the first time in the budget for 1975. It was declared that such forecasts had not been given previously mainly because such forecasts might in themselves contribute to a higher rate of inflation. However, this argument was considered no longer to carry so much weight because the rate of inflation was now forecasted in so many other connections by various institutions and organizations, including institutions of a rather official character. In this situation the Government found the useful effects of having explicit and openly official forecasts more important than the negative effects. As important considerations were stressed the fact that price and wage forecasts would help to see the links between various monetary magnitudes and volume aggregates in the National Budget, and the fact that such forecasts would provide the Parliament with a more complete and realistic picture of the state and trends of development of the economy. (In the end the forecast given – an increase in the price level of some 11 percent in 1975 over 1974 – turned out to be reasonably accurate.)

Another field in which forecasts are usually given, but often in a biased way, refers to foreign trade. In many countries there has been a rather consistent tendency to give forecasts which are biased in the pessimistic direction. This applies both to the volume of export and to price forecasts. (For Norway, see *T. Hersoug* and *L. Johansen*.) One possible explanation may be that the Central Authority may prefer the various non-central decision-makers to underestimate the extension of the set of possible states of the economy because this may help to make them more restrained in putting forward claims of various sorts or in taking actions which aim at capturing results for themselves which when added together for all parties cannot be realized within the actual set of possible states.

Similar considerations might also bear upon the strategy of influencing income settlements. In Norway the degree of coordination of income settlements has varied through recent years, but usually the

Government has initiated at least some degree of coordination by establishing a group of experts which should provide information as a background for the negotiations. As a part of this apparatus an economic model has been constructed (the first version of which is described by *O. Aukrust* and by *F.C. Holte*) for the purpose of providing conditional forecasts of prices, real wages and disposable income for various income groups such as wage-earners, farmers, fishermen and "owners" as consequent upon alternative assumptions about nominal wages, prices of farmers' and fishermen's products, direct and indirect taxes and subsidies in addition to exogenous elements, primarily export and import prices. Such calculations have undoubtedly influenced the outcome of negotiations very much, and are generally believed to have had an "educational" influence which has helped to reach agreements. An interesting question which sometimes comes up is, however, whether an excessive impression of determinism is built into the model. A crucial assumption of the model is that there is a stable proportion between entrepreneurial income and total income earned in "sheltered" industries, i.e., industries which are not subject to competition from foreign producers. This assumption is not well underpinned theoretically, but it is justified by reference to observations which suggest that it holds as an "empirical law". If this is accepted as an unalterable fact, then a nominal wage increase will appear to have much less favourable impact upon disposable real income of workers in these industries than if wages could be increased at the cost of entrepreneurial income since it appears to contribute to larger increases in prices of goods and services which are important in workers' consumption. Whatever the realities are in this special case, it is clear that the form of the set of possible outcomes displayed by the analysis may influence the chances of reaching agreement, and it is at least conceivable that a distorted picture in the direction of displaying a narrow range of possibilities may promote the acceptance of a result which would not have been accepted by all parties if the full real range of possibilities had been displayed.

As a final point concerning the possibilities of influencing the nature of the game we may consider the order in which decisions are taken. A strictly non-cooperative game assumes that all players decide on their actions simultaneously, or at least in such a way that none of them knows about the decisions taken by the others when he makes his own decision. On the other hand, a cooperative game assumes communication and possibly joint decisions about the various actions. As we have already suggested in connection with Figure 4 one may also have games where the decisions are taken in a certain order. The first one to take his decision will then know that the other decision-makers will know his decision when they make theirs, and he (the first one) will take their rational responses to his possible decisions into account when he decides about his own as illustrated by the curve RS and the decision a^* in Figure 4. The second decision-maker will know the decision taken by the first one, but will have to go through a similar analysis of the responses of his followers when he makes his decision, and so on. In economic planning and policy in a game situation the order of decisions by the various players will very often not be predetermined, and especially the Central Authority may be in a position to choose where to place itself in such a sequence of decisions. It may try to induce a fully cooperative solution with joint decisions as we have discussed before; if this fails or is for some reason not desired, then the Central Authority may often choose whether to announce its decisions first or postpone its decisions until the other players have taken theirs. In connection with income settlements in Norway different patterns have been shown illustrating these various possibilities. In some cases the Government has announced steps which it will take concerning subsidies or other arrangements influencing real incomes in advance of the negotiations between the organizations in the labour market; sometimes it has postponed the announcement of such possible steps until it has seen the outcome of the negotiations. The income settlements between farmers, fishermen and the Government, determining product prices, subsidies and other sorts of transfers to these sectors, sometimes take place before the negotiations for wage settlements, sometimes afterwards and sometimes parallel and coordinated. It is not easy to say in general what is a good strategy when such choices are open. By announcing its decisions before the other decision-makers take theirs, the Central Authority may prepare the ground for a better coordination of the other dicisions since these will then be based on more complete information. On the other hand, it is very easy to visualize games in which a player will incur great losses for himself by revealing his move before the other players have to take their decisions.

Interesting possibilities are sometimes open if the Central Authority can make *conditional* declarations about its actions before the other decision-makers decide what to do. Consider Figure 5. The Central Authority considers the point designated by W^{max} to be the best possible outcome. It could now induce the other decision-maker to choose d corresponding to this point by issuing a declaration saying that "if you choose $d^{(1)}$, we (the Central Authority) will choose $a^{(1)}$, if you choose $d^{(2)}$, we choose $a^{(2)}$, . . . ,", and so on, relating a specific action a to every decision d that the other decision-maker may choose. This could be described as a response (or retaliation) function $a = \rho(d)$. If the function ρ is constructed in such a way that the highest value of the preference function U of the other decision-maker along the curve corresponding to $a = \rho(d)$ is reached at $W^{\max}$, then the other decision-maker will choose a d corresponding to this point.

This suggests that a conditional declaration can be a powerful means of influencing the outcome. An interesting example of such an idea in an economic policy context is *B. Hansen's* discussion of wage policy. His idea is that the Government could issue conditional statements about taxes, subsidies etc. so as to induce the trade unions to choose a nominal wage increase which is consistent with the Government's targets. The case is suggested in Figure 6. In this example a is the level of taxation and d the nominal wage level chosen. $W^{\max}$ is the best point according to the preferences of the Central Authority. The curve representing the conditional announcement of the Central Authority is indicated by $a = \rho(d)$. This

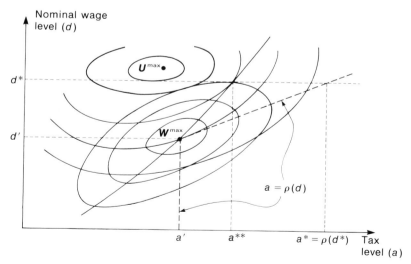

Figure 6

curve indicates a certain tax level a' corresponding to all nominal wage levels lower than d' which corresponds to W^{max}; if d increases beyond this level the tax level will be increased, and the more so the more the nominal wage increases. If this conditional statement is accepted at face value by the trade unions, then the trade unions will choose the wage level d' which conforms with the solution yielding W^{max} since this gives the maximal value of U along the kinked curve $a = \rho(d)$. (In B. Hansen's discussion the employers, or their organization, play a rather passive role. This is justified by reference to conditions prevailing under a high level of effective demand where the employers, according to B. Hansen, do not put up a strong resistence against wage increases.)

A policy somewhat similar to this is attempted by the Norwegian government. In connection with wage negotiations in 1975 the Government offered certain tax reductions as part of a package deal which involved a modest increase in nominal wages. It was furthermore announced that, unless a similar settlement, involving only a moderate increase in nominal wages, is reached in 1976 the Government will withdraw the tax concessions given in 1975. The State Budget is formulated with a rather high tax level with room for later reductions in case of a wage settlement which conforms with the Government's intentions.

At a first glance such a strategy of using conditional policy declarations may seem to hold the key to a strong and efficient policy in a game situation. This is however somewhat deceptive. There is a serious *problem of credibility* involved. To illustrate this, consider again Figure 6. When a decision about d has been taken, then the best decision of the Central Authority is not necessarily to adhere to the declaration represented by $a = \rho(d)$, if it feels free to deviate from it. Suppose that $d = d^*$ is chosen. Then the Central Authority, in order to follow up its previous declaration, should choose a^*. The result is a^*, d^*, which is very bad according to both preference scales. It may be tempting for the Central Authority to abandon the policy represented by $a = \rho(d)$ and instead make the best out of the situation and choose a^{**}. The result then is a^{**}, d^* which is better according to $U(a, d)$ than a', d'.

Now, even if $a = \rho(d)$ has been declared, the opposite player may anticipate this temptation for the Central Authority not to stick to its proclamation. Then in spite of the declared strategy $a = \rho(d)$ the decision d^* may be chosen in the hope that the Central Authority will put up with it and choose a^{**} instead of carrying out the costly retaliation a^*. Thus we see that there is a credibility problem involved. The policy of the Central Authority will be successful only if the opposite player believes in the declaration. In such situations it may pay for a player to take steps which will reduce his own possibilities of deviating from his declarations in order to increase the credibility of the declaration. Games where two or more players try to commit themselves more and more in a contest for credibility relating to their declared strategies may easily lead to an escalation which brings both (or all) parties beyond the point of no return and finally brings results which are disastrous to all players. A policy using such conditional statements is therefore not an easy and simple policy, but often something of a gamble.

(From the discussion of game concepts discussed above we see that the order in which decisions are taken may be very important. On the other hand, very much of game theory appears to assume simultaneous decisions. This type of game theory is however more general than appearance might suggest. This generality is achieved by letting the simultaneous choice refer to *strategies* rather than direct actions. Then games with different assumptions about simultaneity or non-simultaneity of specific decisions can be subsumed under the same general theory. This important point in game theory goes back to *J. von Neumann* and *O. Morgenstern*. We shall return to the concept of strategy later on, but it would take us too far to go further into the theory of games.)

Enough has now been said to show that economic planning and policy in an economy which involves a game structure rather than a simple decision-theoretic scheme are very complicated matters, and they would remain so even if we invoked everything which exists of game theory. This is so partly because of the size of the problem, but also because the game in which economic planning and policy take place does not usually fall into a pre-determined class of games with a reasonably transparent structure. Precisely the influencing of the nature of the game is one of the important aspects of economic planning and policy. As we have seen there is here plenty of scope for activities by the Central Authority which go beyond the preparation of the decisions strictly under its own authority. In a general sense most of these activities can be described as attempts to coordinate decisions. As already suggested some of them may also be considered as parts of "indicative planning", a sort of "soft planning" which does not work by strict decisions by the Central Authority or commands to other agents in the economy, but primarily by announcements of intentions, dissemination of information and coordination of decisions which are taken by other agents. A philosophy of planning comprising such activities has been developed particularly in France. I think further analysis along the game-theoretic lines suggested in this section might help to further clarify the nature of indicative planning, a concept which has remained somewhat obscure to many observers. In a decision-theoretic approach to economic planning it is hard to find any place for these soft forms of planning; in a game situation, and particularly when imperfect information and practical possibilities of reaching and implementing joint decisions are taken into account, many activities associated with the concept of indicative planning fall into place in a natural way.

References for Section 2.3

K.J. Arrow and F.H. Hahn, *General competitive analysis* (Holden-Day, San Fransisco, 1971). Especially Chapter 8.

O. Aukrust, "PRIM I. A model of the price and income distribution mechanism of an open economy", *The Review of Income and Wealth*, Series 16, No. 1 (1970). With some additional material also available as *Artikler* No. 35 (The Central Bureau of Statistics of Norway, Oslo, 1970).

W. Buckley, T. Burns and L.D. Meeker, "Structural resolution of collective action problems", *Behavioral Science* (1974).

B. Hansen, *The economic theory of fiscal policy* (Allen and Unwin, London, 1958). Original Swedish edition in 1955. Especially Chapter XVII, Section 9.

J.C. Harsanyi, "A general theory of rational behaviour in game situations", *Econometrica* (1966).

T. Hersoug and L. Johansen, "Optimal use of forecasts in economic policy decisions: An empirical test", *Journal of Public Economics* (1975).

F.C. Holte, "A model for estimating the consequences of an income settlement", in *Economic planning in Norway: Methods and models*, edited by L. Johansen and H. Hallaråker (Oslo University Press, Oslo, 1970).

R.D. Luce and H. Raiffa, *Games and decisions* – See reference under Section 2.2.

E. Malinvaud, *Lectures on microeconomic theory* (North-Holland, Amsterdam and London, 1972). Especially Chapter 6, "Imperfect competition and game situations", and Chapter 7, "Economies with an infinite number of agents".

J.F. Nash, "Equilibrium in N-person games", *Proceedings, National Academy of Sciences* 36 (1950).

J.F. Nash, "Non-cooperative games", *Annals of Mathematics* (1951).

J. von Neumann and O. Morgenstern, *Theory of games and economic behaviour* – See reference under Section 2.2.

G. Owen, *Game theory* – See reference under Section 2.2.

J.T. Schwartz, *Lectures on the mathematical method in analytical economics* (Gordon and Breach, New York, 1961). Especially Lecture 5.

J. Tinbergen, *Central planning* (Yale University Press, New Haven and London, 1964).

2.4. *The Relevance of a Decision-theoretic Scheme in a Game Situation*

Most systematic approaches to economic planning proceed along lines, and on the basis of formalizations which correspond to the simple decision-theoretic scheme presented in Section 2.1. On the other hand, games such as those discussed in Sections 2.2–2.3 seem to give more realistic descriptions of the situations in which a central authority will often find itself. Since it is very difficult to construct formal methods suitable for facing such game situations squarely and explicitly, it seems that we shall have to live with this discrepancy between the real situations and the formalized planning schemes. In this situation I think it is important to have been through the game considerations given above because it may help to put the decision-theoretic scheme in the proper perspective. It will help to perceive its limitations correctly and to interpret the outcome of analyses based on this scheme in a relevant way. It is a fact that communication between planning experts and politicians has often not been very good. The experts have often been inclined to consider the politicians to be irrational, and the politicians have considered the theoretically oriented experts to be naive. I think one reason for this has been that the planning theorists have insisted on a decision-theoretic scheme while the politicians have perceived the game nature of the situation (but perhaps failed to explain it explicitly and systematically). The considerations given in the preceding and the present section may help to bridge the gap.

Let us now see what differences it makes to the decision-theoretic scheme or to its interpretations and scope for applications if the actual situation corresponds to a game as illustrated in Figure 3.

We then consider the scheme in Figure 3 and raise the question as to what simplifications can be introduced in the analysis of this situation so that a scheme like in Figure 1 can be applied. In principle there are two different avenues towards such a simplification: First, the Central Authority may take actions which alter the situation so as to make it more amenable to analysis in terms of decision theory;

secondly, it may neglect certain game aspects and employ an analysis which only approximately reflects the true situation. The following possibilities seem to be present.

(1)   The Central Authority and the non-central decision-makers are not symmetric players in the game. The Central Authority possesses power to influence the sets of possible actions $D_1, \ldots, D_N$ of the various non-central decision-makers and may use this power to reduce these sets when the game situation is too awkward and threatens to produce unfavourable outcomes. Laws and prohibitions, and commands within boundaries set by law, are of course common means of influencing the sets of possible actions of other players. In Norway such a change took place in 1965 in the fields of monetary and credit policy. The previous system based on negotiations, guidelines and other game types of interactions between the State and private credit institutions was then replaced by a law which provides the State with a number of instruments that may be used to limit the D-sets of the credit institutions. Sometimes it may also be natural to interpret changes in grants and appropriations and perhaps also certain tax rules in similar terms. In Norway for instance the municipalities have formally rather wide scopes for independent actions, but various types of financial regulations determined by the State in practice limit these scopes considerably so that the game element in the relationship between the State and the municipalities gets very much reduced.

(2)   In principle every agent in the economy, whether they be households, enterprises, financial institutions or other organizations, are "non-central decision-makers" in the sense of Figure 3, and could accordingly be included on the list $1, \ldots, N$. However, it would never be practical nor theoretically important to treat all households and all enterprises in this form. It is hard to give a precise criterion, but something like the following might be tentatively suggested: The set of specified decision-makers nos. $1, \ldots, N$ is such that each decision-maker on this list – say no. i – is, in his decisions and behaviour, influenced by considerations as to what at least one other decision-maker on the list thinks about his – no. i's – intentions. A test might be this: If I believe that by announcing alternative intentions on my part I would induce different behaviour on the part of other agents, and this would be of importance to me, then I should in principle be on

the list of specified decision-makers. According to this criterion ordinary households should clearly not be on the list. Even if a (single) household should announce its preference function or its intentions in other ways, this would not influence decisions of other agents in the economy perceivably. The same consideration might apply to a large number of small enterprises. For big enterprises, big financial institutions and organizations of various sorts this would be different. They should accordingly be entered on the list of specified decision-makers.

When the "players" $1, \ldots, N$ have been specified, then the behaviour of all the "small" agents will be represented by behavioural relationships included in the model symbolized by $x = f(a, d_1, \ldots, d_N, z)$. The behaviour of the specified decision-makers will be determined by the structure of the game.

Now the criterion suggested will not give a sharp distinction between agents which should be placed in each of the two categories. For analytical simplification one may transfer more of them into the category represented by the "passive structure" f than strict considerations of realism should dictate. This is very customary in economic analysis where producers which are large enough to have some market power as conscious players, are, as an approximation, treated as if they behave according to competitive assumptions.

(3)   Some decisions which should strictly belong to $d_1, \ldots, d_N$ may in the analysis be transferred to the set of exogenous factors represented by z in Figure 3. This may be particularly convenient when the theoretical or empirical basis for letting these decisions be taken care of through the structure f is weak, and at the same time the positions of these decisions in the game are more or less obscure. When these elements are transferred to being included in z, then it implies that they should, in the preparations of a plan, be predicted alongside with the truly exogenous factors. However, in spite of the fact that we are not able to treat them as endogenous elements or as moves in a game, we may have some ideas about the behaviour of these elements and about the conditions which influence their behaviour. After a full solution has been calculated there would therefore always be a need for reconsideration of the original predictions for these elements, in contrast to the truly exogenous elements. Having seen the complete calculated outcome we may find the original predictions unrealistic and wish to change them. In this way we may proceed until we have a

set of predictions and calculated outcomes which, when seen in relation to each other, do not run counter to the more or less vague ideas we have about the strategic position and the behaviour of the elements in question. This is a very common procedure in economic analysis as a basis for planning.

(4)   As explained in the preceding section the Central Authority may sometimes be in a position to decide the timing of the announcement of its decisions in relation to decisions taken by non-central decision-makers. If it decides to announce its intentions at an early stage, then the other players are in a simpler situation and their decisions can then be more easily described by behavioural relations. Figure 4 gives an illustration of this point. If the Central Authority announces its decision about a before the other decision-maker takes his decision about d, then the Central Authority may base its considerations on the assumption that the other decision-maker will respond according to the curve RS in the diagram. The behaviour corresponding to this curve, i.e., the decision d as a function of the decision about a, may then be included among the behavioural relationships in the model f. On the other hand, if the decision about a is postponed until after the decision about d is taken, then the model can at this stage be used with d as a given datum. If none of these cases apply, then any treatment which tries to simulate the situation by means of a decision-theoretic model will do more violence to the real situation. The relation of government decisions about taxes and subsidies to negotiated wage changes as discussed in the preceding section, may illustrate all cases suggested here.

(5)   To the extent that the game takes a cooperative character the Central Authority will, during the planning process, be in contact with non-central decision-makers and may settle for agreements with some of them. These agreements may take the form that the non-central decision-makers involved consent to restrictions on their decisions d_i while the Central Authority commits itself concerning the use of some components of a. To the extent that these agreements take the form of direct fixation of some components of the various d_i and a these components can for the further analysis (for the determination of the not yet committed components of a) be treated similarly to the truly exogenous factors.

Out of the five avenues listed above of transforming the game scheme in the direction of a simpler decision-theoretic scheme, points 1, 4 and 5 represent interference with the actual situation, while points 2 and 3 are purely analytical simplifications.

To the extent that these steps have not brought us back to a pure decision-theoretic scheme, the Central Authority should in principle find the best decision a (among the possibilities remaining after having taken into account the consequences of point 5) by considering itself as a player in a game. Since theoretically well-founded and analytically practicable methods for solving such game problems are not available, rougher and simpler methods must be used. Series of calculations which treat the decisions by other players as if they were predetermined, but make alternative assumptions about these so as to find out about their consequences, may then be the most useful procedure. This means that we use the model in the form of a decision-theoretic scheme, but the consequences of the fact that the actual situation corresponds to a game is that we have to perform a series of alternative calculations based on alternative assumptions about the decisions taken by other players. In this way we explore the structure of the game, including the consequences of alternative compositions of actions by the various decision-makers, before the Central Authority settles for a specific plan. It also means that one should be prepared for frequent reconsiderations and revisions of the plan as decisions of other players are gradually revealed and possibly deviate from the tentative assumptions made by the Central Authority. In such a process a model which formally looks like a pure decision-theoretic model may be a very important and useful tool, but there is clearly, on the background of the preceding discussion, no reason to be dogmatic about the way of using it. Economic planning would remain very much of an art even if very precise and comprehensive economic models and very efficient computational implements were available, and is in fact even more so when we realistically admit that available models are far from being perfect representations of the real mode of functioning of the economy and far from being able to elucidate all the kinds of questions which come up in connection with economic planning.

2.5. Some Remarks on the Roles of Planning Experts and Political Authorities

In economic planning in an economy corresponding to the simple decision-theoretic scheme outlined in Section 2.1, there would be a fairly clear line of division between the tasks of planning experts and political authorities. The elaboration of the representation $x = f(a, z)$ of the structure and functioning of the economy is a question about facts, about how the economy really functions. It is a matter for experts. Similarly the forecasting of exogenous factors is also a matter of establishing and processing relevant facts. (If only "point forecasts" are to be given, then subjective elements will have to be invoked in order to determine these on the basis of information that is insufficient to yield unique and absolutely reliable forecasts. However, if the forecasts are given in a more complete form, involving a description of the degree of uncertainty involved, then subjective elements can be excluded to a larger extent.) Coming to the set of possible decisions, A, perhaps both experts and politicians might have a say. On the positive side there is in the first place the question about what sorts of policy instruments that are actually available under prevailing conditions in the economy. This is, in the first place, a question about information which may be shared by politicians and planning experts, but where one might perhaps expect the expert to be able to give a more complete and systematic overview. Next, it is a question about policy instruments which may not be available under prevailing conditions, but which are "known" from previous history or from experience in other countries. Finally, on the positive side, there is always scope for innovations, i.e., proposals for instruments and types of policy actions which have not been tried before. There is of course no reason to expect only the experts to get good ideas in this direction. On the negative side, some conceivable instruments and types of policy actions may be ruled out on political grounds even before the experts have analysed the consequences of using them. We should conclude, accordingly, that the establishing of the set of possible decisions A is a joint concern of both experts and the political authorities.

The extension of the set of possible states of the economy, X, is a result of the elements already discussed. The politicians can influence the extension of X by their participation in the delimitation of A, but for the rest it is a matter about facts and analysis which should belong to the realm of the experts.

On the other hand, the preference scale $W(x)$ should be the exclusive domain of the political authorities. This is a matter of desires or preferences of the political authorities, not of something which can be found out by observations and analysis.

This kind of division of tasks between experts and politicians is explicitly or implicitly adopted in most of the more technical or theoretical planning literature. *R. Frisch* has been quite explicit on this in several papers, and it may be illuminating to quote from one of them (from 1963). In discussing methods of selecting a best plan, he points out that "Certain things that come into the picture ... are of such a sort that their elucidation depends solely on the work of *scientific experts*.... The questions that occupy these experts concern objective facts. They are of such a sort that any statement regarding these questions can in a scientific way be qualified as either 'correct' or 'not correct'." Frisch admits, of course, that there are fields of disagreement between experts, but then considers this to be part of a dynamic process in which there is convergence "towards something which can be looked upon as a 'correct' and 'objective' characterization of the outer world. This characterization is something which man has to accept *whether he likes it or not*.... All these things which man can't do anything about is what I mean by the *structure* of the problem one has chosen to consider at a given point of time .... When describing the structure of the economy one must rid one's mind completely of the concepts 'desirable' or 'not desirable'."

Proceeding to consider the preferences Frisch sees these in sharp distinction to the structure of the economy. "What is essential to retain in this connection is that now we are *not* speaking of the structure of the economy – those things which man cannot change –, but we are speaking of precisely the opposite, namely of what man – represented by the responsible authority – would *like* to see realized, disregarding provisionally the question of whether it is structurally feasible or not .... We now have to rid our minds completely of any considerations of what is structurally feasible, and concentrate only on what is desirable or not desirable if it could be obtained." Frisch is aware of the fact that we usually, in our everyday life, do not think in terms of such sharp distinctions. This is, however, mainly due to the fact that we are in need of deciding on some action, small or great, nearly every minute. Intuition, habits and short-cuts will then have to be used. "But when it comes to a *systematic* analysis of the complex alternatives of choice that are open to us in economic planning, . . . the *truly realistic* approach is to segregate the preferences completely as a special point of view distinct from that of the structural elements of the problem."

Anyone who has been in touch with actual planning knows that realities do not correspond strictly to this scheme. Politicians often interfere with spheres which, according to the scheme, should strictly belong under the experts; at the same time politicians often want advice from the experts before they decide what to prefer. There are many reasons for this blurring of the borderline between the two spheres. A factor of paramount importance is the fact that the elements which belong to the "objective" structure are only imperfectly known. If competing hypotheses and theories remain even after all available information and expert knowledge have been utilized, then it is not a matter only of objective analysis to choose the hypothesis on the basis of which one will proceed in the further elaboration of a plan. In such a case strict adherence to the division of tasks suggested by the simple scheme might result in actual policy-decisions which would depend as much upon the experts' subjective assessment of the situation as upon the politicians' preferences. Another important fact is that political authorities have rarely gone through all the hypothetical considerations that must underlie the determination of the preference function in advance of the more concrete elaboration of a plan.

When experts disagree even after having scrutinized all available information on a certain point, then there are approaches which may be more advantageous than simply letting politicians choose between rival hypotheses on the basis of their intuition and impressions. In management science, technological forecasting and related fields, there are developed systematic methods (such as *the Delphi method*) of organizing exchange of information between initially disagreeing experts for trying to make opinions converge towards some sort of consensus or unbiased compromise. There are many cases where it has been demonstrated convincingly that such systematic use of *groups* of experts with different views gives better results than reliance on some single expert opinion held before the experts have been through such a process. In cases where such methods have been systematically used the problems are generally simpler and more well-defined than the problems encountered in connection with national economic planning. Nevertheless, there may be something to be gained by making some attempts in this direction.

Another approach, undoubtedly often used in practice, is to take the consequence of the difficulty of upholding the strict division of tasks between experts and politicians by using experts who are known to share the basic views and preferences of the political authorities. This must more or less implicitly be the view of *W.A. Jöhr* and *H.W. Singer* in their well-known discussion of "The Role of the Economist as Official Adviser". They first point out "how complicated a task it is to judge a problem of economic policy, how many factors have to be weighed against each other." From this they draw the conclusion that "the scientist is undoubtedly better equipped to perform the task of weighing and to reach a conclusion. Not only because it is possible for him to spend more time on the problem, in order to work out all these various factors, but also because, as a scientist, he bears no direct responsibility for action taken and can therefore look at it from a distance. Nor is he caught up in the day-to-day business of administration; he is therefore more likely to have at his command the leisure indispensable for such a careful consideration." For these reasons "any intelligent policy-maker" will, according to Jöhr and Singer, ask his experts not only about facts, arguments and analysis, but also for their *opinions* and the reasons for these. Then the policy-maker can decide whether or not to accept the advice of the experts. From the viewpoint of the politically responsible decision-maker this would hardly be an efficient procedure unless there is some agreement between the politician and the experts, at least where basic aims and values are concerned.

To the problems discussed above, which stem mainly from incomplete information, knowledge, and analytical capacity we should add the fact that the real situation will often be more realistically described as a game situation as discussed in the previous sections and, moreover, a game situation which does not correspond to a clear case convincingly solved in the theory of games. One might try to separate the term economic "policy" and economic "planning" by letting "policy" refer to the game aspects which are analytically rather intractable and require quick actions, negotiations, threats, promises and obscure compromises, and letting "planning" refer to the more tidy aspects which can be dealt with more systematically. This may be a reasonable distinction for some purposes, but it implies that the planning problem will be conditioned by many more political elements than those which are represented by the preference function.

In addition to the actors mentioned in the discussion above, there is a "third party", the general public. When the politicians have to seek support for their decisions and plans among the general public, then this may further contribute to blurring the distinction between the tasks of the politicians and the tasks of the experts. Since imperfect knowledge prevails, the debate on economic policy will have to be concerned not only with preferences, but also with questions about how the economic system really functions. Furthermore, when both these aspects have to be involved, and no objective factor can determine the weights attached to these two aspects in the debate, then convenience and tactical considerations will often dictate. It then seems to be an empirical fact that disagreement about preferences are often (but of course not always) played down while there are heated arguments about elements which could in principle be investigated by objective analysis and which should, according to the simple scheme, belong to the domain of the experts. It clearly also happens that politicians withdraw from the field assigned to them in the simple scheme and leave to experts problems which involve preferences. This happens especially when the general public – perhaps as a result of prior political debates – holds exaggerated beliefs about the ex-tension of the set of possible results. Politicians who usually disagree may then agree that "unpopular" measures are necessary, and may call upon experts to work out a plan for the "necessary" steps and present it with an appearance of objective necessity.

In Section 1.4 we quoted a description of planning by *J. Kornai* which emphasized planning as "a process of cognition and com-promise." Furthermore, Kornai underlined that the planning process itself "helps in understanding our own desires, wishes, goals; and helps to confront them with the reality. It is a framework for exchange of information (and) a device to understand the inter-dependencies and to reconcile the conflicting interests." The elements of our planning scheme are not there in advance, nicely sorted out into categories which fall under the expert and under the politician respectively, but emerge gradually during a process as described by Kornai.

One should not conclude from this that the distinctions drawn by *R.*

Frisch as quoted at the beginning of this section, are futile. We should clearly be prepared for factors which tend to blur these distinctions in practice, but this does not imply that we should give up all attempts to keep different things apart. There is a fundamental distinction between preferences on the one hand and elements which can be investigated by objective analysis and by recourse to observed facts on the other hand, and only confusion can result from giving up this distinction *completely* in response to the factors which tend to make it less sharp in practice.

Whether or not one tries to draw a line of division between the tasks of experts and of responsible political authorities there will always be a communication problem involved. We shall return to some aspects of this in Chapter 3. In the present context we shall only emphasize the importance of the point by quoting the Polish economist *J. Pajestka*, who possesses a large amount of experience from planning in Poland and other countries. According to Pajestka it often happens that planning work by experts remains separated from practical decision-making because of this problem: "The policy-makers quite often do not participate in the planning process in a sufficient way, preferring to leave it to the planning experts. The experts then perform the function which should be performed by the policy-makers (in a more or less wider scope). As a result, the plan may become a document representing rather the expert opinions than the policy choices. Consequently, the policy tends to develop along its own ways, not availing itself of the advantages presented by planning. Planning becomes inefficient and the policy unplanned." To avoid such failures Pajestka recommends that the policy-makers themselves should take part in the planning process to a considerable extent, but this again requires that the planning techniques and procedures should be so devised as to make it possible for the policy-makers to do so.

References for Section 2.5

G. Báger and A. Hajnal, "Organizational aspects of social planning", in *Progress in cybernetics and systems research*, Vol. II, edited by R. Trappl and F. de P. Hanika (Wiley, New York, 1975).

The Delphi method: Techniques and applications, edited by H.A. Linstone and M. Turoff (Addison-Wesley, Reading, MA, 1975).

R. Frisch, "An implementation system for optimal national planning without detailed quantity fixation from a central authority", in *Proceedings of the 3rd International Conference on Operational Research* (English Universities Press, London, 1964).

L. Johansen, "Planlegging og spill" – See reference under Section 2.2.

W.A. Jöhr and H.W. Singer, *The rôle of the economist as official adviser* (Allen and Unwin, London, 1955). Especially p. 71.

J. Kornai, "The place of mathematical planning in the control of the economic system" – See reference under Section 1.4.

J. Pajestka, "Dialogue between planning experts and policy makers in the process of plan formulation", in *Essays on planning and economic development*, Vol. 3 (PWN, Warsaw, 1968).

2.6. Dynamic Interpretation of the Planning Scheme – The Concept of Strategy

The planning scheme set out in Figure 1 and the game scheme in Figure 3 have no explicit time dimension. The most straight-forward interpretation of these schemes is then a static interpretation, i.e., an interpretation pretending that we consider decisions for one period of time which can be treated as unrelated to other periods. This would limit considerably the range of applicability of such schemes and the lines of thought which we have presented in connection with these schemes. However, by a suitable interpretation of the various elements (and at the cost of some complications) the schemes may also be taken to represent a planning situation with a time dimension. For an elaboration of this point we shall consider mainly the simple case given in Section 2.1, and next only add some remarks on the complications which arise in a game situation as explained in Section 2.2.

We now consider a series of time periods designated by $t = 1, 2, \ldots, T$, where T is the "horizon" – the last time period under consideration. In most of what follows we shall not specify this explicitly.

In Section 2.1 a policy was represented by the symbol a, and the set of all possible policies by A. An element a could be thought of as a vector indicating the values assigned to all available instruments of policy, perhaps supplemented by qualitative descriptions if not only quantitatively different policies were under consideration. We shall now interpret an element a to be a description not only of a policy for one specific period, but a complete description of policies – i.e., values assigned to the various instruments – for all time periods under consideration. We may thus think of the element a as made up of components $a_1, a_2, \ldots$ and write:

$$(22) \qquad a = (a_1, a_2, \ldots, a_t, \ldots),$$

where now a_t describes the policy in period t, for $t = 1, 2, \ldots$. For instance, in an element a a specific tax rate which may vary from one period to another will now be represented by one rate included in a_1 and applied in period 1, another rate included in a_2 and applied in period 2, and so on.

Similarly the exogenous factors represented by z and the results or states of the economy represented by x may be decomposed into components referring to the various time periods, i.e., we may write:

$$(23) \qquad z = (z_1, z_2, \ldots, z_t, \ldots), \qquad x = (x_1, x_2, \ldots, x_t, \ldots).$$

Now in z for instance the level of some export price will be represented by one figure included in z_1, another figure included in z_2, and so on, and in x for instance total private consumption will be represented by different figures included in the various components $x_1, x_2, \ldots$.

Thus a policy a is now a set of time sequences for the various instruments in use, z a collection of time series for the various exogenous factors, and x a collection of time series for the various variables describing the state of the economy.

In the simple exposition in Section 2.1 the mode of functioning of the economy was represented by $x = f(a, z)$ as explained in (7). This representation is still valid and should be interpreted as saying how the time series of results or states of the economy depend on the development through time of the policy and the exogenous factors. However, assuming that the results in each period depend only upon the policy and exogenous factors in the same and in preceding periods, we may write this in a somewhat less condensed and more informative way:

$$x_1 = f_1(a_1, z_1),$$
$$x_2 = f_2(a_1, a_2, z_1, z_2),$$

$$\vdots$$

$$(24)$$

$$x_t = f_t(a_1, a_2, \ldots, a_t, z_1, z_2, \ldots, z_t),$$

$$\vdots$$

The history before $t = 1$ is of course also of importance, but this is a given fact, uninfluenced by exogenous factors and policies dated $t = 1, 2, \ldots$. It is therefore not explicitly specified.

The assumptions underlying the structure (24) would obviously be valid for a mechanical system. However, in a system involving the behaviour of conscious individuals, formulation (24) might be questioned. In particular, the behaviour of some agents may depend upon expectations about the future. For the exogenous factors included in z this is perhaps not serious, since such expectations must depend upon observations from the past. When this formation of expectations is taken into account, then the effect of expectations can be represented in the form as given in (24). The problem may appear to be somewhat more serious for the components of the policy a. If all components $a_1, a_2, \ldots$ where announced right at the beginning, then all these would clearly influence the behaviour already for the first period, and all components should in principle be entered in all relations in (24). However, this is a matter of interpretation. If the Central Authority prefers to commit itself to specific policy actions for several periods already at the beginning of the first period, then we could include all these elements of policy into a_1. In general, for any period t we could let component a_t represent those actions to which the Central Authority commits itself by decisions in period t regardless of whether they be concretely implemented in this or in later periods. If the Central Authority announces intentions which are not binding, then these announcements may be considered as part of the policy in the period in which the announcements take place. The actual execution, which may deviate from the announced intentions, is subsequently taken as part of the policy in that period. By such interpretations we may consider (24) to be generally valid.

The various possibility sets A, Z, and X now need some more elaboration. Consider first the set of possible policies A. This should now be considered as the set of all possible time sequences $a_1, a_2, \ldots$. This set may have a special structure in that the possible actions in a certain period t may depend upon the previous history. We may introduce A_t as the set of possible policies in period t, i.e., symbolically write:

(25) $\quad a_t \in A_t,$

where A_t depends on $a_1, \ldots, a_{t-1}, z_1, \ldots, z_{t-1}, x_1, \ldots, x_{t-1}$. For brevity we may introduce $H(1, t-1)$ for the "history" from period 1 through

$t - 1$:

(26) $H(1, t - 1) = (a_1, \ldots, a_{t-1}, z_1, \ldots, z_{t-1}, x_1, \ldots, x_{t-1})$,

and indicate the dependency of A_t on this history by writing:

(27) $A_t = A_t(H(1, t - 1))$.

There is some redundancy in these formulations since the series of elements $x_1, \ldots, x_{t-1}$ depends on the series $a_1, \ldots, a_{t-1}$ and $z_1, \ldots, z_{t-1}$ by (24). However, we write this as by (26)–(27) to indicate that A_t depends, in general, on the whole history up to and including $t - 1$ regardless of how we prefer to describe this history.

There are plenty of examples of such a dependency. If some production activities are under the direction of the Central Authority, then the possible scales of these activities in some period depend upon investments and other actions taken in previous periods. The scope for foreign borrowing in one period may depend upon borrowing in previous periods. The possibilities of expanding education in some direction in one period depend upon the education of teachers in previous periods, and so on.

The relation between the full set of possible policies A and the sets of possible policies referring to the individual periods $A_1, A_2, \ldots$ may now be given in the following way:

(28) $A = \{a_1, a_2, \ldots, a_t, \ldots \, | \, a_1 \in A_1, a_2 \in A_2, \ldots, a_t \in A_t, \ldots\}$,

where A_1 is given and A_t, for $t = 2, 3, \ldots$, depends on the history up to $t - 1$ as indicated by $A_t = A_t(H(1, t - 1))$.

The notation in (28) means that A is the set of all series $a_1, a_2, \ldots, a_t, \ldots$ which are such that the statements after the bar are true.

From the dependency of A_t on the history up to $t - 1$ it appears that the set A is now in general not independent of the realizations of the exogenous factors.

This means that, if a full plan covering all the time periods under consideration has been worked out on the basis of a provisional forecast of the exogenous factors, then it may not only be undesirable, but *impossible* to adhere to the plan for the policy actions if the forecasts of the exogenous factors prove to be wrong.

For the correct understanding of the decision problem in a dynamic context a closer look at the sets of possible actions at the various points of time is interesting. Consider a fixed period θ. At the point of time where the decision about a_θ is to be taken, the set of possible decisions is A_θ which depends upon the history up to and including period $\theta - 1$. The extension of A_θ is thus determined by, inter alia, the decision $a_{\theta-1}$. Let us next consider the set of possible decisions for period θ as seen from the beginning of period $\theta - 1$, i.e., from a point of time where $a_{\theta-1}$ is not yet fixed. Let us denote this set by $A_{\theta(\theta-1)}$. This set is then larger than A_θ. In fact, viewed from the beginning of period $\theta - 1$ any decision a_θ for period θ which belongs to some possibility set A_θ that can be generated by some permissible decision $a_{\theta-1}$, is possible. Neglecting now the influence of the exogenous elements, and writing the dependence of any set A_t on the previous history of decisions as:

(29) $A_t = A_t(a_1, \ldots, a_{t-1})$,

we may express $A_{\theta(\theta-1)}$ as the union of all sets A_θ which can be generated by variation in $a_{\theta-1}$, i.e.:

(30) $A_{\theta(\theta-1)} = \bigcup_{a_{\theta-1} \in A_{\theta-1}} A_\theta(a_1, \ldots, a_{\theta-2}, a_{\theta-1}) = A_{\theta(\theta-1)}(a_1, \ldots, a_{\theta-2})$.

The set here defined will evidently depend upon decisions up to period $\theta - 2$ as indicated to the right in (30). We may now proceed to consider the set of possible decisions in period θ as viewed from the beginning of period $\theta - 2$, i.e., $A_{\theta(\theta-2)}$. This is again a union of such sets as defined in (30), or a union of all sets $A_\theta(a_1, \ldots, a_{\theta-2}, a_{\theta-1})$ which can be generated by some decision $a_{\theta-2} \in A_{\theta-2}$ for period $\theta - 2$ and, for each such decision, some decision $a_{\theta-1}$ which belongs to the set $A_{\theta-1}$ consequent upon $a_{\theta-2}$ (and previous history). Symbolically we have:

(31) $A_{\theta(\theta-2)} = \bigcup_{a_{\theta-2} \in A_{\theta-2}} A_{\theta(\theta-1)}(a_1, \ldots, a_{\theta-2})$,

or

(32) $A_{\theta(\theta-2)} = \bigcup_{a_{\theta-2}} [\bigcup_{a_{\theta-1}} A_\theta(a_1, \ldots, a_{\theta-2}, a_{\theta-1})]$,

where the union in the last expression is formed for all $a_{\theta-2} \in$ $A_{\theta-2}(a_1, \ldots, a_{\theta-3})$ and, for each such $a_{\theta-2}$, for $a_{\theta-1} \in A_{\theta-1}(a_1, \ldots, a_{\theta-2})$. In the same way we may proceed step by step and end up with a set of possible decisions for period θ as viewed from the beginning of the first period, i.e., when no decisions $a_1, a_2, \ldots$ have yet been taken. This last set is $A_{\theta(1)}$. It follows from the construction of these sets that:

$$(33) \qquad A_\theta \subset A_{\theta(\theta-1)} \subset A_{\theta(\theta-2)} \ldots \subset A_{\theta(1)},$$

which is a symbolical statement of an obvious fact. Considering the set of possibilities for a given period θ this set appears larger and larger [if we have proper subsets in (33)] the earlier is the period from which we view the possibilities for θ because we are then not committed for the intervening periods. When we move in the natural direction through calendar time, implementing the decisions taken as we move along, then the set of possible decisions for a fixed period θ will gradually narrow down. We end up with the set A_θ first defined as the set of possible decisions for θ when we are at the beginning of this period. As an example we might think of the possible decisions embodied in the State Budget for 1980. Viewed from today (1976) there is a wide range of possible budgets for 1980. As we approach the year 1980 more and more decisions will be taken which commit the Cental Authority by legislation and contracts, by moral and political commitments and so on. The narrowing down will also be due to physical factors in the form of plant and equipment invested in various branches such as health, education, communication, etc. which take a rigid form. Thus, at the end of 1979, when the State Budget for 1980 is to be determined, one may feel that there is not much freedom for choice among alternatives. This effect is an important reason for carrying out planning for a wider horizon than one year. In connection with the Norwegian State Budget the Government now outlines every year main trends of the budget for three additional years beyond the first. These budget figures for the additional years are not formally adopted in the same way as the budget for the coming year, but they help to see the current budget in the longer perspective and possibly to see whether the immediate changes, confined within rather narrow bounds, are conducive to larger changes which may be desired in the longer run.

The connections between the various concepts introduced above are

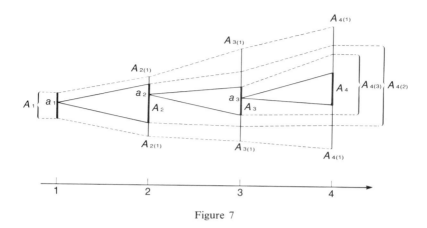

Figure 7

suggested by Figure 7 for a simple case where the possibility sets are intervals, i.e., where there is only one quantitative instrument.

Considerations similar to those above also hold for the set of possible states of the economy. The set of possible states in any year θ as viewed from the present may be very large, but gradually narrow down as we move through time and approach the beginning of period θ, taking decisions and becoming more and more committed as we move along. Thus, a state x_θ which is attainable when viewed from the first period may become unattainable from a certain period on as a consequence of decisions already taken.

With the time dimension introduced the preference function $W(x)$ is now an "intertemporal" preference function, ranking not only alternative situations in one period, but alternative developments over a sequence of periods for the economy. Many analytical problems related to dynamic models get simpler if this preference function can be written in an additive form, i.e., as:

$$(34) \qquad W(x) = W(x_1, x_2, \ldots, x_t, \ldots)$$
$$= W_1(x_1) + W_2(x_2) + \cdots + W_t(x_t) + \cdots.$$

However, for a general discussion this specification is not necessary.

There are many interesting and important problems related to the form of an intertemporal preference function. Besides the problem about the permissibility of the additive form, there are problems about the relative weights attached to the near and the more distant future ("time preference") and about the termination of the function (the "horizon"). These problems will however not be pursued here since they are extensively treated in economic welfare theory, optimal growth theory and the theory of cost–benefit analysis.

Having discussed the time aspects of the various elements of the problem we now go on to consider the optimization. We shall not, at this point, go into technicalities, but only give some general observations relevant to the time aspect.

Under full information the maximization of the preference function $W(x)$ subject to the constraints given by (24) and the various restrictions on the sets of possible decisions may be carried out by methods similar to those which are used in static problems. Whether two variables in a problem are different variables referring to the same period of time or the same kind of variable referring to different periods of time is in principle of no consequence for solution techniques. The "only" problem is that we get a very large problem when the same types of variables are repeated for every time period. It is then important to look for structural characteristics which can be used to devise more efficient solution algorithms. For getting a clear view of the structure of such dynamic problems the utilization of socalled *decision trees* is often useful. These are systematic methods of exhibiting the points of time at which various decisions have to be taken, the sets of possible decisions at each point of time, and the consequences of each decision for the sets of possible decisions at the following points of time as well as the gain accruing as one moves from one stage to another. This technique is most useful when there is a finite (and not too large) number of possible decisions at each point of time. Examples of decision trees are found in many books on decision theory, game theory and operations research. (See e.g., *H. Raiffa.*) An analytical technique which is often useful for optimization in a dynamic setting, and which exploits the special structure of $x = f(a, z)$ set out in (24), is *dynamic programming* as developed by *R. Bellman* and others. *Optimal control theory* as developed by *L.S. Pontryagin* and others ("the maximum principle") is also a powerful tool.

These techniques are surveyed and further references are given for instance in *M.D. Intriligator, Mathematical Optimization and Economic Theory.* Examples of the use of control theory abound in the literature from recent years. Examples using dynamic programming to solve an illustrative planning model are given by *R. Radner*. The "classical" optimal control theory is developed for continuous time, but corresponding techniques have more recently been developed also for the case of discrete time. An example of the use of the "discrete maximum principle" is briefly described by *I.P. Iwanilow* and *A.A. Petrow*. In spite of these technical developments, exact solutions can very rarely be found to dynamic optimization problems of sufficient size and complexity to be of practical relevance in economic planning. We have set out the dynamic scheme above in a rather general form as a frame of reference. In practice many sorts of simplifications have to be introduced.

Let us now consider some consequences of uncertainty or incomplete information.

We have pointed out that a set of possible actions A_t for period t may depend on the realizations of the exogenous factors up to and including period $t - 1$. This has important consequences. If we have initially worked out a plan on the basis of provisional forecasts of the exogenous elements, and these subsequently turn out to be incorrect, then it may be not only desirable, but also *necessary to revise the plan for the following periods* – and this may of course happen in every period. The general praxiology referred to in Section 1.4 allows for such problems and recommends as a remedy "flexible planning" which tries to avoid decisions which narrow down the range of future possibilities too much. *Kotarbinski* expresses the idea in the following way: "Thus, a plan should be flexible, which means two things: first, that it ought not to recommend rigidly that a definite step be taken when such a step will have to depend on circumstances to be known only at a later time; secondly, that it ought not to recommend an earlier stage which would unnecessarily narrow the amplitude of later possibilities. Thus, a plan should not even indirectly recommend measures which would restrict the scale of future possibilities. By way of example, it is better, *ceteris paribus*, to choose a route which provides for arrival at a railway station from which there are several trains to one's destination, than a station from which there is only one train to that destination." Knowing right from the beginning that the forecast will not necessarily prove to be correct, we might already in advance work out a plan for how the tentative plan should be revised on various occasions in the future on the basis of information which has accrued up to that time. This is suggested by Kotarbinski in the following terms: "If a plan is characterized by adequate precision, it

ought in certain cases to provide for the various alternative modifications of action according to certain circumstances, given that the full
or even partial range of such alternatives can be foreseen in advance." The idea is more explicitly developed by *I. Svennilson* in the
work referred to in Section 1.4.

More generally, the idea of planning possible revisions of original
plans may be developed into the idea of using a *strategy*. This means
abandoning the idea of working out *now* a plan for what actions
should be taken at various points of time in the future. Instead one
works out *rules* which say how one should, at each point of time in
the future, respond to information gathered up to that point of time.
In general, we may let action a_t depend on the whole history up to
and including period $t - 1$ by functions δ_t, i.e., set:

$$(35) \qquad \begin{aligned} a_t &= \delta_t(a_1, z_1, x_1, a_2, z_2, x_2, \ldots, a_{t-1}, z_{t-1}, x_{t-1}) \\ &= \delta_t(H(1, t-1)), \qquad\qquad t = 1, 2, \ldots. \end{aligned}$$

In this formulation there is again some redundancy as in connection
with the formulation (26)–(27). For $t = 1$ the formulation (35) is
degenerate in that no variables enter on the right-hand side.

The problem now contains a_1 – the first period action – and the
functional forms $\delta_2, \delta_3, \ldots$ as the unknowns. These should be determined so that they, when applied to the economic system as defined
by the structural relations (24) and the sets of possible actions as
recurrently determined by (27)–(28), yield a value of the preference
function as high as possible. The way of using the solution would be
first to implement the calculated solution for a_1, then let time pass for
one period, next observe the realized values of z_1 and x_1 and insert
these together with a_1 in the functional form δ_2 so as to obtain the
solution a_2; then implement this a_2 and move one period further in
time, observe the realized values of z_2 and x_2, insert in δ_3 to obtain a_3,
and so on.

It is important to understand that a strategy in general results in a
series of actions which are

1) *not* the same as the actions which would be taken if, in the
   presence of uncertainty, everything had to be decided in an initial
   planning period; and
2) *not* the same as the actions which would be taken if all future
   exogenous factors were known with certainty already in the initial
   period.

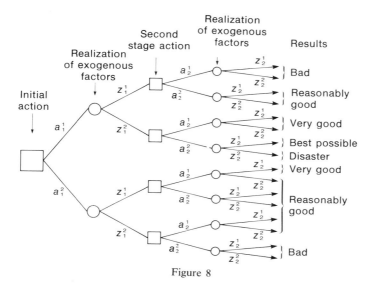

Figure 8

These facts are illustrated by means of a simple example in Figure 8.

In this example there is first an initial action to be taken. The set of possible actions consists of two elements, a_1^1 and a_1^2. Then exogenous factors are realized, in alternatives z_1^1 or z_1^2. At the second stage there is a choice between action a_2^1 and a_2^2, and thereafter exogenous factors are realized, either as z_2^1 or as z_2^2. The results now appear as $x_1 = f_1(a_1, z_1)$ and $x_2 = f_2(a_1, a_2, z_1, z_2)$ and are evaluated by $W(x_1, x_2)$. For every sequence a_1, z_1, a_2, z_2 in the figure we can imagine the values of W indicated at the arrow-heads to the right. We have simplified the matter by characterizing the results as "Best", "Very good", "Reasonably good", "Bad" and "Disaster".

Now suppose, corresponding to 1) above, that everything, i.e., both a_1 and a_2, should be decided in the initial period, when neither z_1 or z_2 is known. We assume that we are not gamblers in our attitude towards uncertainty. Then we would not choose (a_1^1, a_2^1) as our plan, since we might get z_1^1 for z_1, thus ending up with a bad result, and we assume this to outweigh the possibility of the lucky case of z_1^2 for z_1, yielding a very good result. Nor will we choose (a_1^1, a_2^2) as our plan. For the exogenous realizations (z_1^2, z_2^2) this would lead to disaster. We would instead choose the plan (a_1^2, a_2^1). This would be bound to give a reasonably good result. The final possibility, (a_1^2, a_2^2), might again lead to a bad result.

Suppose next that we knew z_1 and z_2 right from the beginning, and that $z_1 = z_1^2$ and $z_2 = z_2^1$. Then the plane would be (a_1^1, a_2^2), leading to the best possible result.

Now finally suppose, realistically, that we do not know z_1 and z_2 in advance, but we know that, when the second stage action shall be determined, then we will know whether $z_1 = z_1^1$ or $z_1 = z_1^2$ came up. Then a good strategy is evidently to start with a_1^1, and then follow up with:

$$(36) \qquad a_2 = \begin{cases} a_2^2 & \text{if} \quad z_1 = z_1^1, \\ a_2^1 & \text{if} \quad z_1 = z_1^2. \end{cases}$$

This strategy, which is a special case of a strategy function δ_t as represented in general by (35), yields at least a reasonably good result, and may yield a very good result. If actually $z_1 = z_1^2$ comes up, then this strategy produces a very good result regardless of z_2. This strategy is therefore better than the policy (a_1^2, a_2^1) selected above for the case where both a_1 and a_2 should be determined immediately, since the latter would only produce reasonably good results under all circumstances, never very good results.

Comparing the strategy with the case of full information from the beginning we see that we miss the opportunity of reaching the best possible result because we do not want to take the chance of disaster. On the other hand, comparing with the case of committing ourselves to a fully specified plan from the beginning in spite of uncertainty, we see that we can opt for the very good result by deciding on $a_1 = a_1^1$ because we postpone the actual decision about a_2 until we have seen whether z_1 turns out to be z_1^1 or z_1^2, thus avoiding the danger of disaster by choosing a_2^1 if $z_1 = z_1^2$ occurs.

To find an optimal strategy in general means to optimize with respect to functional forms. This appears simple in our small example, but is usually a more demanding task than ordinary maximization with respect to a limited number of variables. Optimal strategies are developed in the literature only for rather simple problems, and often with a priori restrictions on the types of strategy functions which are permitted. The general idea is, however, very valuable and can be used as a guideline also when exact optimal solutions cannot be established.

We have not yet taken into account the decisions by other players, represented by $d_1, d_2, \ldots, d_N$, which were introduced in Sections 2.2–2.3. These could also be decomposed into decisions to be taken in the different periods of time, and the sets of possible decisions could again be generated similarly to (28)–(30). Now the sets of possible actions by the Central Authority would in principle depend also upon previous decisions taken by non-central decision-makers, and the sets of possible decisions by non-central decision-makers might depend upon previous decisions by the Central Authority.

We saw above that uncertainty about the future development of exogenous elements may make it advantageous to develop a strategy rather than a strict plan. When we recognize the existence of other players in the game, then thinking in terms of strategies becomes even more important.

If there were no limitations on capacity of thinking, establishing models and analysing problems, then all players could sit down and determine their strategies before the commencement of the actual playing. As soon as the game had started no more thinking would be necessary: All players would only in every period have to insert the observations made up to that point of time into the strategy functions in order to determine their next moves. This is of course an unrealistic picture of how it can be done in practice, since the range of possible situations which may arise in the future is too large. Kotarbinski states explicitly that, provided one plans so as to keep a rather wide range of possibilities for future actions open, then "it is often more economical . . . to leave the future agent the task of undertaking the appropriate measures when it is known which of the many possibilities has actually occurred." However, it is important to be aware of the logic of the problem and the strategy concept, and it is not unlikely that progress in the methodology of planning will in the future partly be achieved by more conscious and explicit use of these ideas.

We have abstained here from giving a precise meaning to the optimization involved in determining the strategies; we have only suggested that these should be determined so as to yield a high value of the preference function and avoid the possibility of very bad results. For rigorous analysis something more must be said. We leave this point here with the suggestion that the best way of achieving precision is to introduce probabilities and replace the idea of maximizing $W(x)$ by the maximization of the *expected value of* $W(x)$. We shall return to this point in a later chapter.

References for Section 2.6

R. Bellman and R. Kalaba, *Dynamic programming and modern control theory* (Academic Press, New York, 1965).

M.D. Intriligator, *Mathematical optimization and economic theory* (Prentice Hall, Englewood Cliffs, NJ, 1971). Especially Chapter 13, "Dynamic programming", and Chapter 14, "Maximum principle".

I.P. Iwanow and A.A. Petrow, "Optimierungsaufgaben in dynamischen mehrsektoralen Produktionsmodellen", in *Mathematik und Wirtschaft*, Band 8 (Verlag die Wirtschaft, Berlin (GDR), 1972).

T. Kotarbinski, *Praxiology* – See reference under Section 1.4.

L. Pontryagin et al., *The mathematical theory of optimal processes* – See reference under Section 1.3.

R. Radner, *Notes on the theory of economic planning* (Center for Economic Research, Athens, 1963).

R. Radner, "Dynamic programming of economic growth", in *Activity analysis in the theory of growth and planning*, edited by E. Malinvaud and M.O.L. Bacharach (MacMillan, London, 1967).

H. Raiffa, *Decision analysis* (Addison-Wesley, Reading, MA, 1968).

I. Svennilson, *Ekonomisk planering* – See reference under Section 1.4.

2.7. *Some Further Notes on Concepts and Terminology Related to the Planning Scheme*

In the previous sections we have used several concepts and terms which may be in need of some further discussion and clarification. In particular we may try to distinguish between various types of statements about future developments which are used in connection with economic planning. Although there is no unequivocal and generally accepted terminology in the literature, we are in conformity with quite widespread usage if we distinguish between the following three main types of statements:

(1) A *projection* is a description of a future *possible* state or development, with no further reference to the likelihood or desirability of the described state or development and no indication of intentions to reach the described state or development.

(2) A *forecast* is a description of a future state or development which is considered by the forecaster to be *expected, probable or most probable.* Further precision can be given to these concepts by means of statistical and probabalistic concepts. A forecast may be a simple "point forecast" describing only one state or development, or take the form of a more complete statement describing also the degree of uncertainty attached to the forecast in the form of probability distributions, standard deviations, intervals, etc.

(3) A *plan* is a description of a future state or development which expresses an *intention* by the authority by whom, or on whose behalf the plan has been elaborated. In a complete plan both the desired results (in the form of a description of a state or development) and the actions intended to be taken in order to achieve these results should be explicated. The intended results may be called *targets* so that a complete plan consists of targets and a plan for actions.

To these basic concepts may be added two further concepts, the meaning of which will be more fully explained further on:

(4) *Conditional forecasts* which are intended to be valid (in the sense
     of giving expected or probable states as under point 2 above)
     only on certain conditions without implying anything about the
     likelihood of these conditions being fulfilled.
(5) *Indicative forecasts* which are intended to influence – through the
     very elaboration and announcement of the forecasts – the state
     or development which is being forecasted.

If we use the term forecast as a general term comprising points 2, 4,
and 5 above we may use the term *pure forecast* for forecasts which
are neither conditional nor indicative.

The concepts introduced by the first three points above correspond
more or less with the terminology of *J.R. Stone, P. Massé* and several
other writers in the field. *J. Tinbergen* (*Central Planning*, 1964) uses a
somewhat different terminology, defining a forecast as "an estimate
of the future economic situation under the assumption that there will
be no change in economic policy." He then questions the usefulness
of distinguishing between forecasts and projections. He points out
that any forecast must be based on a large number of assumptions
about the operation of the economy and about the probable course of
exogenous variables, and draws the following conclusion: "Everybody making a forecast chooses these assumptions as realistically as
possible, but even so forecasts will as a rule not coincide with the
actual course of events. There does not seem to be any reason
therefore to make a distinction between forecasts and so-called
projections."

Tinbergen is probably right that no projection will in practice be
made with no explicit or implicit reference to what is realistic or
probable, since there are generally so many possible projections
which can be made, and they are not all equally interesting. Any actual
projection will therefore be based on some degree of forecasting in
the sense that some elements of the projection and its underlying
assumptions are based on considerations about what is probable.
However, one may purposely deviate from making all elements on the
projection subject to such considerations. For instance, a "forecast"
in Tinbergen's sense, assuming that there will be no change in
economic policy, may be a useful exercise for investigating certain

problems which may arise in the future, but may not qualify as a forecast in the sense defined above since "no change in policy" may be considered to be a very unlikely event.

Also *H. Theil* uses a terminology somewhat at variance with the one we have proposed above. Theil observes that "a forecaster will usually predict a variable over which he has no direct control", but notes that there are exceptions to this. More specifically, "a forecast of a value taken by a variable which is directly controlled by the forecaster himself is called a *plan*."

Thus, while Tinbergen tends to play down the distinction between a forecast and a projection, Theil tends to play down the distinction between a forecast and a plan. (Theil does, however, restore the distinction to some degree by proposing to use the term anticipations for forecasts of variables over which the forecaster has no direct control. Thus plans are forecasts which are not anticipations.)

In our treatment of planning methods it seems useful to retain all the concepts and distinctions given above and use separate terms for them.

The term conditional forecasts introduced under point 4 above, may be used to describe more precisely statements which are intermediate between projections and forecasts as defined above. A statement about the future must be based on assumptions. We then remain within a realm of pure forecasting to the extent that these assumptions are chosen on the basis of assessments of what is probable. For some assumptions we may, however, avoid such assessments of what is probable and replace them by arbitrary assumptions, by assumptions chosen for convenience, or assumptions chosen because we find it interesting to study their consequences. The forecast will then be conditional upon these assumptions. The distinction between the two cases is reflected by the fact that the pure forecast will be meaningful without any further explanation, whereas a conditional forecast is only meaningful when supplemented by some "if-statements".

Conditional forecasts are now intermediate between projections and pure forecasts defined above in that a conditional forecast is nearer to being a pure projection the more it rests upon assumptions chosen on other grounds than assessments of what are the most probable developments. In practice projections are often presented without the full set of necessary "if-statements", but such explanations would form part of the evidence if the question is raised whether the projection really describes a *possible* future state or development.

Let us now relate this discussion more directly to the planning schemes used in previous sections.

Considering the decision-theoretic scheme presented in Section 2.1, a complete projection would be a set of elements a, z and x for which $a \in A$, $z \in Z$ and a, z and x are compatible in view of the structure $x = f(a, z)$ so that $x \in X$. For the game-theoretic scheme in Section 2.2 the elements $d_1, \ldots, d_N$ would have to be added and taken into account. In a dynamic interpretation as explained in Section 2.6 all the elements mentioned here would represent time series for the various variables involved. Most projections presented in practice are, however, not as complete as this suggests. In many cases only the resulting state or development x is presented. In order for such a presentation to qualify as a projection one should have reasons to be confident that x belongs to the set X of possible states, but one may perhaps sometimes feel confident about this without spelling out in detail the full set of elements including a, z and possibly $d_1, \ldots, d_N$.

A natural type of conditional forecast within these schemes would be forecasts which rely on probability statements about the exogenous factors z, and then gives forecasts for x conditional upon assumptions about a and possibly $d_1, \ldots, d_N$ which are not necessarily deemed to be probable. A usual type of conditional forecast would be forecasts based on the assumption of "no change in policy" (if this can be defined in a natural manner). Such forecasts will be particularly interesting because they may reveal problems which are not felt very urgently at the moment, but which may develop gradually if policy continues to follow habitual lines.

In relation to our planning scheme one might raise the question if it is at all meaningful to ask for *pure* forecasts of the elements involved. This is clearly possible for the exogenous factors z which are beyond the influence of the planner or other agents in the economy. A forecast for all elements including a and x might be meaningful, in the sense of being the most probable development of these factors, if it is worked out by some expert or observer not involved in the decision-making. A statement about a would then represent his evaluation of what is the most likely decision by the Central Authority. For the Central Authority itself (or planners working for this authority) a forecast of a in the same sense would not be that meaningful (unless we follow *H. Theil*'s terminology as suggested above). For decisions which I am just about to make I do not work out the probabilities that I will make this or that decision; I prepare the decision and take it. However, for decisions which need not necessarily be taken immediately, it may be useful to work out a non-committing plan which I am prepared to revise at a later stage on the basis of new information. It is then logically meaningful to speak about forecasts of own decisions. This is particularly clear if we consider the policy in the form of a strategy. When strategy rules have been worked out as symbolized by (35), and the probability distribution of the exogenous elements are known, then the Central Authority can in a meaningful way speak about probability distributions for its own later actions.

A plan in the most rigid sense would be a statement about the future concerning both a, z and x in such a way that a and x represent intentions, as explained above. When we admit that there is uncertainty, then the most rational behaviour is not to cling to the a first selected regardless of what happens, but rather to consider all plans as in a sense provisional, subject to revisions in the light of new information. Then intentions and forecasts in a probabilistic sense get inseparably intertwined.

In Norway (and probably in many other countries) there has been a discussion as to whether the National Budgets represent plans or forecasts. Clearly the elements that can be referred to our category z are pure forecasts. On the other hand, the elements represented by x are partly influenced by exogenous elements and partly by actions of the Central Authority, the latter being chosen so as to help to achieve a state x which is partly influenced by exogenous elements about which we can do nothing but forecast them, and partly by purposive actions. Whether the figures published in a national budget for such items as national product, private consumption, etc. are plans or forecasts, is then a question which cannot be answered in this form. But we might perhaps speak about the degree of "planned-ness" and "forecasted-ness" of the various components of x. If a component of x would be highly influenced by changes in z within the possible range Z, but relatively little influenced by variations in policy a within the set of possible policies A, i.e., the component in question is very sensitive to changes in z and not very sensitive to changes in a, then we might say that this component has a high degree of "forecasted-ness". Correspondingly a component which is more sensitive to changes in policy a and less sensitive to changes in exogenous elements z has a higher degree of "planned-ness". In a national budget there should then be some elements which are pure forecasts and some elements which are fully and directly planned, whereas the bulk of the elements would be somewhere in between with some degree of "forecasted-ness" and some degree of "planned-ness".

The attitude towards these terminological questions in the Norwegian National Budget seems to be rather relaxed. It may be observed, in the first place, that the term "budget" already implies some degree of intention or commitment. The term "plan" is not used explicitly. The section describing the development of national product and its components, for instance for 1975, is titled "Forecast of the development of the Norwegian economy in 1975", and refers very neutrally to the main figures as describing the development which is "assumed as a basis for the National Budget for 1975". There is, however, no doubt about the intentional character of many of the figures contained in the National Budget. On several points, particularly concerning fiscal policy and monetary and credit policy, main lines for the use of important instruments are indicated and related to the description of the "assumed" development of national product, consumption, investment and so on. It is also indicated where the Government feels particular needs for more efficient instruments. Another indicator of the plan character is the fact that later in the term the Government regularly publishes a revised national budget, and halfway through the term a report which compares actual developments with the budgeted ones, and significant deviations often induce changes in the use of the policy instruments.

Besides the annual national budgets the Norwegian government works out and presents to the Parliament documents which describe the development of the economy over a period of four years. These documents are officially called "Long-Term Programmes". In addition to very much of descriptive material they also contain several more or less clear announcements of intentions. They are, however, more weakly related to planned use of instruments of policy than the targets in the national budgets although there is now some coordination between the long-term programmes and the elaboration of the State Budget in a four-year perspective. On this basis one might perhaps draw a terminological distinction between a "programme" and a "plan", a programme expressing intentions or goals but being less explicit with regard to how the goals should be achieved. However, the distinction is not clear. In the long-term programme for

1954–57 it is for instance explained that "this programme is a continuation of the long-term *planning* which has previously been carried
out" – and it is referred to the previous "economic long-term *plan* for
the period 1949–52." On the other hand, the so-called "Perspective
Analysis of the Norwegian Economy" which was presented as a
supplement to the long-term programme for 1970–73 and which describes the development of the Norwegian economy up to 1990, is
explicitly stated to contain projections rather than plans or forecasts.
For some presumably exogenous factors such as the development of
population one has tried to make realistic forecasts, but on many
other points assumptions are chosen which are not necessarily meant
to be the most probable. The projection for the main macroeconomic
categories is described as a "neutral projection", which is a projection based on the assumption of a smooth continuation of present
trends of economic policy. It is explained that the purpose of such
projections is to study the consequences of these assumptions, not to
present a picture of the most likely development. Without itself being
a plan (or a forecast) the projection in the Perspective Analysis is
seen as a tool for planning, and the preface to the Perspective
Analysis announces the extension of the *planning* perspective or
horizon as the objective of the analysis. It is indicated that such
analyses of the really long-term perspectives will gradually become "a
systematic and regular part of the economic planning." (In the same
connection it is pointed out that "the really operational plans in the
Norwegian planning system" are found in the National Budget and
the State Budget. We shall return to the concept of an "operative"
plan below.)

In Norway national budgets, four-year programmes and perspective
analyses are worked out in the Ministry of Finance, i.e., the work is
done on behalf of the Government and directly integrated into the
decision process forming the economic policy. The division responsible for the four-year programmes and the perspective analyses is
officially named "The Planning Division".

In the Netherlands the document which corresponds more or less
to the Norwegian National Budget is called "The Central Economic
Plan", and is worked out by a "Central Planning Bureau". This
Planning Bureau is, however, not directly subordinate to the
Government and the "plan" does not possess the official status of a
Government document as is the case for the Norwegian national
budgets. In the prefaces to the Central Economic Plans for the

Netherlands it has been stressed several times that the document does not represent a plan in a strict sense. For instance, the preface to the document for 1961 says that "no more than its predecessors this 'plan' comprises recommendations for economic policy. Consequently the figures for 1961 constitute a forecast and not a plan. Only policy measures already inacted or announced have been taken into consideration." In the terminology introduced above the "plans" in the Netherlands can probably best be described as conditional forecasts, worked out by an institution not subordinate to the Government, but conditioned by what is known or assumed about policy actions to be taken by the Government.

In France, to take another example, four-year programmes have played a much more prominent part right from the beginning after World War II than in most other Western countries. They have been directly integrated in the political process and have clearly been important for Government decision-making, and they have been unabashingly presented as "plans".

As mentioned in Section 1.1 there have however been periods in which a gap has evolved between plans and planners on the one side and actual policy and politicians on the other side.

In the socialist countries in Eastern Europe the term "plan" has of course been in regular use, and there has been no doubt about the plan character of the documents, although in the early experimental phases of planning in the USSR such terms as "control figures" and "orientations" were cautiously used about documents which had not yet gained full status as officially adopted plans.

In the USSR in this early period there was a discussion on planning concepts and methodology between adherents of "genetic planning" and of "teleological planning". The debate had many facets, but one of the most important ones can be interpreted as referring to the rôle of forecasts versus active shaping of the development according to chosen targets. To the geneticists the future was determined to a very large extent by "hidden objective tendencies of development." The main question was to discover those tendencies and to forecast their manifestations in the future. To the teleologists the future was much more rich in possibilities; determination, mobilization of the forces of society and conscious transformation of the structure of the economy played a much larger part. Referring to concepts used before we may perhaps say that the set of possible states X was thought to be small by the geneticists, accordingly analysis and forecasting took a central place. The teleologists believed X to be very large; accordingly decisions and actions were more important. The teleologists came out on top in the debate and their attitude characterized the first five-year plan periods. (*S.G. Strumilin*, mentioned in Section 1.3, was a leading teleologist, while *V.G. Groman* was perhaps the leading geneticist. For a discussion, see e.g., *E.G. Dolan*.)

There may be a need for some further considerations of the concept of a forecast in a social context. For a system consisting of other things than conscious individuals, a forecast is a simple and obvious concept. In a social system the concept of forecasting is more problematic. Since the system consists of individuals who act on the basis of information and expectations, the forecast itself may interfere with the operation of the system by providing information and influencing expectations. The forecast may accordingly influence the course of the events being forecasted. One may then even raise the problem if it is at all possible to work out correct forecasts for such systems. If one simply works out a forecast without taking into account the fact that the forecast itself influences the course of events, and then announces the forecast, then the forecast will prove to be wrong. The way around this is of course to try to take into account the effect of the forecast already in working out the forecast, but without further assumptions it is not necessarily true that the situation admits a correct forecast. Such problems were recognized by *O. Morgenstern* in a book *Wirtschaftsprognose* already in 1928. He pointed out that in the fields of social sciences there would often be a causal relationship between a forecast and the events being forecasted, and perceived clearly the problems this raises for forecasting in such contexts. Morgenstern was especially concerned with forecasting related to business cycles, and drew the conclusion that forecasts might destabilize the development rather than stabilize it. He arrived at the recommendation that forecasts of trade cycle developments should not be published. Institutes investigating the trade cycles should restrict themselves to publishing only the most up-to-date and precise information on the current situation, but not give any further interpretations or forecasts on this basis.

The relevance of the problem raised by Morgenstern is illustrated by the fact that for instance Norwegian national budgets have until quite recently avoided publishing figures concerning expected rates of inflation. The National Budget for 1975 was, however, quite explicit, making an assumption about a rise in the consumption price index of about 11 percent from 1974 to 1975. This forecast was worked out by means of the National Budget model MODIS on the basis of intended changes in excise taxes, subsidies, and some prices directly regulated by the Government, some known results of wage settlements and agreements between the Government and the farmers' organizations about prices of farm products, and pure forecasts of some exogenous variables such as import prices. In the introduction to the National Budget it was pointed out that such price forecasts had not previously been published in the national budgets because one had feared that such forecasts might in themselves contribute to enhancing the rate of price increase. This consideration was however now considered to be of lesser importance since price forecasts of a more or less official status were published in many other contexts. The decisive consideration was then that the integration of explicit price forecasts into the National Budget would help to provide a better basis for the Parliament in its debates on economic policy. (Ex post the forecast mentioned proved to be quite accurate.)

From the description of the basis for the calculation of the assumed price increase of 11 percent it is clear that this item represented some degree of "planned-ness" in the sense defined above since it was influenced by some Government instruments. Formally it might well have been called a "target". By feasible variations in policy the price increase could certainly be curtailed to some degree or pushed somewhat higher up. When the budget adopted an expected rate of inflation of 11 percent, this was because other alternatives were considered worse when effects on other variables were also taken into account. A lower rate of inflation might for instance be achievable only at the cost of a more moderate growth in employment and national product, a lower share of Government expenditures, or a more unfavourable (from the Government's viewpoint) distribution of income. A higher rate of inflation has well-known undesirable consequences. The rate of 11 percent chosen represented a sort of optimal balancing between the various concerns and was in this sense a target. The Government however emphasized that it did *not* represent a target. This may perhaps be justified by the fact that the degree of "forecasted-ness" is higher than the degree of "planned-ness" because of the large influence of exogenous variables on the rate of inflation in a country like Norway. (It is also highly influenced by variables which might be classified as d-variables in our scheme, such as prices of farm products, which take an intermediate position with regard to the distinction between policy influences and exogenous influences.) When the Government hesitated to call the 11 percent of inflation a target it referred, however, to another consideration: "As far as possible the Government will try to achieve a lower rate of inflation than shown by the figures presented." This terminology is of course politically understandable. However, for quite many figures which are explicitly declared to be targets one could adduce similar considerations to the effect that if some exogenous variables take a more favourable course than expected, or if instruments turn out to be more efficient, then one will seize the opportunity to try to achieve more favourable values for the target variables.

The publication of the price level forecast by the Government has not been much criticized. This does however not apply to the accompanying forecast of the increase in the level of nominal wages. The National Budget for 1975 assumed an increase of around 17 percent in the level of nominal wages, and this forecast was widely publicized and commented on in newspapers, radio and television. The publication of this assumption or forecast was criticized in the journal of the Employers' Union which held that this forecast had created difficulties for wage negotiations at various levels because it was adopted as more or less binding, and while many groups raised claims of larger than average wage increases in order to make amends for relatively unfavourable positions inherited from the past, no groups seemed to be willing to accept less than the average wage increase forecasted. On this background it was claimed that the publication of the forecast for the wage increase contributed to the inflationary development, and that such forecasts ought not to be published in the future.

Trade cycles and inflations as mentioned above represent fields where published forecasts may clearly have harmful effects. Regional migrations of people and economic resources is another field where similar concerns may be justified. However, it should of course not be concluded that, because forecasts in a social context may influence the course of the events being forecasted, such forecasts are always harmful. As we have touched upon particularly in Section 2.3 various sorts of forecasts may be important elements in the Central Authority's attempts to coordinate decisions taken by various agents in the economy. In indicative planning precisely the power of the forecasts to influence the course of the events is one of the main elements relied upon. We shall return to some problems in this connection in a special chapter on the role of macroeconomic planning in an economy with a high degree of decentralized decision-making.

We have distinguished above between different kinds of forecasts. One may also distinguish between various kinds of plans.

In the general definition above we indicated that a complete plan should contain both targets and a plan for actions. Especially long-term plans do often not contain very much of specification of actions to be taken by the Central Authority, it being left to a series of short-term plans to specify these in due course. A plan which specifies in some detail the action to be taken is often called an *operational plan.* A fully operational plan should contain specifications of all actions necessary for the implementation of the plan in the form of statements which are meaningful as messages to the agents subordinate to the Central Authority whose task it is to execute the various parts of the plan. A figure indicating the magnitude of the gross national product is of course not such an operational message – there is no agent to whom this figure would be a meaningful instruction of what it has to do. A figure for the production of steel is not yet operational if steel production is carried out by independent firms. If the steel producers are directly subordinate to a Government ministry, then such a figure is nearer to being operational. However, since there are many types and qualities of steel, a fully operational plan must break down this figure into many more specific components before it gives a complete and unequivocal instruction to the managers of steel plants of what to do.

It follows from these considerations that an operational plan will look very different in economies with a highly centralized decision structure and economies with highly decentralized decision-making. Planning in these two different types of systems is often characterized as *direct planning* versus *indirect planning.*

In a system of direct planning an operational plan must be very detailed and in the end give rise to instructions which contain the "names" of the variables which it is intended to influence, such as the rate of production of various goods, investments of various sorts and so on. For indirect planning this is not so. Indirect planning works by influencing the conditions and/or motivations under which *other* decision-makers determine the magnitudes which the Central Authority intends to influence. For instance, the Central Authority may have some concern for the production of specific goods and wish to influence this production by means of taxes, subsidies and/or price regulations. The operational plan of the Central Authority will in this case imply specific instructions about taxes, subsidies and/or prices, but not instructions to anybody about the rate of output of the commodities concerned.

As a result of such differences an operational plan for e.g., a socialist country in Eastern Europe will generally contain much more of details concerning production, investment, foreign trade, etc., than operational plans in a country like Norway where the typical operational plan is the National Budget together with the State Budget and a plan for various sorts of interference in the credit market. On the other hand, plans which are not meant to be fully operational, particularly really long-term plans, may not be that different in scope and appearance in countries with different systems of management.

Similar distinctions between direct and indirect planning are widely used, though not often precisely defined. The United Nations publication *Economic Planning in Europe*, referred to already in Section 1.1, introduces the distinction in the following terms: "*Direct planning* applies where the Central Authority responsible for the plan has powers of disposition over the preponderant share of national resources. It can therefore assume the functions of both owner and entrepreneur and planning then becomes the explicit technique for economic management; *indirect planning* prevails where such powers are diffused among members of the community in individual or corporate entities and the state is restricted (outside the limited area of its own direct activity as investor, consumer or banker) mainly to measures influencing the use of these rights." It is pointed out that "market economies apply some elements of direct planning and socialist economies use indirect methods of planning." Nevertheless, it is argued that "the differences between the premises and the corresponding types of planning are so profound as to set limits to the possibilities of useful comparison of techniques of planning – and particularly of plan implementations – used in the two groups of countries . . ." This points to a difficulty also for the present lectures. Many topics of planning cannot be treated jointly for such different systems. For instance, although we have tried to remain in this chapter at a rather high level of generality, it is clear that many of the topics treated in the previous sections of this chapter are more relevant to a country in which indirect planning predominates than to a country with extensive direct planning. This applies to our stressing the game nature of the problem, as well as several aspects of coordination and forecasting in relation to planning. The very scheme distinguishing between actions or decisions a and results x is perhaps most useful when indirect planning is of some importance. Comparing the system of strict direct planning to a Robinson Crusoe economy it is clear that the parts of our planning schemes representing pre-ferences W and sets of possible states X are still relevant, and the planning problem may be formulated by means of these elements, whereas there is not so much need for the concepts represented by a and A. However, once it is recognized that there are exogenous elements as represented by z, then the scheme retains more of its relevance since then the resulting state x is not directly and uniquely determined by some action taken by Robinson, but influenced also by elements not under his control. We may then for instance consider inputs into a production process to be the direct decisions represented by a, and these inputs jointly with exogenous factors such as weather conditions determine the outputs represented by x. Similar inter-pretations may be appropriate for some elements of planning in socialist economies. The direct decisions may refer to inputs, whereas outputs are somewhat uncertain results influenced by other factors as well. (Or the direct decisions may refer to outputs, but then with the consequence that required inputs are somewhat uncertain.) For foreign trade direct decisions may refer to quantities of exports and imports, whereas prices are uncertain or determined by other de-cision-makers.

In spite of the striking differences *some* elements of indirect planning are always present for the internal economy even in socialist economies; for instance various sorts of taxes and subsidies are used to influence non-central decision-makers, bonus schemes of various sorts are used to influence management, labour productivity and so on, and of course occasionally the wage and price system is changed so as to influence decisions taken. These indirect means are rarely used as the *only* means of governing the course of production, but rather as means of providing incentives which support the direct decisions about quantities of output. The consequences of the economic reforms in Eastern Europe since the 1960's have however been to extend the scope for indirect planning.

Coming to more technical details concerning the structure of investment and production, and perhaps also the structure of consumer demand, there are of course many aspects which are rather independent of the type of economic system for which one is planning. Furthermore, considerations which are more or less generally valid in one system may be relevant to planning or management in some sectors in other systems.

In view of these observations we have found it interesting and convenient not to separate the treatment of planning under different systems completely, although we have to do so in some contexts.

References for Section 2.7

E.G. Dolan, "The teleological period in Soviet economic planning", *Yale Economic Essays* (1970).

L. Johansen, "Prinsipielle betraktninger om prognoser og langtidsplanlegging", *Memorandum* from the Institute of Economics at the University of Oslo (12 May 1970).

L. Johansen, "Prognoser i samfunnsmessig sammenheng", *Sosialøkonomen*, No. 8 (1971).

P. Massé, "The French plan and economic theory", *Econometrica* (1965).

O. Morgenstern, *Wirtschaftsprognose* (Verlag von Julius Springer, Vienna, 1928).

R. Stone, "Consistent projections in multi-sector models", in *Activity analysis in the theory of growth and planning*, edited by E. Malinvaud and M.O.L. Bacharach (MacMillan, London, 1967).

H. Theil, *Applied economic forecasting* (North-Holland, Amsterdam, 1966). Especially pp. 3–4.

J. Tinbergen, *Central planning* (Yale University Press, New Haven and London, 1964).

United Nations, Economic Commission for Europe, *Economic survey of Europe in 1962* – See reference under Section 1.1.

Chapter 3

VARIOUS WAYS OF SIMPLIFYING THE PLANNING PROBLEM AND THE PLANNING SCHEME IN PRACTICE

3.1. Introduction

In the previous sections we have on several occasions referred to our planning schemes as models which for practical reasons have to be approximations rather than complete and precise descriptions of realities. However, since we have up to now been concerned mainly with principles, concepts, and ways of posing the planning problem, we have not been much concerned with practical problems. We have most of the time been thinking of actions or decisions a, states of the economy x, the structure or mode of operation of the economy represented by f, and the preference scale W (and sometimes also exogenous elements z and decisions by other decision-makers $d_1, \ldots, d_N$) as being complete representations of the relevant elements of the planning problem. It is clear that no practical planning can tackle the problem in this all-embracing form and aim at perfect optimization within the set of possibilities thus generated. Many sorts of simplifications and short-cuts have to be applied in practical planning. The subject of this chapter is to set forth and discuss some such simplifications which are used in practice or recommended in the planning literature. The simplifications can largely be classified under the following categories:

(1) reduction of the size of the problem by neglecting some aspects and/or narrowing down the range of possibilities to be considered without changing the form of the problem;

(2) reduction in the size of the problem by compressing it without changing its form;

(3) simplifications in analyses and calculations achieved by lowering the level of aspiration somewhat with regard to accuracy and perfection in the optimization involved in the basic planning scheme;

(4) splitting of the overall problem into a series of smaller problems between which the interrelationships are relatively simple and easy to handle;

(5) modifications in the form of the problem.

Since some of the simplifications which we shall discuss refer to more than one of these categories at the same time, we shall not proceed strictly in the order suggested by this classification. However, for the evaluation of the various kinds of simplifications and for keeping the contact between practice and the "ideal" theoretical scheme it is useful in each case to consider the procedures in relation to the "ideal" schemes and indicate to which category of simplifications they largely belong.

The reasons for the necessity of relying on simplified analyses as a basis for decisions are of course numerous. They are related to limited insight and imagination, limited possibilities of observation, limited capacity and time for analysis and computations, limited capacity for absorbing information, and so on. The question of how far to go in the direction of perfecting the analyses is in itself an optimization problem, but a peculiar one in that it can itself not be subjected to analysis. This holds at least in the last instance. Should one try to analyse the question of how to strike an optimal balance between perfection and simplification, then the same question could be raised in relation to *this* question, and so on. At some point a decision must be taken on intuitive grounds. It is like going in a big forest to pick mushrooms. One may explore the possibilities in a certain limited region, but at some point one must stop the explorations and start picking because further explorations as to the possibilities of finding more and better mushrooms by walking a little bit further would defeat the purpose of the hike. One must decide to stop the explorations on an intuitive basis, i.e., without actually investigating whether further explorations would have yielded better results.

The costs of data-gathering, analysis, etc. create a sort of paradox for attempts at rational behaviour since an important decision must be taken on intuitive grounds, with no possibility of checking whether it is "rational" without violating the idea of rationality. In the literature such problems are referred to as the "limits of rationality", and decisions and behaviour which reflect limitations and costs of information, analysis, etc. are often referred to as "bounded rationality". (Some key references to discussions by *R. Radner, L.J. Savage, H.A. Simon*, and others are given below.)

The upshot of these viewpoints for the problem of the "optimal degree of simplification" along the lines mentioned above is that we cannot expect to find an analytical method of locating this optimum.

The decision must be taken on the basis of intuition combined with insight from theory and experience from practice.

In principle the problem of obtaining simplified models which match the realities to a reasonable degree, thus forming a sound basis for decisions, is not only a problem of constructing good models, but also of changing the realities. If it is felt or experienced that the actual economic mechanism surrounding us is too complicated to be simulated and understood in a sufficiently simple way, then economic planning and policy will not be of much use. One might then try to *simplify the realities*. In the terminology of the following section this would often be a matter of qualitative policy. Such attempts at simplifying mechanisms are well-known from organizational planning. (See for instance *J.C. Emery.*) They are often described as "decoupling". These are devices by which mutual dependencies between sub-units are weakened. The full system can then be represented by more self-contained subsystems, and the need for coordination is diminished. Larger buffer stocks, the creation of "excess" capacity and slack, flexible multi-purpose tools instead of highly specialized equipment, standardization and limitations of assortment are examples of devices which help in decoupling a system to some degree. When realities are changed by such devices it is clear that central decision-makers can do with a less detailed and less accurate model than when stocks are small, when there is no excess capacity, when equipment is highly specialized, and so on. In the field of national economic planning the choice of instruments in economic policy may be influenced by such considerations, and the grand question of centralization versus decentralization of decision-making may to some extent be seen on the same general background.

References for Section 3.1

J.C. Emery, *Organizational planning and control systems* (Collier–MacMillan, London, 1969).

J. Lesourne, *Cost–benefit analysis and economic theory* (North-Holland, Amsterdam, 1975). Chapter 7, "Information cost and decision cost".

J. Marschak, "Economic planning and the cost of thinking", *Social Research* (1966).

R. Radner, "Satisficing", in *Optimization techniques: IFIP Technical Conference – Lecture notes in computer science 27*, edited by G.I. Marschuk (Springer-Verlag, Berlin, 1975).

L.J. Savage, *The foundations of statistics* (Wiley, New York, 1954).

H.A. Simon, "Theories of decision-making in economics and behavioural science", *American Economic Review* (1959).

H.A. Simon, "Theories of bounded rationality", in *Decisions in organizations*, edited by C.B. McGuire and R. Radner (North-Holland, Amsterdam, 1972).

3.2. Qualitative and Qantitative Aspects of Planning – Economic Systems

A complete description of an economic policy involves qualitative as well as quantitative aspects. Two policies are only quantitatively different if the difference between them can be described in a natural way by the values of a number of quantitatively measurable indicators of the use of policy instruments. Two policies are qualitatively different if the difference between them cannot be described in this way.

Examples of policies which are only quantitatively different are policies which differ with regard to the values of tax parameters, government expenditures on various accounts, the indicators describing monetary and credit policy, and so on. Similarly policies in a highly centralized economy are only quantitatively different if they differ only with regard to for instance production plans assigned to the various branches and enterprises and the values of parameters describing the wage and bonus system. Examples of qualitatively different policies are policies permitting free price movements versus policies including state regulation of prices; policies permitting free imports of commodities versus policies of direct trade regulations; policies where enterprises are given detailed production plans from a central authority versus policies where only a few indicators are given to the enterprises while the details are determined in decentralized ways.

These definitions do not resolve all cases of doubt. For instance, if some sort of tax has not been in use, we might formally say that it has been applied with a zero rate. A change from zero rate to some positive rate is then a quantitative change in policy. But it might also be described as a qualitative change, introducing a new kind of instrument. In several countries the introduction of even a very modest income tax on incomes above a certain limit was considered to bring something essentially new into the economic system and provoked bitter political struggles; on the other hand, the gradual increase in taxation to some ten times the original rate or more has been considered more as a matter of degree and has not given rise to similar confrontations.

A more formal definition than the one given above is perhaps the following: *Two policies are quantitatively different, but qualitatively similar, if the minimal sufficient set of instructions to the executing bodies for the first policy can be applied also for the second policy, only with some figures replaced by others, and vice versa.* By means of the clause "minimal" in the definition this resolves such questions as whether the change from a zero rate for some instrument to a positive rate is a qualitative or a quantitative change. When the instrument is not used (used at zero rate) no further description of this instrument is necessary in the instructions, i.e., it does not belong to the "minimal" sufficient set of instructions. But then the same verbal instructions cannot be used for a policy using the instrument at a positive rate. Consequently, according to this definition, the taking into use of an instrument previously not used represents a qualitative change.

For convenience we shall follow the terminology of *J. Tinbergen* (*The Theory of Economic Policy*) and speak about "qualitative policy" instead of using the heavier expression "choice among policies which may be qualitatively different." In the same way we shall use the expression "quantitative policy" when we consider policy alternatives which are only quantitatively different.

Now qualitative policy will in principle involve everything from a full-scale revolution which changes the pattern of ownership, replaces traditional instruments of policy by a completely new set of instruments, changes the information system, and so on, to a modest change in the form of the tax system. The first type of change might be called changes in the basic premises of the economy or in the economic system, whereas the second type of change might be called qualitative changes within the framework of the prevailing system. Many introductions to the study of economic systems do, in my opinion, tend to blur the distinction by considering the economic system as something chosen by "society", by some collective decision on the basis of rational economic considerations. For instance, a well-known book by C. Landauer, *Contemporary Economic Systems*, defines an economic system in the following terms: "An economic system may be defined as the sum total of the devices by which the preference among alternative purposes of economic activity is determined and by which individual activities are coordinated for the achievement of these purposes. The central problem of any

economic system is the allocation of the resources." Another widely
used book, *A.G. Gruchy*'s *Comparative Economic Systems* presents
the concept of an economic system in the following way: "An
economic system is an evolving pattern or complex of human
relations which is concerned with the disposal of scarce resources
for the purpose of satisfying various private and public needs for
goods and services" – and goes on to assert that such systems have
historical origins and undergo development in such a way as to "move
towards the various goals set by individuals and groups." In my
opinion such definitions tend to assume too much of common purpose
and to assume away too much of power and conflicts. They tend to
neglect the possibility that an economic system may not be established by some sort of collective will, but that it may rather
represent the result of the interplay of all sorts of forces in an
historical process. A system established in this way may very well be
some sort of non-cooperative equilibrium which does not serve any
sort of common purpose. (By most economists and politicians
Sweden is considered to be one of the most firmly planned and
governed countries in the West. Nevertheless an economist, *A. Leion*,
who is by no means an outsider, recently wrote as follows in *"The
Swedish Model"*, "We may accordingly ask ourselves: Who does in
fact govern the development? What is the correct answer? No-
body? No. The answer is that the system governs itself. It moves on
without rudder. Surely, there are officers who *think* they are
navigating . . ." This is obviously pushing things to extremes, but it is
interesting to contrast this viewpoint with the definition of economic
systems found in most text-books.) All the same there will of course
in most systems be some central authority with more or less specific
preferences and purposes guiding its policy. In a broad sense this
central authority will, apart from specific transitional periods, be
interested in status quo with respect to the basic qualitative and power
aspects of the situation and in a smooth functioning of the existing
system.

On the basis of the considerations adduced above I think we may
fruitfully distinguish between the following two types of qualitative
changes:

(1) *Basic qualitative changes which will generally not be contemplated as possible policies by any central authority under the
prevailing power structure.* Such changes will not be evaluated

and compared with ordinary quantitative changes within the same preference structure. They will only be instigated by a change in the power structure of society and the replacement of the previously ruling preference structure by an entirely new one.

(2) *Minor qualitative changes in policy which may be contemplated by a central authority and compared with quantitative changes with regard to costs and benefits, and implemented by the same central authority if the benefits are found to outweigh the costs.*

Although the distinction is of course not absolutely clear, I think it is better to have than not to have it since the clear cases within the two categories are fundamentally different. It would be completely unrealistic to think of changes in policy under the first category to be planned and executed in a systematic way as assumed by the methodology of economic planning. It would not even be clear how to formulate the problem since such changes are bound to happen only when new preference structures are replacing old ones as the governors of the various moves. However, qualitative changes of the second category could in principle be treated similarly to other contemplated changes in policy, "only" with some more technical complexity.

I shall from now on reserve the term "changes in the economic system" for qualitative changes belonging to the first category above, while the term "qualitative policy" will be reserved for changes belonging to the second category.

In economics *J. Tinbergen* has perhaps gone further than any other in trying to use economic theory, and more especially welfare theory, to draw conclusions about an optimal type of economic system, originally in his paper *"The Theory of the Optimum Regime"* (1959), and since then in many other papers. His conclusions are based on a preference function which evaluates the quantitative results of the operation of the system, independently of how the quantitative results are obtained. Patterns of ownership, centralization versus decentralization etc., are considered only as means of obtaining the quantitative results. (The idea that there is an "optimum regime" together with the idea that an economic system is chosen only as means of obtaining good quantitative results has lead to Tinbergen's much debated proposition about the convergence of the various economic systems towards a common system which combines the best aspects of the various existing systems.) The way in which I have drawn the distinction between changes in the economic system on the one hand and qualitative policy on the other implies a somewhat sceptical attitude towards the philosophy underlying these attempts. However, there is no doubt that economics, without necessarily nurturing the ambition of pointing out an "optimal economic system", can contribute very much to the analysis of the operation of various economic systems, and thereby furnish some elements for a comparison of economic systems and accordingly also contribute to the set of factors which may determine changes in economic systems.

This last remark is in the spirit of some suggestions by *R. Frisch.* In discussing problems which involved qualitative changes he often considered preference functions which contained only quantitative descriptions of the state or development of the economy as arguments. However, he was not quite as explicit as J. Tinbergen in drawing conclusions about an optimal economic system. In connection with the problem of whether or not to use certain instruments (often of such importance that he spoke about what type of economic institutions one should establish) he suggested the following type of exercises. First consider the optimization problem in a rather free form in which no assumptions are made about institutional constraints. Next consider the same optimization problem when institutional constraints are taken into account. A comparison between the value of the preference function obtained in the two cases would, according to Frisch, "furnish a sound piece of information," as it would "visualize the penalty we have to pay for restricting the list of politically permissible means of implementation."

In relation to the simple planning scheme introduced in Section 2.1 the "sound piece of information," representing the difference in what can be achieved under a wider and a narrower set of feasible policies, could be expressed as:

$$(1) \qquad \max_{a \in A^{**}} W(f(a, z)) - \max_{a \in A^{*}} W(f(a, z)).$$

Here W is a function evaluating the quantitative aspects of the resulting state $x = f(a, z)$, A^{**} is a set of permissible policies when a wide range of instruments can be used, while A^{*} is the set of permissible policies when there are more restrictions on which instruments can be used. The set A^{*} is accordingly a subset of A^{**}.

The difference in (1) must then clearly be positive, or at least non-negative.

An exercise as suggested by (1) is meaningful if the preference function W can be used to represent preferences with regard to the quantitative aspects of the resulting state x independently of whether the state obtains under a regime characterized by the set A^{**} or the set A^* of permissible policies. The difference in (1) then indicates "the penalty we have to pay for restricting the list of politically permissible means of implementation" (Frisch) from A^{**} to A^*. If the use of instruments permitted by A^{**}, but not by A^*, are in themselves considered to create undesirable conditions for other reasons than the quantitative economic results they generate, then one may still prefer to remain within the boundaries of A^* in spite of a positive difference (1). In principle one may of course think of a more general preference function including also preferences with regard to qualitative aspects, but this is hardly a feasible procedure in practice. Even the characterization of the choice problem involved in qualitative policy in such terms as given by the difference in (1) is a task which in most cases would go beyond what economic analysis can presently furnish. It is hard enough to establish reasonably reliable models for the working of an economy influenced only by variations in a *given* set of instruments. It might appear possible to calculate the results of abandoning the use of some instruments, but perhaps more difficult to calculate the effects of introducing new instruments. The introduction of a new type of tax which influences investment behaviour, may for instance have effects which are difficult to forecast quantitatively, lacking empirical evidence from actual use of the specific type of tax in question. However, sometimes new instruments may have fairly predictable effects and perhaps bring an otherwise uncertain situation under control. This applies particularly when instruments for straight forward direct regulations are introduced for variables which would otherwise be market determined. Conversely, the abandoning of such an instrument might have rather unpredictable effects.

The basic difficulty in this field is that observations generated under one regime do often not permit reliable estimation of what would happen under another regime. Experimentations might be a way out of this difficulty, and there are now some examples of experimentation in economics with the aim of studying what would happen under alternative regimes. In the United States experiments have been conducted with different tax and social benefit schemes for selected groups of people in order to find out for instance about the effects on rates of labour force participation and other aspects of labour supply. (See e.g., the book on *Work Incentives* in the series of *Brookings Studies in Social Experimentation*, and *K. Dickinson* and *H.W. Watts* and further references given there.) In the USSR in the 1960's there were experiments with new forms of planning and management and extended degrees of enteprise independence before decisions about reforms in the economic system on a larger scale were taken. First a limited number of enterprises were selected for the experiments, and gradually as experience and evidence accumulated modified experiments were carried out for larger samples of enterprises. (See for instance *V.G. Afanasyev.*) In Germany (West) a series of books is being published on experimental economic research. These experiments, in which gaming is often used as a tool, are mainly concerned with microeconomic problems. Such experiments and others will probably play a more important part in the future than in the past, and this may help to extend the range of qualitative policies which can be subjected to economic analysis and integrated into the planning schemes alongside with quantitative aspects. (For some thoughts on the possible role of experiments in economics, see *O. Morgenstern* and *J.G. Zielinski.*)

However, for the time being economics is definitely much stronger in studying and evaluating effects of quantitative policy than for the case of qualitative policy. Formalized methods which more or less correspond to the schemes discussed in Chapter 2 are therefore in most cases restricted to quantitative policy. Comparing with the classification of types of simplifications given in Section 3.1, the limitation to studying only quantitative policy is a reduction in the size and complexity of the problem, but it does not in itself change the form of the problem as an optimization problem containing such elements as defined and described in connection with the planning schemes of Chapter 2. In other words, it is a type 1 simplification. The full planning problem will then so to speak have to be solved in two steps. First qualitative policy decisions are taken on the basis of political considerations, intuition, and other forms of less systematized insights, anticipating more or less clearly the quantitative results to be obtainable on the basis of the qualitative decisions. Next the quantitative aspects of the planning problem are worked out in a more systematic way corresponding to the schemes discussed previously, on the basis of a set of possible actions A now restricted by the qualitative decisions already taken. If the results of the quantitative explorations fail to meet some of the anticipations tentatively made at the qualitative stage, then one might return to that stage and try other qualitative decisions. Thus by a rough iteration one may try to approach what should in principle be the solution of a complete and simultaneous model for both qualitative and quantitative aspects. This does however entail the solution for the quantitative aspects of the plan under at least some alternative qualitative conditions (reflected in different structures of A and f in each case) with such difficulties and uncertainties as suggested above.

A book by *W.A. Jöhr* and *H.W. Singer* on *The Rôle of the Economist as Official Adviser* contains an appendix with an explicit criticism of *J. Tinbergen*'s approach to economic planning and policy as outlined in his book *On the Theory of Economic Policy*. One of the main points made here is that a theory of economic policy which is mainly applicable to quantitative policy is very deficient in practice. In order to emphasize the point the authors compare the elaboration of economic policy with the design of a house. In this case it would, in principle, be possible to formalize the problem, introducing all sorts of conditions which refer to the way in which rooms of various sorts should be separated or placed adjacent to each other, how doors and windows should be placed, conditions relating to heating arrangements, and so on. For constructing the complete set of feasible house designs very many complicated indicators and constraints would have to be taken into account, and the optimal choice from this almost intractable set would be a very demanding task. In spite of the perplexing size and degree of complexity of the problem when one thinks of it in these terms, houses are constructed every day, and most of them turn out to be reasonably satisfactory and useful. Jöhr and Singer refer to intuition and judgement combined with a trial and error procedure as the superior method which solves the problem in practice in spite of the fact that a complete formalization would involve almost insurmountable difficulties.

These considerations provide a useful warning and a reminder of the limitations of the use of formalized methods of planning which are able to treat mainly quantitative aspects. However, the allegoric description of the design of a house definitely exaggerates the qualitative aspects as compared with the problem of formulation of economic policy as usually encountered in practice, perhaps apart from special transitional periods of system changes.

Before leaving the subject of qualitative versus quantitative planning, let me briefly suggest a simple method which may be of some help in modest attempts to handle quantitative and qualitative aspects jointly. Let us consider a small market model which is part of a larger planning model. For the specific market under consideration there are two qualitatively different alternatives open; either we may let price and quantity be determined by demand and supply at an equilibrating price, or we may introduce direct price regulation. In the latter case, quantity produced and traded may be determined in different ways. Let it first be determined by demand.

For this market let q be quantity produced, q^D quantity demanded, and q^S the quantity which equates marginal cost to price, i.e., quantity supplied if producers are free to adapt output to a given price. Let the price of the product be p, and let in general y be a vector of other variables influencing the conditions in this market. The vector y may stand for other endogenous variables in the model, exogenous variables and instrument variables. They are included here only to symbolize the fact that the market under consideration is part of a larger system.

Demand and supply functions are denoted by:

(2) $q^D = F(p, y)$,

(3) $q^S = G(p, y)$.

Under free market conditions quantity produced and price would be determined by:

(4) $q = F(p, y) = G(p, y)$ [free market],

while under price control as described above we would have

(5) $p = \bar{p}, \quad q = F(p, y)$ [price control].

Here $\bar{p}$ is the price set by the Central Authority.

If now both these alternatives should be encompassed by the same planning model, then we could formally manage this by introducing a new variable λ defined in the following way:

(6) $\lambda = \begin{cases} 0 & \text{by price control,} \\ 1 & \text{by free market.} \end{cases}$

By means of this variable a general description of the market under consideration can be given in the following way:

(7) $\lambda[F(p, y) - G(p, y)] + (1 - \lambda)(p - \bar{p}) = 0, \qquad q = F(p, y).$

If $\lambda = 1$, the conditions in (7) are equivalent to the description (4) of the conditions of a free market, while, if $\lambda = 0$, the description (7) is equivalent to the description (5) of the conditions under price control. We would then introduce the equations in (7) alongside with all the other conditions of the complete model. The variable λ would then be an instrument which could be used to switch this market between free market conditions and price control. The price fixed under price control, i.e., $\bar{p}$, is another instrument. The variables λ and $\bar{p}$ (the latter being relevant only when $\lambda = 0$) are then components of the full policy description generally denoted by a. [The use of such zero–one variables to represent qualitative aspects of an economic mechanism was suggested by *J. Marschak* (1953).]

If the Central Authority were able and willing to specify in advance the degree of its preference for one of these qualitative alternatives over the other, then an element $k\lambda$ might be added to the preference function W. Apart from the quantitative differences between the situations under free market and price control this term would raise the value of the preference function by k under free market conditions as compared with price control. If $k > 0$ this reflects a preference for free market conditions, and by a maximization of W price control would be chosen (i.e., $\lambda = 0$) only if it results in a quantitative constellation which is sufficiently superior as evaluated by the component of the preference function which has the quantitative variables as arguments.

The variable λ might perhaps also appear in other equations than (7) and the preference function. For instance, if the case of free market and the case of price control entail perceivably different inputs of labour or other resources for, e.g., administration, then a term involving the variable λ should be included in the equations describing the balance between available and utilized amounts of these resources.

By introducing more such variables one could describe several qualitatively different alternatives. For instance, if in addition to price control of the type given by (5) we also have the possibility of introducing price control with quantity determined by the supply function, i.e., the case:

(8) $p = \bar{p},\quad q = G(p, y),$

then the general description could be given by:

$$\lambda[F(p, y) - G(p, y)] + (\mu + \nu)(p - \bar{p}) = 0,$$

(9) $$(\lambda + \mu)[q - F(p, y)] + \nu[q - G(p, y)] = 0,$$

$$\lambda + \mu + \nu = 1 \quad (\lambda, \mu, \nu = 0 \text{ or } 1).$$

The conditions on the last line of (9) imply that one and only one of the variables λ, μ and ν can be equal to 1. If $\lambda = 1$, then we have a free market; if $\mu = 1$, then we have the same case as given by (7); if $\nu = 1$ we have price control with quantity produced determined by the supply function, i.e., there may be unsatisfied demand. In this case all variables λ, μ, ν and $\bar{p}$ would be components of the full policy vector a, and the conditions on the last line of (9) would be parts of the description of the set A of possible policies.

Still another variant that might be described in such terms in the case of price control where quantity produced is determined by the smaller of the values of the two functions F and G, i.e., $q = \text{Min}[F(p, y), G(p, y)]$.

Apart from the choice between price control and free market adaptation of prices and quantities, such devices could be used to introduce the choice between direct import regulations and free import, fixed or floating exchange rates, free or regulated interest rates, etc. A large number of such binary variables (variables which can only take the value zero or one) would have to be introduced. There seem to be no macroeconomic models used in practice which have introduced such variables for making optimal choices between qualitatively different policies. Computationally optimization in models involving both continuous variables and such binary variables is very cumbersome and requires large computational capacities.

However, computations for optimization of more limited, but formally similar models for combined decisions about production and location of enterprises and models integrating decisions about investment projects into a somewhat broader framework have been successfully solved, at least approximately. In such cases binary variables are used to indicate whether a project is included in the full plan or not, and to indicate the choice of location of activities from among a finite number of discrete alternatives. Such choices may also be considered as qualitative policy. Interesting examples of models of this type are found in the references to *D. Kendrick* and to *Multi-level Planning* below. In the literature on operations research, programming and optimization relevant techniques and algorithms are treated under the titles integer (or discrete) programming, when some variables are restricted to taking integer values; zero–one, binary or Boolean programming, when some variables are restricted to taking only the values zero or one; and mixed integer programming when both integer variables and continuous variables enter the same problem. Such devices furnish some possibilities for expanding the generality and range of applicability of planning models somewhat into the sphere of qualitative policy.

As suggested previously one may, however, easily run into problems of estimation of the relevant functions. For instance, if price control has prevailed and the demand function has been suppressed, then it would not be easy to introduce this into the more general model encompassing also the case of free market in a reliable way. The housing market in several countries where there has been rents control is a case in point. It is not easy to estimate what the rents would be, and what the profitability and rate of new residential construction would be, if controls were abandoned and free markets established.

The preceding discussion has been concerned with the introduction of qualitatively different *policy* alternatives. "Artificial" variables like those introduced above are present for instance in the Norwegian national budgetting model MODIS, but for a somewhat different purpose. This refers to the assumptions of the model, particularly to the problem of which variables should be considered as exogenously and which as endogenously determined. For instance, for some production sectors there may be a choice between assuming quantity produced to be exogenously determined (for instance through the availability of some necessary natural resources) or assuming quantity to be determined by demand. For some sectors there is also a choice between, on the one hand, to let output price be exogenously determined (by conditions on the "world market") and profits be endogenously determined, or, on the other hand, to let output price be determined by a mark-up relation for profits. Such choices between alternative assumptions are represented, in the model, by a large number of binary variables, ordered in certain vectors so that it is easy to keep track of the combinations of assumptions in each calculation. Here the qualitative differences refer to assumptions about the actual structure and are not subject to choice for the purpose of optimization. When the assumptions have been chosen from the set of qualitatively different possibilities, then the remaining calculations are purely quantitative. Thus the task is much simpler than in the case of a choice concerning qualitatively different policies. However, lowering the level of ambition from full and perfect optimization, similar techniques can be used for exploring the consequences of alternative qualitative policies by specifying a sample of qualitatively different policies and in each case optimizing with respect to the remaining quantitative aspects.

Also in the French planning model FIFI such binary variables are used so as to keep open different possibilities with regard to exogeneity or endogeneity of various prices.

In econometric literature there are now quite many studies which involve "dummy variables" to represent the switching between different "regimes" in economic policy, for instance in studies of the Phillips curve with, respectively without, various sorts of incomes policy. *S. Gupta et al.* have extended the use of such variables somewhat in the direction of analysis for policy purposes by studying the "optimal coordination of aggregate stabilization policy and price controls." In this study a binary variable is used to represent the turning on and off of a general price control. When price control is turned on, then this is assumed to affect the behaviour of the system also through the effects of price controls on expectations about future prices which again influence actual behaviour in various ways. The "optimal coordination" sought is explored by means of experimental simulation calculations.

Although it is still true, as pointed out above, that economics is stronger in connection with quantitative than in connection with qualitative policy, the brief survey of ideas given above shows that there are several trends which point in the direction of extending systematic analysis also into the field of qualitatively different policies.

References for Section 3.2

V.G. Afanasyev, *The scientific management of society* (Progress Publishers, Moscow, 1971). Especially pp. 213–216.

Beiträge zur experimentellen Wirtschaftsforschung, edited by H. Sauermann (J.C.B. Mohr (Paul Siebeck), Tübingen). The first volume of this series appeared in 1967.

K. Dickinson and H.W. Watts, "The experimental panel data resources at the poverty institute data center", *American Economic Review, Papers and Proceedings* (May 1975).

R. Frisch, "Preface to the Oslo Channel Model", in *Europes future in figures*, edited by R.C. Geary (North-Holland, Amsterdam, 1962).

R. Frisch, "General outlook on a method of advanced and democratic macroeconomic planning", *Memorandum* from the Institute of Economics at the University of Oslo (14 December 1965).

H. Greenberg, *Integer programming* (Academic Press, New York and London, 1971).

A.G. Gruchy, *Comparative economic systems* (Houghton Mifflin, Boston, 1966).

S.K. Gupta et al., "Optimal coordination of aggregate stabilization policy and price controls: Some simulation results", *Annals of Economic and Social Measurement* (1975).

W.A. Jöhr and H.W. Singer, *The rôle of the economist as official adviser* – See reference under Section 2.5.

D. Kendrick, *Programming investment in the process industries* – See reference under Section 1.3.

C. Landauer, *Contemporary economic systems* (J.B. Lippincott, Philadelphia and New York, 1964).

A. Leion, *Den svenska modellen* (Rabén & Sjögren, Stockholm, 1974).

J. Marschak, "Economic measurements for policy and prediction", in *Studies in econometric methods*, edited by W.C. Hood and T.C. Koopmans, Cowles Foundation Monograph 14 (Yale University Press, New Haven, 1953).

O. Morgenstern, "Experiment and large scale computation in economics", in *Economic Activity Analysis*, edited by O. Morgenstern (Wiley, New York, 1954).

Multi-level planning: Case studies in Mexico – See reference under Section 1.3.

J. Tinbergen, *On the theory of economic policy* – See reference under Section 1.3.

J. Tinbergen, "The theory of the optimum regime", in his *Selected papers* (North-Holland, Amsterdam, 1959).

Work incentives and income guarantees: The New Jersey negative income tax experiment, edited by J.A. Pechman and P.M. Timpane, Brookings Studies in Social Experimentation (The Brookings Institution, Washington, DC, 1975).

J.G. Zielinski, "The rôle of economic experiments in improving the economic management mechanism", *Soviet Studies* (1973).

3.3. Aggregation

Up to now we have most of the time thought of the elements involved in the planning scheme as being specified in all details, without being worried about the number of variables and the size of the model and of the analytical and computational tasks. In practice one will have to do with a less perfect representation. In a paper from 1933, in which the term "macro" was used probably for the first time in connection with economics, R. Frisch pointed out that it will always be possible to give an economic analysis full of details if we confine ourselves to a purely formal theory, and continued: "Indeed, it is always possible by a suitable system of subscripts and superscripts, etc., to introduce practically all factors which we may imagine: all individual commodities, all individual entrepreneurs, all individual consumers, etc., and to write out various kinds of relationships between these magnitudes, taking care that the number of equations is equal to the number of variables. Such a theory, however, would only have a rather limited interest . . . . In order to . . . explain the movement of the system taken in its entirety, we must deliberately disregard a considerable amount of the details of the picture. We may perhaps start by throwing all kinds of production into one variable, all consumption into another, and so on, imagining that the notions 'production', 'consumption', and so on, can be measured by some sort of total indices." R. Frisch put down these observations in connection with the need for numerical solutions based on empirical data in connection with economic analysis rather than economic planning in particular. The need to go beyond purely formal analysis is of course even more obligatory in connection with economic planning, and accordingly some aggregation is necessary, although not to the extreme degree suggested at the end of the quotation from R. Frisch.

Referring to the types of simplification listed in Section 3.1, aggregation is the most typical example of type 2, i.e., reduction of the size of the problem by compressing it without altering its form.

The degree of aggregation will have to be different for different kinds of plans. In particular, if a plan is intended to be an operational plan as defined in Section 2.7, then special considerations apply as will be further discussed below.

In discussing the use of aggregation we shall relate the considerations to the simple planning scheme presented in Section 2.1 and illustrated in Figure 1 of that section. It will be obvious how similar considerations could be applied to the extended scheme of Section 2.2 which includes more decision-makers in addition to the Central Authority.

We now consider the elements a (the policy), z (exogenous factors), x (the state of the economy), $x = f(a, z)$ (the model of the structure of the economy) and $W(x)$ (the preference scale), all defined at the beginning of Section 2.1, as a true representation of the underlying realities in all conceivable and relevant details. In practice the scheme can, however, not be used in this form. The natural idea then is to construct an analogous scheme in more aggregated terms. We designate the elements of this scheme in the following way:

(10)
$\bar{a}$: the policy described in aggregated terms;
$\bar{z}$: exogenous factors described in aggregated terms;
$\bar{x}$: the state of the economy described in aggregated terms.

Analogously with the form $x = f(a, z)$ we now tentatively write:

(11) $\bar{x} = F(\bar{a}, \bar{z})$,

to indicate that the resulting state of the economy described in aggregated terms depends on the policy and the exogenous elements, also specified only in aggregated terms. It is very questionable whether this is permissible; this is one of the main points to be discussed below. The preference function is also problematic. We tentatively put it down as:

(12) $\bar{W} = \bar{W}(\bar{x})$.

This will also be further discussed below.

The relationships between the detailed description and the aggregated description of policy, exogenous factors, and resulting states of the economy are represented by:

(13) $\bar{a} = g_a(a), \quad \bar{z} = g_z(z), \quad \bar{x} = g_x(x).$

This means that there are rules of aggregation so that, to every conceivable detailed description of a policy a there corresponds a description of the same policy in aggregated terms, and similarly for the exogenous factors and the state of the economy. If only quantitative policy is considered so that the elements in the formulas in (13) are vectors, then aggregation means that there are fewer components in $\bar{a}$, $\bar{z}$ and $\bar{x}$ than in a, z and x, respectively. The functions g_a, g_z and g_x symbolize the rules of aggregation. In general, these functions cannot be inverted. For instance, while there exists a unique $\bar{a}$ corresponding to every a, there will in general exist many different a's corresponding to the same $\bar{a}$. In other words, if we know the detailed description of the policy we can infer the aggregated description of the same policy; on the other hand, if we know the aggregated description of the policy we can in general not infer a unique detailed description of the policy. Thus there is a loss of information implied by going from a detailed description to an aggregated description. The same applies to exogenous factors and the states of the economy.

The most obvious examples of aggregation are simply *summations*. For instance, if we have several detailed categories of public expenditures indicated in the detailed description a of an economic policy, then we will have fewer categories in the aggregated description $\bar{a}$. The summations of the relevant detailed categories so as to obtain the aggregated categories are parts of the rules of aggregation represented by the function symbol g_a. Similarly the summation of various categories of exports may be parts of the rules of aggregation represented by g_z if volumes of exports are taken as exogenous factors. The formation of national accounting aggregates on the basis of more detailed information are parts of g_x.

In many cases not ordinary summations, but rather *weighted sums* are used, for instance in forming aggregated volume categories by using a set of fixed base prices. *Averages* will also often be represented in the rules of aggregation. In the aggregated description of policy we may for instance use some average tax rates which are formed as averages of detailed tax rates represented in the description a of a policy. The ways in which the averages are formed are then parts of the symbolic representation g_a of the rules of aggregation. For the exogenous factors we may have individual prices of commodities traded on world markets in the detailed description z whereas averages or indexes are represented in the aggregated description $\bar{z}$. In describing the state of the economy individual internal prices may be involved in x while only averages or indexes are represented in $\bar{x}$.

For the major part the functions g_a, g_z and g_x will, as suggested by these examples, represent linear functions transforming many variables in the detailed description into a smaller number of variables in the aggregated description. But non-linear functions may also be involved. In particular, when both prices, volumes, and values are taken into account in the description of the state of the economy, then there may be ways of aggregating from the detailed description to the aggregated description which involve non-linearities stemming from the fact that value is equal to price multiplied by quantity.

Aggregation in the ways suggested above, comprising only quantitative variables, is not very problematic. The case of qualitative differences is more problematic. This refers particularly to the description of the economic policy. For instance, consider the problem of whether or not there should be direct import regulation. In the detailed description of the policy, we may describe the qualitative choice between direct regulation or free import referring to each individual import commodity. Thus we may have import regulation for some groups of commodities and free import for others. These choices could be represented for instance by a set of binary variables in the way illustrated in the preceding section. If we now construct an aggregated model analogously with the detailed description, aggregating for instance to such a degree that there remains only one category of imports, then there would seem to be a choice between only two possibilities, either full-scale free imports or full-scale import regulation. This would conceal policy possibilities to an intolerable degree. One should somehow, in the aggregated description of the policy, try to represent intermediate cases with import regulation for some commodities and free import for others. This would entail some sort of quantitative indicator of the extent of regulation of imports (perhaps formed as a sort of index of the binary variables describing the actual policy in detail). It is, however, less obvious than in the purely quantitative cases suggested above how this should be done. In general, aggregation is easier and works more satisfactorily in connection with quantitative planning than for qualitative planning.

We now turn to the somewhat deeper problems involved in aggregation. For convenience we have put together the various elements introduced above in Figure 9. In this figure we have, in addition to the

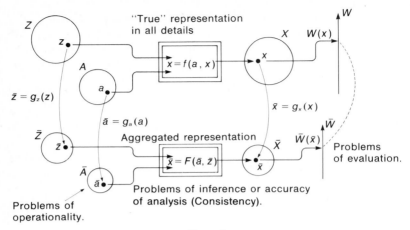

Figure 9

elements introduced by (10)–(13), also indicated the set of possible policies $\bar{A}$, the set of possible constellations of exogenous factors $\bar{Z}$, and the set of possible states of the economy $\bar{X}$, all expressed in aggregated terms. The set $\bar{A}$ is the set of all possible $\bar{a}$, i.e., the set which can be generated by $\bar{a} = g_a(a)$ when a varies over the set A of possible policies described in all details. Similarly $\bar{Z}$ is generated by g_z and Z, and $\bar{X}$ generated by g_x and X.

The problems encountered in planning by means of a representation of the economy in aggregated terms can now be grouped in the following categories: Problems of *operationality*, problems of *evaluation*, and problems of *inference or accuracy of analysis*. Although there are some overlappings, we shall discuss these fields of problems one by one. In this discussion we assume that the underlying structure is represented in a true and accurate way by means of the elements a, A, z, Z, x, X, f, and W. In this form the structure is, however, unknown or unmanagable, and planning is accordingly performed by means of an aggregated representation in terms of $\bar{a}$, $\bar{A}$, $\bar{z}$, $\bar{Z}$, $\bar{x}$, $\bar{X}$, F, and $\bar{W}$. Statistics for the aggregated categories must of course be based on a larger number of observations of the detailed elements, but they are aggregated so to speak before the planners get in touch with them. The aggregation functions g_a, g_z and g_x may exist in a statistical bureau and administrative offices in the form of explicit mathematical formulas, in the form of computational programmes, or in the form of statistical and administrative routines used in producing figures at the level of aggregation used by the planners.

Operationality.   In Section 2.7 we defined a fully operational plan as a plan which contains "specifications of all actions necessary for the implementation of the plan in the form of statements which are meaningful as messages to the agents subordinate to the Central Authority whose task it is to execute the various parts of the plan." If a plan is to be operational, this clearly sets limits to the degree to which the elements of the policy description a can be aggregated. Take for instance the granting of licenses for imports, building licences, or the extension of loans from state banks. In all these cases the concrete execution of the policy consists in the granting of the individual licences or loans. However, a plan which operates with aggregated figures in the form of total amounts of licences and loans, perhaps subdivided into categories according to certain criteria, will still qualify as an operational plan since such totals will be meaningful as instructions to the executing administrative bodies. On the other hand, a plan including tax policy which specifies only the total amount of direct taxes to be collected, the total amount of indirect taxes to be collected, etc. is not operational since these figures are not meaningful as instructions to the tax assessing and collecting authorities. It is of course conceivable that the details of the tax schemes might be determined by administrative bodies so as to aim at reaching the total figures indicated in the plan. The main point is, however, that these administrative authorities would be unable to predict a total tax revenue generated by the various schemes since revenue will depend upon the repercussions in the whole economic system. It will also be influenced by other policy parameters than those characterizing the tax system. In many countries policy proposals involving the use of the total quantity of money as an important instrument fail to be operational because the "total quantity of money" is not clearly defined, or is itself not determined directly by any political or administrative body, but only indirectly linked to such decisions through relationships that are only partly understood. Thus an instruction to set aggregate money supply at a specified level does not always meet the requirement of operationality.

The use of highly aggregated indicators of economic policy rather than operational specifications has often left plans or planning models suspended in the air. This is perhaps particularly true for many developing countries, but it applies also to many other countries. In Norway, for example, the usefulness of the National Budget was for many years undermined by the fact that the aggregate indicators of the economic policy in the National Budget did not correspond well with the figures on the revenue and expenditure sides of the State Budget which forms the basis for the administrative execution of many parts of the economic policy of the Government. This was remedied to some extent by a statistical regrouping of the items on the State Budget so as to conform somewhat more closely with the categories of the National Budget. More recently the situation has again become somewhat better, partly by reformulation of the national budgetting model, construction of special computational programmes that provide the link between aggregate tax figures and the detailed decisions on rates, exemptions, and so on, and finally by a rearrangement of the standard form of the State Budget. But there are still considerable problems referring to the detailed definitions of the items in the State Budget as compared with the National Budget aggregates, and to the detailed timing of revenues and expenses. Monetary and credit policy represents another important channel for the execution of the Government's economic policy. Here the operationality of the National Budget still suffers from missing or weak links between the aggregate indicators in the National Budget and the concrete, detailed execution of this part of the policy, although a partial link is provided by the stipulation, in the National Budget, of figures for loans to be extended by the State banks. (A special research project has been initiated in the Central Bank of Norway in order to improve the situation in this policy.)

As suggested previously the requirement of operationality is particularly important for short-term plans. In medium or long-term plans one may be less restrained in working with an aggregated description of economic policy.

Evaluation. When we first, in Section 2.1, introduced the symbol x for the description of the state of the economy, we pointed out that in principle "the description has to be as detailed as required by the Central Authority in order to judge about the desirability of the state." Aggregation of the components of x beyond this will imply a loss of information that will make evaluations of the state more uncertain. The actual situation would, on the basis of complete information, be evaluated by the preference scale $W(x)$. When we only know the states as described in aggregated terms by $\bar{x}$, then we want the preference function $\bar{W}$ to be such that it ranks the possible states in approximately the same way as the correct and complete preference scale $W(x)$. More precisely: Consider two alternative states x' and x''. In aggregated terms these states are represented by $\bar{x}' = g_x(x')$ and $\bar{x}'' = g_x(x'')$. By means of the preference function in the aggregated representation these two states are evaluated by:

$$(14) \qquad \bar{W}(\bar{x}') = \bar{W}(g_x(x')) \quad \text{and} \quad \bar{W}(\bar{x}'') = \bar{W}(g_x(x'')).$$

We now want this evaluation to be compatible with the evaluation based on the detailed descriptions, i.e., we want the following condition to be satisfied:

$$(15) \qquad \bar{W}(\bar{x}') \gtreqless \bar{W}(\bar{x}'') \quad \text{according as} \quad W(x') \gtreqless W(x'').$$

This would hold good, for any pair x', x'' in X, if the following relation holds identically in x over the set of possible states X:

$$(16) \qquad \bar{W}(g_x(x)) \equiv W(x).$$

This means that we would like to have aggregation functions g_x which are such that the preference function $W(x)$ can be arranged with these as kernel functions.

In trying to get relation (16) at least approximately fulfilled we are in practice not free to let the aggregation functions g_x be determined only by this requirement. The aggregation functions must be of such a form that they are statistically and administratively manageable and interpretable. To what extent is it possible to get (16) satisfied with "natural" aggregates is crucially dependent upon the price system. The ideal price system, from this point of view, is a set of prices which reflect marginal rates of substitution in preference functions. For instance, if consumers are price-takers and markets are balanced, then economic theory furnishes good reasons to consider total volume of consumption calculated by means of such prices as a good "kernel" in the preference function of consumers over a range of variation around the base point which is not too wide. If the preference function of the Central Authority exhibits "consumers' sovereignty", then the Central Authority may on such grounds be justified in neglecting information about details of the composition of private consumption and evaluate the results of policy, as far as private consumption is concerned, only on the basis of aggregated figures. At least, this might be acceptable if all consumers were on approximately the same level of income. Otherwise the Central Authority might stop short of this complete aggregation, and instead use figures for the total consumption of groups of consumers, the groups being defined by criteria which the Central Authority finds relevant for its evaluations. Another example: The detailed description of the results of economic policy may contain information on exports and imports of all commodities. For the evaluation of the results this is probably superfluous. The evaluation of this aspect will probably be concerned mainly with the balance of payment effects, and these can be expressed conveniently by suitable aggregates of exports and imports. Such aggregates accordingly form convenient kernels of the total preference function.

The calculation of volume indexes by means of a set of base prices is useful also on many other points than private consumption. Such volume indexes are, however, in general only of a rather "local" validity, base prices reflecting the marginal rates of substitution in the underlying more detailed preference structure only in a certain neighbourhood around a base point. The form of the set of possible states X is therefore of great importance for the validity of evaluations based on aggregated figures. If the set of possible states X is such that certain variables remain in rather constant proportions over the full set X, then these variables can be aggregated without much loss in the accuracy of relevant evaluations regardless of whether or not the marginal rates of substitution in the more detailed preference structure would change considerably if it were possible to move outside the set X. For instance, if incomes of various groups tend to move in approximately constant proportions regardless of how the instruments of policy are used, then there is no great loss as far as accuracy of evaluations are concerned by aggregating incomes of these groups.

From the discussion of possible losses of relevant information by aggregation it should not be concluded that one should always aggregate to the smallest degree possible, i.e., only to the degree that other considerations than those presently being discussed impose upon us. Evaluating alternative results is in itself a complicated task, and if alternative results are described in too much detail, then no human being would be able to compare and rank them without access to simplifying devices. Already a model like the Norwegian national budgetting model MODIS produces so much of detailed results that Government officials and politicians are in need of aggregated descriptions of the results in order to evaluate them.

Problems of Inference or Accuracy of Analysis. We now come to the problem which is often described as *the* aggregation problem. It is concerned with the question of whether or not it is possible to infer correctly about the state of the economy in aggregated terms, $\bar{x}$, from aggregated information about $\bar{a}$ and $\bar{z}$, not knowing the details contained in the underlying a and z. This is the same as the question whether or not there really exists a function F as tentatively introduced by (11) and indicated as a function from the sets $\bar{A}$ and $\bar{Z}$ to the set $\bar{X}$ in Figure 9. In general, the answer is in the negative. This is visualized by Figure 10. We start the consideration from a given

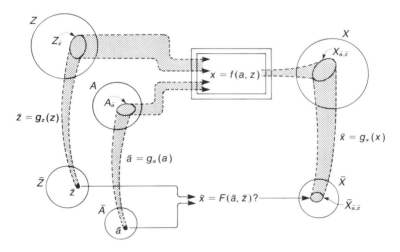

Figure 10

macro description of policy $\bar{a}$, and a given constellation of exogenous factors in aggregated description, $\bar{z}$. We are interested in finding out what conclusions can be inferred from this about the state of the economy in aggregated terms, $\bar{x}$. This must be done via the correct underlying structure as represented in all details by $x = f(a, z)$.

We then first observe that, to a given macro description of the
policy $\bar{a}$, there corresponds a set of policies a described in details.
This is indicated in Figure 10 as a subset of A and consists of all
elements a which are such that they produce the given element $\bar{a}$ by
aggregation, i.e., by $\bar{a} = g_a(a)$. In the same way there is a subset of Z
which is compatible with the given constellation $\bar{z}$ of exogenous
factors in aggregated terms, i.e., a subset of elements z which are
such that $g_z(z)$ produces the given constellation $\bar{z}$ in aggregated terms.
In the figure these subsets are denoted by $A_{\bar{a}}$ and $Z_{\bar{z}}$ respectively.
Now let a vary over $A_{\bar{a}}$ and z vary over $Z_{\bar{z}}$. Through the correct
detailed description of the structure of the economy $x = f(a, z)$ these
variations generate a set of states of the economy which is a subset of
X. In the figure this subset is denoted by $X_{\bar{a},\bar{z}}$. This is the set of
possible states of the economy, described in all details, which are
compatible with the given aggregated policy description $\bar{a}$ and the
given aggregated description of the constellation of exogenous factors
$\bar{z}$. The final step in order to see what this implies for the resulting
state of the economy in aggregated terms, is to consider the ag-
gregation function $\bar{x} = g_x(x)$. When x now varies over $X_{\bar{a},\bar{z}}$, then this
aggregation function generates a set of possible states as described in
aggregated terms. This is a subset of $\bar{X}$ which is, in the figure,
denoted by $\bar{X}_{\bar{a},\bar{z}}$.

The reasoning presented above represents the inference about the
resulting state of the economy in aggregated terms which can be
correctly drawn from an aggregated specification of policy and ex-
ogenous factors. The crucial question clearly is how large the set $\bar{X}_{\bar{a},\bar{z}}$
will be. If this set is very large, then there is a loss of accuracy due to
the aggregation of the description of policy and exogenous factors
which will make planning in aggregated terms a dubious matter. Any
attempt to describe the structure of the economy in terms of a
macro model as symbolized by $\bar{x} = F(\bar{a}, \bar{z})$, tentatively introduced by
(11), will involve chances of gross errors. (Logically there is of course
the possibility that all elements of the set $\bar{X}_{\bar{a},\bar{z}}$ are almost indifferent
according to the preference function $\bar{W}$, or even better, that all
elements of $X_{\bar{a},\bar{z}}$ are indifferent according to the preference scale W.
Then the indeterminacy would be of no consequence with regard to
the preference level reached. There is, however, no reason to expect
that this should be so.) On the other extreme the set $\bar{X}_{\bar{a},\bar{z}}$ may collapse
into containing only one element $\bar{x}$. If this holds good for every
specification of $\bar{a}$ in $\bar{A}$ and $\bar{z}$ in $\bar{Z}$, then there exists a function F as

introduced by (11) and there is no loss in accuracy due to the aggregation. This does not require that the set $X_{\bar{a},\bar{z}}$ collapses in this way. Even if the set $X_{\bar{a},\bar{z}}$ is quite large the aggregation functions $\bar{x} = g_x(x)$ may "collect" all the elements of this set into one element $\bar{x}$ in $\bar{X}$.

In working with aggregated concepts we do of course wish the loss in accuracy to be small. In trying to meet this requirement we have at our disposal the degree and form of aggregation as represented by the aggregation functions; these are "man-made" for analytical purposes and not descriptions of given realities. There is, however, no complete freedom. As emphasized before it is desirable that the aggregates are administratively and statistically convenient and rather easily interpretable, and for the aggregation of x into $\bar{x}$ we must also take into account the concern for the evaluation problem. For the aggregation of the description of policy a into $\bar{a}$ we have to bear in mind the requirement of operationality, particularly in short-term plans. The latter consideration does however not often run counter to the concern for accuracy of inference if administrative divisions are reasonably formed.

Usually there are two different bases for aggregation when we want the loss in accuracy to be small. Roughly the first condition, which might be called the case of *restricted domain*, says that variables which always vary according to a rather fixed pattern in relation to each other may be aggregated. The other condition says that variables which have always approximately the same comparative effects on the variables representing the "output" of the analysis may be aggregated. This may be called the case of *equivalent effects*. We have an example of the case of restricted domain if some world market prices included in the detailed description z of exogenous factors always vary in approximately the same proportions. They may then be well represented by an index. Looking at Figure 10 this means that the bunch from $\bar{z}$ to the set Z is narrow so that $Z_{\bar{z}}$ is a small set, and correspondingly the effects from variations within this set do not contribute much to making the set $X_{\bar{a},\bar{z}}$ large. An example of approximately equivalent effects may be the granting of building licences or import licences. If the total amounts of licences granted are contained in the description $\bar{a}$, then these totals may be composed in many different ways so that the set $A_{\bar{a}}$ is quite large. Correspondingly the set $X_{\bar{a},\bar{z}}$ may also be large, but when it comes to the aggregated description of the resulting state of the economy, in terms of gross national product, total employment, balance of payment, etc., then this may nevertheless narrow down to a small set $\bar{X}_{\bar{a},\bar{z}}$.

The last statement holds true if the effects of all types of building activity included under the licence regulations have almost the same macroeconomic effects, and similarly for imports. Whether this will be so or not is partly a question about the form of the aggregation functions g_a. For instance, in the case of building licences, the total amount of licences may be measured in different ways, and not all of them may be equally good for all purposes. Aggregation works best when the comparative effects are the same with regard to *all* variables used in the aggregate description of the resulting state of the economy.

The rearrangement of the system of the State Budget of Norway, mentioned under the discussion of operationality above, is relevant also for the accuracy of analysis. Under the traditional system state expenditures were mainly classified according to administrative criteria. Under the new system several kinds of groupings are used, with aggregate classification into such categories as current expenditures on goods and services, expenditures for new buildings and plants, transfers to the private sector and municipalities, repayment of debt, etc., as the most useful one for analysing the macroeconomic effects of a certain budget. This classification is an example of constructing aggregation functions g_a on the basis of the criterion of approximately equivalent effects.

In order to discuss aggregation problems more fully it would be necessary to specify the structure of the economy in more basic terms than the "reduced form" which we have been using in representing it symbolically as $x = f(a, z)$. It should also be noticed that our discussion is somewhat limited by the fact that we have assumed that there is a stable structure $x = f(a, z)$ when all details are included. It may happen that there is no such stable detailed structure. Then aggregated relationships may sometimes be more stable than the micro relationships. For instance, a total demand relation for cheese may be more stable than demand relations for individual types of cheese. However, such "favourable" effects probably apply only up to some rather moderate level of aggregation.

There is now a large body of specialized literature on problems of aggregation in economics. A good survey is provided by *H.A.J. Green*. See also *Y. Ijiri*. A brief exposition of some aspects is given in *R.G.D. Allen*'s *Mathematical Economics*. Most of the literature is concerned with problems which, in our classification above, fall in the category "problems of inference or accuracy of analysis". The problem is often referred to as the problem of "*consistent aggregation*". Criteria for aggregation which are above roughly suggested by reference to the restrictedness of the domain are often discussed in a terminology referring to the "degrees of freedom". Such restrictions are often deduced from optimizing behaviour. Criteria corresponding to our term "equivalent effects" often end up by requiring linearity of some functions. Analyses relevant to what we have called the problem of "evaluation" are found under phrases referring to "functional separability", "two-stage maximization", the theory of "utility trees", and perhaps also other terms. In addition there is of course very much to be found in economic welfare theory and the theory of price indices that is relevant to the problem of evaluation.

Much of the theoretical literature is concerned with exact consistency, and generally finds that the conditions for this are so strict that they can rarely be expected to be fulfilled in practice. This does not always give a good guide to practice where approximate consistency would be sufficient. A practical approach is taken by J. *Kornai* and other Hungarian economists. From a large, detailed, and accordingly not quite transparent model they have calculated a large number of feasible and rather widely dispersed solutions and fitted macro functions to the corresponding aggregates. This is found useful in gaining insight into the mode of operation of the more detailed model and in perceiving the range of possibilities involved in the detailed structure.

In this section we have treated one level of planning – planning on behalf of a central authority – and discussed aggregation problems encountered in the elaboration of a plan at this level. In a hierarchical system where there are exchange of information and plans and some scope for independent decisions at various levels, some further problems related to aggregation may be encountered. We shall touch upon some such problems on various occasions in the following, particularly in the discussion of decentralization. A brief discussion of some such problems is given by M. *Ellman*.

References for Section 3.3

R.G.D. Allen, *Mathematical economics* (MacMillan, London, 1965) Chapter 20.

M. Ellman, "Aggregation as a cause of inconsistent plans", *Economica* (1969).

R. Frisch, "Propagation problems and impulse problems in dynamic economics", in *Economic essays in honour of Gustav Cassel* (Allen and Unwin, London, 1933).

H.A.J. Green, *Aggregation in economic analysis* (Princeton University Press, Princeton, 1964).

Y. Ijiri, "Fundamental queries in aggregation theory", *Journal of the American Statistical Association* (1971).

J. Kornai, *Mathematical planning of structural decisions*, 2nd enlarged edition (North-Holland, Amsterdam, 1975). Especially Section 29.6.

3.4. *Planning in Stages*

The need for aggregation in connection with economic planning described in the preceding section clearly raises a dilemma: on one hand considerations concerning the sheer size of the planning model may compel us to aggregate variables and relations to a considerable degree; on the other hand concern for the operationality of the ensuing plan requires quite much of detailed specifications. There may be no level of aggregation which is satisfactory from both these points of view at the same time. "Planning in stages", a term coined by *J. Tinbergen*, is a method of resolving this dilemma. The idea is that a complete plan should be worked out in a series of "stages" which refer to different levels of aggregation. First a highly aggregated model should be used in order to work out a plan in terms of a few key aggregated variables. The information contained in the specification of the aggregated variables should next be used as a starting point, and as frames or conditions for working out more detailed, i.e., less aggregated aspects of the plan. The process should continue through stages until one reaches a degree of detailedness which is satisfactory from the point of view of operationality of the plan. (Tinbergen did not emphasize the requirement for operationality as I have done here, but this seems to me to be a major point of view.) In one of his early expositions of "planning in stages" (1960) Tinbergen distinguished between a *macro stage* in which such key variables as gross national product and its rate of growth, total investment, total consumption, total exports and total imports were determined; a *sector stage* in which these variables were split up according to production sectors; a *project stage* in which individual projects were appraised and ranked, and finally a *regional stage* in which at least some of the variables, particularly those emerging from the project stage, were given a regional designation. The variables determined at each stage should be compatible with plan figures worked out at the preceding stages. [Tinbergen had suggested the necessity of planning in stages already in his *On the Theory of Economic Policy* (Chapter VIII). A series of stages deviating some-

what from those suggested above is given in J. Tinbergen's and H.C.
Bos' *Mathematical Models of Economic Growth* (Section 1.4), and an
again slightly different system is suggested in J. Tinbergen's *Central
Planning* (Chapter 4). The differences refer particularly to the order
of the regional and the project stage.]

In order to elucidate the idea of planning in stages let us briefly
consider a very simple example. We consider the problem of demand
management within the framework of a multiplier model. In the
detailed description of the economy we distinguish between n branches. We neglect input–output relations so that total value of output
in each sector consists of wages and profits, in proportions which may
be different as between sectors. Total demand towards each sector
consists of consumption demand and investment goods demand.
Consumption demand depends upon wage income and profits, with
possibly different demand coefficients, and there is also an exogenous
element. Investment consists of an endogenous element determined
by profits and an exogenous element. The exogenous elements in
consumption and investment may contain both non-controlled elements and elements determined by the Central Authority, i.e., instrument variables, but for the present purpose it is not necessary to
distinguish these symbolically.

The complete model then consists of the following equations:

(17) $x_i = c_i + j_i,$ $i = 1, \ldots, n,$

(18) $c_i = \alpha_i W + \beta_i P + \gamma_i + c_i^0,$ $i = 1, \ldots, n,$

(19) $j_i = \lambda_i P + \mu_i + j_i^0,$ $i = 1, \ldots, n,$

(20) $W = \sum_{k=1}^{n} w_k x_k,$

(21) $P = \sum_{k=1}^{n} (1 - w_k) x_k$

(22) $X = \sum_{k=1}^{n} x_k, \qquad C = \sum_{k=1}^{n} c_k, \qquad J = \sum_{k=1}^{n} j_k.$

All magnitudes are values in constant prices. Macro variables are
distinguished by capitals. The value of output from sector no. i is x_i,

consisting of consumption goods c_i and investment goods j_i. Equations (18) represent demand functions with demand for commodity no. i depending upon total wage income W and total profits P with α_i, β_i and γ_i as constants. The symbol c_i^0 represents exogenous consumption demand. Equations (19) give investment demand as functions of profits with λ_i and μ_i as constants and j_i^0 representing exogenous investment demand. In equation (20) w_k is the wage share in sector no. k, and the summation indicated in the formula then gives total wage income W. Similarly equation (21) gives total profits P. In equations (22) we define total output, which is the same as total income, as X, total consumption as C, and total investment as J.

We might now consider equations (17)–(21) as a set of $3n + 2$ equations in the same number of variables, viz. x_i, c_i, j_i for $i = 1, \ldots, n$, W and P. This system can be solved when the exogenous elements c_i^0 and j_i^0 are specified. As suggested above the latter elements may contain instrument variables. When this system has been solved the totals in equations (22) can be calculated by simple summations. The policy problem is to specify the instrument elements in c_i^0 and j_i^0 in such a way that certain macroeconomic goals concerning total output, consumption, and investment, and perhaps also concerning the income components W and P, are reached. There may be a preference function with these variables as arguments, which is to be maximized, perhaps constrained by capacity limitations. However, we need not consider these problems further for the present purpose. We limit ourselves to considering the problem of solving the equations for specified values of the exogenous elements, including instruments. Whether or not there is a preference function in the background, the plan figures must as a minimum requirement for consistency satisfy the equations.

As mentioned above we have a system of $3n + 2$ equations. However, there is a rather simple structure which permits some simplifications. We may insert from (20) and (21) into (18) and (19), and further insert from these equations into (17). We then have a system of n equations in the n unknowns $x_1, \ldots, x_n$. When this system is solved as a simultaneous system, we can insert back and obtain all the other variables.

This describes the complete and exact solution in the present case. For illustrating the idea of planning in stages let us now see whether we can arrange the solution of the model in such a way that we first use a pure macro model, and next find the values of the variables referring to the various sectors in a simplified way by using the information already contained in the solution from the macro model. In general we cannot obtain the exact solution in this way. What we look for is a procedure which gives us sufficiently good approximations by such a two-stage calculation, and which is simpler than the elaboration of the exact solution as described above.

From equations (17)–(19) we obtain by summation:

(23) $X = C + J,$

(24) $C = \alpha W + \beta P + \gamma + C^0,$

(25) $J = \lambda P + \mu + J^0,$

where α, β, γ, λ, and μ are defined by summation of the corresponding coefficients referring to sectors, i.e., $\alpha = \Sigma \alpha_i$, etc. Furthermore $C^0 = \Sigma c_i^0$ and $J^0 = \Sigma j_i^0$. From (20)–(22) it furthermore follows that:

(26) $X = W + P.$

When C^0 and J^0 are specified we now have four equations to determine the five macro variables X, C, J, W and P. We still miss one equation. This evidently refers to the determination of the distribution of income between wages and profits. This aspect cannot be determined from pure macro analysis if the distribution share w_k varies as between sectors. This is the key point where we have to introduce an approximation which simplifies the analysis so that all the macro variables can be determined without determining at the same time the internal structure, i.e., sectoral composition of the various aggregates. The simplification which suggests itself is to put:

(27) $W = wX,$

where w is the wage share in total income. This specification would be correct if all wage shares $w_1, \ldots, w_n$ were equal. Equation (20) could then be written in the form of (27). In general w is not constant independent of the sectoral composition. On the basis of equations (20) we may consider w as an average of the wage shares in the individual sectors since we have:

(28) $$W = \frac{\Sigma w_k x_k}{\Sigma x_k} X = wX,$$

i.e.,

(29) $$w = \frac{\Sigma w_k x_k}{\Sigma x_k}.$$

Now the introduction of w as a symbol in (27) does not help to make the macroeconomic model determinate as long as w is not a constant independent of the sectoral composition. However, we may, as an approximation, pretend that w is constant and thus solve the macro model (23)–(27) with regard to all macro variables X, C, J, W and P. This is easily done (but it is not necessary for our purpose to put down the solution).

Planning in stages (of which there are now two) would consist of the following steps.

First stage. Solve the macro model (23)–(27) for specified values of C^0 and J^0, treating the wage share w as a constant. As already suggested there may be a preference function which we want to maximize by means of the instrument elements contained in C^0 and J^0. The calculations at this stage may therefore consist of more than a simple solution of the equation system. The system is however small and transparent, and it would be easy to vary the instrument components so as to achieve a satisfactory constellation of the endogenous variables.

Second stage. Having obtained the values of all macro variables in the first stage, we can now calculate the sector variables in a very simple way. First of all we have of course to break down the aggregate values of C^0 and J^0 into sectoral components c_i^0 and j_i^0. The sums of these should be compatible with the values of the macro variables, but the compositions may reflect preferences with regard to the more detailed structure. Once these elements are specified we can calculate consumption demand c_i and investment demand j_i from equations (18) and (19), using the values already obtained in the first stage for wage income W and profits P. Next we simply add c_i and j_i so as to obtain sectoral output x_i according to (17), for $i = 1, \ldots, n$.

A remarkable thing about this procedure is that we need to solve only the small macro system as a system of simultaneous equations (five equations and variables in the present illustrative case). The sectoral composition of the various aggregates can be found in the second stage, using information from the first stage, by very simple calculations involving nothing like a solution of a system of simultaneous equations of the order n.

The problem involved, which makes this an approximation rather than a correct detailed solution, is related to the use of the average wage share w. In the first stage, where we have to specify a value for this wage share, we may for instance use the observed wage share in total income from a previous year, or perhaps this value extrapolated according to a trend (which in our case might be due to trends in the composition of output). When the calculations in the second stage have been performed, an average income share is implied since we have now calculated all sectoral outputs x_i; an average wage share can then be calculated according to formula (29). If this wage share should happen to be equal to the one from which we started out in the first stage, then all equations of the complete model are satisfied, and we have reached a correct solution by the two-stage procedure. This would happen only by coincidence. We may however hope for a good approximation. If the wage share implied by the detailed calculations at the second stage is very near to the wage share from which we started out in the first stage, then this is an indication that the full solution for all variables is approximately correct since the model is so simple that there is nothing which could cause discontinuities. If there is time and practical possibilities it would always be desirable, at the end of this second stage to calculate the implied average wage share and compare it with the one originally assumed in the first stage. If there is a disturbing discrepancy, we might revise the value of the wage share and repeat the calculations at the first stage, and consequently also repeat the calculations at the second stage. There are now good reasons to expect the implied wage share emerging at the end of the second stage to be nearer to the one now assumed at the first stage. In this way we might proceed with an iteration, repeating calculations at the first and second stage and correcting the assumed value of the wage share at the first stage in each round. However, with a reasonable structuring of the revision procedure and a reasonable estimate of the initial average wage share one would not expect more than one or two iterations to be necessary, and in many practical cases already the first round would yield sufficiently good approximations. It does of course help if the various wage shares $w_1, \ldots, w_n$ are not too different so that the average wage share w is rather stable even if the sectoral composition of total output changes. Furthermore it helps if the marginal propensities to spend out of wages and profits are not very different since a revision of w, and accordingly of W and P, will then not entail dramatic changes in the composition $x_1, \ldots, x_n$ of X.

In the small example given above we obtained very much by way of simplifications in the second stage because of the special structure of the model. The point is that the variables W and P play a special role in that all simultaneity in the model so to speak operates through these variables. [This point emerges very clearly if we insert from (18) and (19) into (17) and consider the resulting equations jointly with (20) and (21) as a system of $n + 2$ equations in the $n + 2$ variables $x_1, \ldots, x_n, W, P$. The coefficient matrix of this system then reveals the key roles of W and P.] If we for instance had included input–output relations, then there would also be direct links between the various $x_1, \ldots, x_n$, i.e., relationships between these variables not operating via the macro variables as W and P. Then we would face an ordinary input–output system which would have to be solved as a simultaneous system in the second stage. However, this would be a somewhat more straight-forward task than considering the full model in one stage. Particularly if a series of tentative calculations at the macro stage is desired in order to determine the main aspects of the plan, much can still be gained by proceeding by stages.

By means of planning in stages it may be possible to combine concerns for simplicity of analytical tasks and concerns for operationality of the ensuing plan. This was the consideration which was adduced as a motivation for planning in stages at the beginning of this section.

The possibilities for a successful decomposition into stages depends on the structure of the underlying complete system. In practice this will often not be spelt out in details, but at least some intuitive notions about it are necessary in order to judge whether a system of models used at different stages and the types of connections between them together will produce an outcome which is a good approximation to what would have been obtained if the complete underlying system could be used in practice. The problem is clearly related to the conditions for consistent (or approximately consistent) aggregation discussed in the preceding section. As suggested by our small example the existence of averages which are not too sensitive to changes in the internal compositions of the aggregates is a crucial condition. Average labour productivity and average capital/output coefficients are other examples of coefficients which may be useful at a macro stage, and subject to revisions in the light of sectoral results achieved in later stages.

Even if it were not necessary for computational and analytical reasons to decompose the problem into stages, it might still be desirable for other reasons.

The elaboration of a plan is 'in practice never something which can be done at one stroke. Some search in the form of calculation of alternatives, trials and errors, and iterations will always take place. Although it might be possible to perform this process on a full-scale model, there may be a large gain in letting most of this process take place in a "first-stage" macro model before details are worked out. A similar process may be necessary at the second stage, but this will be much more limited if the process is already more or less completed at the macro level, yielding rather definitive information and limitations for the lower-level calculations.

There is also the problem of transparency. If the analytical tasks in connection with planning are performed by experts, it might be much easier to communicate on the basis of a well-designed series of models arranged in stages than on the basis of one large simultaneous model. The example presented above is perhaps too small to illustrate this point convincingly. The decomposition into stages does however make it possible to explain first the economic contents of the small model (23)–(27) (admitting that we are not sure of the correctness of the stipulated value of the wage share w, but this will be checked after the more detailed calculations have been carried out), and next go on to explain the breakdown of total consumption and total investment according to the simple mechanism given by (18)–(19). This may be more transparent and pedagogical than an explanation based directly upon the system (17)–(21). In practice, where many more details enter, the point is of course much more convincing. Even an expert on planning models may feel a need for having a sort of macroeconomic analogue of a full model with many details in order to support his understanding of how the full model works. Such a concern for transparency and ease of communication with people who have political responsibility for the contents of the plan, but no time or capacity to study large and complicated models, was one of

Tinbergen's main considerations in his arguments for planning in stages.

In the Netherlands a combination of a first-stage macroeconomic model and a second-stage detailed input–output system was used in the Central Planning Bureau a long time ago [see, for instance, *Scope and Methods of the Central Planning Bureau* (1956) and *J. Sandee and D.B.J. Schouten* (1953)]. Calculations performed in stages were also used by *C. Almon* in his large forecast calculations for the American economy. In the USSR the practice has been to plan in stages long before formal methods were taken into use. (It is interesting to compare with the quotation from *S.G. Strumilin* given in Section 1.3.) Although a vast number of plan figures have been worked out by the Central Planning Commission, most of them have nevertheless been somewhat aggregated. These figures have been passed down to lower echelons in the planning system, being disaggregated step by step, and finally ended up as detailed plan instructions to individual enterprises. Usually there have been a couple of rounds of iteration up and down in this system. This is a sort of organizational system of planning in stages which goes beyond the scope of "planning in stages" as more narrowly conceived. Also in the more formal use of for instance input–output models in planning in the USSR decomposition into stages has been used. It is for instance reported that the elaboration of the plan for 1966–70 was performed by first determining the total growth rate and other macro indicators on the basis of highly aggregated analyses, next imposing these macroeconomic conditions on a twenty-sector input–output model as an intermediate stage, and finally breaking this down again into much more detailed specifications. (See *United Nations, Macro-Economic Models for Planning and Policy-Making*. See also *A.G. Aganbegjan* and *K.A. Bagrinovsky*.)

Other interesting examples of "planning in stages" are found in price planning in the East European Countries. In these countries prices are generally kept constant for rather long periods, and then subjected to large-scale centrally determined price adjustments affecting almost all prices. (Practice has varied somewhat between countries and become somewhat more flexible as a consequence of the reforms commencing around the middle of the 1960s.) Price calculations in Czechoslovakia in the 1960s were performed in a manner corresponding to planning in stages. The basic analytical tool was input–output calculations in price form. Certain main principles were determined in advance, including concern for the balance between production costs and revenues in enterprises. Since there was a tremendous amount of data to be used, and a very large number of prices to be determined, it could not be done by one operation on a sufficiently large simultaneous system. Instead, price indexes were first calculated for "branches". Next, these were broken down by more detailed calculations for a large number of "product groups"; finally these were again disaggregated into indexes for around 25 000 product groups, which should form the basis for price setting for individual commodities. (See the *United Nations* publication just mentioned.)

The small illustrative model used above contains only two stages. The system as proposed by Tinbergen would consist of several stages. A very important problem then comes up as to which breakdowns should be performed at higher, and which at lower stages. For instance, should a disaggregation according to sectors of production be performed before a disaggregation according to regions, or vice versa? Different suggestions exist in the literature, and if we consider the organization of planning in the USSR as an organizational parallel to the idea of planning in stages, practice has also varied. The structure has usually been that ministries corresponding to industries have taken the level immediately below the top level, but there was an interval (1957–65) in which a regional breakdown occupied this place. No good theory exists as to what would be some sort of optimal arrangement. Factors which should evidently play a rôle in this are the strength or importance of various kinds of linkages between sectors and between regions and the flexibility or slack in these relationships. If any kind of production could take place any- where at the same costs, then there would be no serious problem. However, it is an obvious fact that this is not so. Then preferences or priorities will have to enter the considerations. If there are strong preferences with regard to the compositions of output of the economy, and almost indifference with regard to regional distribution of economic activity, then sector calculations should be performed at the second stage and regional calculations at the third. The con- sequence of this is that we accept the restrictions on the regional distribution which are implied by the decisions made with regard to the sectoral composition of output. If regional considerations count very heavily, then the arrangement might be reversed. Then we would be willing to accept the consequences, in the form of restrictions on the composition of output, of the preferences we have with regard to the regional distribution of activity. In practice neither of these extremes would be realistic, but it gives at least some rough indications if preferences are clearly stronger with regard to one aspect than with regard to the other. If both aspects count roughly to the same degree in the preferences, then it is more difficult to give general suggestions.

If there is easy access to foreign markets, then the ties between sectoral composition and regional distribution will be less strict and the dilemma more easily resolved.

A beginning of an analysis of the problems suggested above is given by *M. Keren.*

In the USSR it seems that the sectoral and the regional aspects are now treated at the same level in a parallel way. This may turn out to be a better solution than trying to determine a unique sequence of stages. Roughly the procedure seems to be that the Central Authority issues broad outlines and guiding principles for the new plan. Then the enterprises work out their plan proposals. These are submitted *at the same time* to regional planning authorities and sectoral planning authorities. The State Planning Commission of the USSR then receives proposals both from regional and from sectoral planning authorities. The information from both sources then cover the same "elementary particles", but it is adjusted and aggregated in each case according to what is relevant in view of the concerns and conditions under control of the regional and sectoral authorities respectively. The proposals and observations are then examined in the State Planning Commission which carries out the complex task of coordinating the sectoral and regional aspects of the plan. Usually more than one round of adjustments are found necessary. (See *United Nations, Multi-Level Planning and Decision-Making,* and *N.P. Fedorenko.*)

At the lowest stage in a full planning system decisions about individual investment projects will normally take an important position. Here some sort of investment criterion, such as the present value criterion, may define the type of calculations. The information from previous stages used in such calculations might consist of interest rates, expected wage rates, prices of raw materials, etc., perhaps with differentiation according to regions. The test for correct relations between the various stages or levels would then consist in checking whether the implications for resource requirements and outputs of all projects accepted according to the criterion used are compatible with plan figures at the more aggregated stages. If not, then revisions at preceding stages might be necessary. Examples of calculation of such "shadow prices" from more aggregated models for use in investment decisions are found for instance in *Multi-Level Planning: Case Studies in Mexico* and in many other books and papers on planning in developing countries.

As originally conceived by Tinbergen planning in stages does not necessarily imply anything about the organizational structure of planning. All stages might be worked out within the same planning institution. As suggested by the references to practice in the USSR one may also have planning in stages where different stages of a plan are elaborated at different organizational levels. We shall return to some such questions in chapters on centralization and decentralization in economic planning.

References for Section 3.4

A.G. Aganbegjan and K.A. Bagrinovsky, "The system of optimal intersectoral models", in *Input–output techniques*, edited by A. Brody and A.P. Carter (North-Holland, Amsterdam, 1972).

C. Almon, *The American economy to 1975* (Harper and Row, New York and London, 1966).

N.P. Fedorenko, "Price and optimal planning", in *Contemporary Soviet economics*, Vol. I, edited by M. Yanowitch (International Arts and Sciences Press, New York, 1969).

N.P. Fedorenko, *Optimal functioning system for a socialist economy* (Progress Publishers, Moscow, 1974). Especially pp. 155–167.

M. Keren, "Industrial vs. regional partitioning of soviet planning organization: A comparison", *Economics of Planning* (1964).

Multi-level planning: Case studies in Mexico, edited by L.M. Goreux and A.S. Manne (North-Holland, Amsterdam, 1973).

K. Porwit, *Central planning: Evaluation of variants* (Pergamon Press, London, 1967). Especially Chapters 3 and 4. Translated from Polish.

J. Sandee and D.B.J. Schouten, "A combination of a macro-economic model and a detailed input–output system", in *Input–output relations* (H.E. Stenfert Kroese, Leiden, 1953).

Scope and methods of the Central Planning Bureau (The Central Planning Bureau, The Hague, 1956).

The Soviet planned economy (Progress Publishers, Moscow, 1974). Especially pp. 140–148.

J. Tinbergen, *On the theory of economic policy* – See reference under Section 1.3.

J. Tinbergen, "Planning in stages", *Statsøkonomisk Tidsskrift* (1960).

J. Tinbergen and H.C. Bos, *Mathematical models of economic growth* (McGraw-Hill, New York and London, 1962).

J. Tinbergen, *Central planning* – See reference under Section 2.7.
United Nations, Economic Commission for Europe, *Macro-economic models for planning and policy-making* (Geneva, 1967). Especially the chapter on "The use of macro-economic models for production and investment planning in the USSR" and the chapter on "The price model and its use in practice" referring to Czechoslovakia.
United Nations, *Multi-level planning and decision-making*, Papers presented to the Sixth Meeting of Senior Economic Advisers to ECE Governments (New York, 1970). Especially pp. 123–124.

3.5. Splitting the Problem in Separate Parts (Partitioning)

The simplified planning procedure described in the preceding section as "planning in stages" is in a way a splitting of the problem in several parts so that the sequential solution of these parts, with possible iterations between them, is simpler than a simultaneous solution for all aspects. In planning in stages the same "things" are however included all the time, either as individual entities at the most detailed stage, or as elements comprised by more and more aggregated categories as we approach the macro stage. Another possibility for simplification (still belonging to type 4 of simplifications listed in Section 3.1) is to see whether the problem can be split in *separate* parts in such a form that one group of variables and conditions can be treated separately from another group of variables and conditions. In contrast to planning in stages which involves a hierarchical arrangement of stages, the splitting of the problem which we now have in mind may be thought of as splitting of the full problem into smaller problems arranged side by side, containing "different things". To introduce a brief term we might call this *partitioning*.

Since mutual interrelationships, directly or indirectly, transcend all traditional barriers between the social sciences and all borderlines between spheres of policy, it is clear that "everything" should in principle be treated simultaneously, in one big decision process. In practice this is of course impossible. Some partitioning always has to take place. It may then be useful to make some explorations into the problem of what sorts of conditions may help to reduce the loss which may be incurred because of less perfect coordination when a big problem has been partitioned. This might inter alia help to draw the lines of division, i.e., to arrange the pattern of partitioning in reasonable ways. We shall consider only partitioning into two parts, but the arguments can easily be extended so as to cover partitioning into more than two parts.

As a mere formality we first rewrite the scheme from Section 2.1 in the following form:

(30) $a = (a_1, a_2),\quad z = (z_1, z_2),\quad x = (x_1, x_2),$

(31) $x_1 = f_1(a_1, a_2, z_1, z_2),$

(32) $x_2 = f_2(a_1, a_2, z_1, z_2),$

(33) $W = W(x_1, x_2).$

We have here split a, z and x in two parts. If we have a purely quantitative problem so that a, z and x are vectors (which we shall assume in this section), then each of them is split into two subvectors. In (31)–(33) we have indicated these subvectors separately as arguments, otherwise the model has exactly the same meaning as in Section 2.1. The maximization problem now takes the form:

(34) $\underset{(a_1, a_2)\in A}{\mathrm{Max}}\ W(f_1(a_1, a_2, z_1, z_2),\ f_2(a_1, a_2, z_1, z_2)),$

corresponding to formula (10) in Section 2.1.

The problem now is whether we could, at least approximately, solve the total maximization problem by considering two subproblems in separation: In one subproblem we make forecasts of z_1 and decide on a_1 with a view to the resulting x_1, so as to contribute as much as possible to the maximization of the preference function W; in the second subproblem z_2 is forecasted and a_2 determined with a view to the effect on x_2 so as to contribute also in this part as much as possible to the maximization of W. It is immediately clear that we cannot, in general, achieve a correct maximization of W in this way. The decision about a_1, which should contribute as much as possible to the maximization of W, cannot be determined independently of the decisions taken in the other subproblem, and vice versa. However, the following simple observation gives a clue as to how to proceed. Suppose that the full solution to the problem of maximizing the preference function W, under correct predictions of z_1 and z_2, is given by a_1^*, a_2^*, x_1^* and x_2^*. Next assume that two "departments" are assigned the tasks of treating the two subproblems separately. Suppose (hypothetically) that Department 1, which is to determine a_1, has been correctly informed about the optimal a_2^* in addition to being informed about z_1 and z_2. The reduced problem of Department 1 is then to solve the following maximization problem:

$$(35) \qquad \underset{\substack{a_1 \text{ such} \\ \text{that } (a_1, a_2^*) \in A}}{\text{Max}} \quad W(f_1(a_1, a_2^*, z_1, z_2), f_2(a_1, a_2^*, z_1, z_2)).$$

The symbolism is intented to express the idea that W should be maximized with respect to a_1, with a_1 limited by the condition that $a = (a_1, a_2^*)$ should be a feasible policy. It is obvious that $a_1 = a_1^*$ solves this problem. This is of course a smaller problem than the original, complete one.

If Department 1 has also been informed about the vector x_2^* expressing the optimal values of the variables under the concern of the other department, then the problem of Department 1 can be written in the form

$$(36) \qquad \underset{\substack{a_1 \text{ such} \\ \text{that } (a_1, a_2^*) \in A}}{\text{Max}} \quad W(f_1(a_1, a_2^*, z_1, z_2), x_2^*).$$

This appears simpler than (36). The solution to (36) is evidently also $a_1 = a_1^*$.

These arguments hold of course also the other way round, i.e., for Department 2 in determining a_2 if a_1, or a_1 and x_1, are correctly known. Thus, if we, in solving one part of the problem have correct information about the values which should be determined in the other subproblem, then we reach a correct determination of the problem in "our" part by solving the smaller maximization problem with respect to the instruments belonging to our department.

Now the problem in practice is that, in trying to solve one part of the problem we do not know the solution of the other part. But we might hope for reasonably good results by an iteration procedure proceeding according to the following steps inspired by the considerations referring to (35) above:

First step. This step is carried out for the first subproblem, i.e., for the determination of a_1. In doing this one makes a preliminary estimate of what a_2 will be in the optimal solution of the overall problem, i.e., one tries to guess at a_2^*. Let this guess be $a_2^{(0)}$. On this basis the maximization problem (35) is solved with the preliminary estimate $a_2^{(0)}$ replacing a_2^*. This results in $a_1^{(1)}$ as the first tentative solution for the instruments of Department 1.

Second step. The determination of a_1 resulting from the first step, i.e., $a_1^{(1)}$, is passed on as information to Department 2 which performs the second step. This is then to determine a_2 by a maximization corresponding, exactly to (35), only with a_2 as the variable and a_1 fixed as determined by the first step, i.e., as $a_1^{(1)}$. This determination yields $a_2^{(1)}$ as a proposal for the stipulation of instrument values for Department 2.

Third step. By the second step is determined a subvector $a_2^{(1)}$ which is in general not the same as the one initially assumed in the first step above, $a_2^{(0)}$. The first step is therefore repeated with the new subvector $a_2^{(1)}$ resulting from the second step replacing the provisional estimate $a_2^{(0)}$ used in the first step.

From the third step comes a new solution $a_1^{(2)}$ for a_1 which is in general different from $a_1^{(1)}$ determined in the first step. This is then passed on and used as information in a repetition of the same kind of calculations as in the second step, and so on. By this iterative procedure one might hope that the solutions for a_1 and a_2 converge towards the correct solution of the complete problem, i.e., towards a_1^*, a_2^*. If this is so, then we have obtained a simplification in that each subproblem is of a smaller dimension (having a smaller vector of unknowns) than the complete problem.

A slightly different procedure is suggested by (36) above. In that case an initial tentative estimate is made for both a_2 and x_2, i.e., $a_2^{(0)}$ and $x_2^{(0)}$. These replace a_2^* and x_2^* when a_1 is determined for the first subproblem as formulated by (36). This gives $a_1^{(1)}$ which jointly with $a_2^{(0)}$ (and z_1 and z_2) may be inserted in $x_1 = f_1(a_1, a_2, z_1, z_2)$ to yield $x_1^{(1)}$, i.e.,

$$x_1^{(1)} = f_1(a_1^{(1)}, a_2^{(0)}, z_1, z_2).$$

The information represented by $a_1^{(1)}$ and $x_1^{(1)}$ is next used to solve the corresponding problem for a_2 and x_2, and so on.

Not much can be said in general about the convergence properties of such procedures, but similar procedures often work well in other connections. (See for instance the formulation of the derivation of maximum likelihood estimates by means of iterative procedures in *J.D. Sargan* and in *W. Oberhofer* and *J. Kmenta.*)

Without attempting a mathematical discussion of the problems involved, let us see in a more intuitive manner what sort of properties or conditions will help to make such a partitioning feasible and useful. We may have two different interpretations in mind. In the first place, the partitioning may be a purely computational simplification, all work being done in the same institution. In the second place, the different parts of the planning problem may be handled by different institutions, as suggested by the use of the term "departments" above. Apart from the organizational difference, the importance of this distinction lies in the fact that the information problem is much more important in the case of the second interpretation. When different institutions are involved, the partitioning has a better chance of being successful if less of information from one problem is needed for solving the other problem.

Conditions which may help to create favourable possibilities for successful partitioning may refer to the shape of the set of feasible policies A, to the form of the preference function W, and to the form of the full structural model f, now partitioned into f_1 and f_2.

The form of the set of possible policies.   In the maximization problem as formulated by (34) it is in general impossible to determine whether a specification of a_1 is feasible without knowing something about the policy a_2 belonging to the other subproblem, and vice versa. This makes the partitioning cumbersome. It increases the need for exchange of information, and it may also happen that the iteration gets stuck in unfavourable constellations. Some sort of independence would therefore be advantageous. We could formulate this requirement by saying that there should exist sets A_1 for a_1 and A_2 for a_2, such that A_1 is the set of feasible policies in the first problem regardless of the specification of a_2, and A_2 is the set of feasible policies in the second problem regardless of the specification of a_1. Formally this may be written as:

$$(37) \qquad A = A_1 \times A_2.$$

This means that the policy $a = (a_1, a_2)$ belongs to A if and only if a_1 belongs to A_1 and a_2 belongs to A_2. (The set A is then called the

Cartesian product of A_1 and A_2.) In this case the condition in the partitioned problem formulated by (35) or (36) which generally says that the permissible policies a_1 are "a_1 such that $(a_1, a_2^*) \in A$", could be replaced by the simpler condition "$a_1 \in A_1$" which does not involve a_2^*.

This holds good for all steps if there is an iteration process; i.e., the domain of variation of policies for one subproblem remains the same regardless of what solutions are arrived at in the other subproblem.

The importance of a condition of the sort (37) is illustrated in Figure 11 for the case of only two instruments. In the upper part of the figure we have depicted a case where a_1 and a_2 are both assumed to be simple quantitative instruments, subject to non-negativity constraints and a common limitation $a_1 + a_2 \leqq K =$ some constant. Thus the set of possible policies A is represented by the triangle OPQ. In this case the set of possible values for a_2 depends on the value of a_1, and vice versa. The curved lines are indifference lines for W corresponding to $W(x_1, x_2)$ when we have inserted for x_1 and x_2 in terms of the instruments, and z_1, z_2 have been forecasted, i.e., $W =$

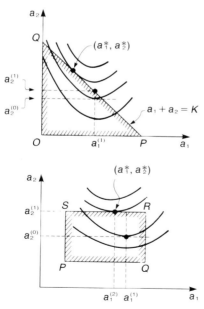

Figure 11

$W(f_1(a_1, a_2, z_1, z_2), f_2(a_1, a_2, z_1, z_2))$. The optimal policy a_1^*, a_2^* has been indicated. Now suppose that we, in solving the first subproblem, tentatively stipulate a_2 as $a_2^{(0)}$. Then the first step, solving subproblem 1, yields $a_1 = a_1^{(1)}$ as indicated. The second step, solving subproblem 2, takes $a_1^{(1)}$ as given and determines $a_2 = a_2^{(1)}$ so as to make W as large as possible. As indicated in the figure this yields a point on the boundary PQ of A in the figure. Next we should again solve subproblem 1 with $a_2 = a_2^{(1)}$ as given. We then clearly fail in increasing W further in spite of the fact that we have not reached the optimal policy.

The next case illustrated in the figure is similar to the first, but now the region of feasible policies is limited by upper and lower limits for a_1, independently of a_2, and upper and lower limits for a_2, independently of a_1. The set A then corresponds to a rectangle like $PQRS$ in the figure. This is an example of independence in the sense symbolized by (37). In this case $a_2^{(0)}$ is first chosen tentatively and $a_1 = a_1^{(1)}$ determined. In the second step $a_1^{(1)}$ is taken as given and $a_2 = a_2^{(1)}$ determined to be on the upper boundary for a_2. Next this value of a_2 is taken as given and a_1 determined to be $a_1 = a_1^{(2)}$. The next step for a_2 yields no change, i.e., it gives $a_2 = a_2^{(2)} = a_2^{(1)}$, and $a_1^{(2)}, a_2^{(2)}$ constitutes the optimal policy a_1^*, a_2^*. The form of the set A was favourable for the iteration procedure.

In many cases it is possible to arrange the partitioning in such a way that condition (37) is fulfilled. For instance, if instruments belonging to the money and credit sector of an economy are separated out as one part, then the ranges of feasible variations of the instruments of this department (interest rates, reserve ratios, limitations on borrowing and lending, etc.) would be independent of tax rates, government expenditures on various accounts, etc. which are specified in the other department. (Observe that we are now only speaking about ranges of feasible variations, not about the desirable constellations.)

In some cases, however, a partitioning that might seem natural from many points of view, would fail to satisfy the above condition completely. For instance, if we wish to consider the planning for the educational system as one part separated from the rest of the economic planning, then the set of possible decisions which can be taken in this department will not be independent of decisions taken in the main department of economic planning. In such cases it would be natural to consider total government grants to the education sector (perhaps split in some main categories like grants for investments, for current expenditures, and for income transfers) as instruments belonging to the main department of planning, say Department 1. The more detailed specifications of these grants according to types of schools, etc. would then be instruments of Department 2. The set of feasible decisions in Department 2 would then be limited by the decisions taken in Department 1 about the total grants. We might write $A_2 = A_2(a_1)$ to indicate that the set of feasible policies in Department 2 depends upon the specification of policy in Department 1. If the relationships are of the simple form mentioned here it would not complicate the partitioning too much. It would then be natural to start the iteration by solving the subproblem of Department 1, yielding a provisional solution $a_1^{(1)}$ for a_1. The set of feasible policies for Department 2 would then have a simple structure, and a tentative a_2, satisfying $a_2 \in A_2(a_1^{(1)})$, could be worked out. Let this be $a_2^{(1)}$. In the following step Department 1 should again solve subproblem 1. In this solution one should now of course not feel committed by the provisional decisions taken in Department 2 of the problem in response to the provisional a_1, but feel free to adjust a_1 with consequences for A_2, even if this should render $a_2^{(1)}$ infeasible, i.e., $A_2(a_1^{(2)})$ should not necessarily contain $a_2^{(1)}$. (This is at variance with the procedure suggested above.) Whether this would be desirable or not should be judged on the basis of information about x_2 (the results of the dispositions in Department 2) as evaluated through the preference function. (The case here suggested could also be treated from the viewpoint of planning in stages.)

The form of the preference function. In general the preference function (33) depends on variables belonging to both subproblems jointly, with the possibility of all sorts of dependencies across the borderline between the two departments. This means inter alia that the evaluation of a change in elements belonging to x_1 cannot be carried out without taking into account the constellation of variables contained in x_2, and vice versa. It would clearly simplify matters if the preference function could be written in the additive form:

(38) $$W(x_1, x_2) = W_1(x_1) + W_2(x_2),$$

where W_1 is a function depending only on x_1, and W_2 is a function depending only on x_2. (In the present context it would suffice if the original function W is such that the additive form can be obtained by subjecting W to a monotonous transformation.) The essential implication of (38) is that the marginal rate of substitution between two variables belonging to one group, x_1 or x_2, is independent of the values of the variables belonging to the other group. This helps to solve each of the two subproblems with less need for information about the constellation of the variables belonging to the other problem since it can be decided without knowing x_2 whether or not a certain change in x_1 is advantageous, and similarly for a change in x_2. There are probably quite many cases in which one would be willing to accept an assumption like (38). For instance, consider the planning of general education, education in arts subjects, cultural activities, etc. as belonging to Department 2, i.e., the levels of the various activities in this department are measured by variables included in x_2. Then there may be many dependencies *within* this group, but we would probably be willing to accept the assumption that the marginal rates of substitution between variables in this group are independent of the levels of the various "more economic" variables contained in x_1, and vice versa. The same might apply to many variables in the health sector. If we tried to treat the transportation sector as a separate part, then the matter would be more dubious. For instance, if we consider the preferences concerning various forms of transportation, then the marginal rates of substitution within this group might depend upon the level of satisfaction of other economic needs.

Various types of conditions and functional forms leading to simplifications in the optimization, including possibilities of partitioning the problem into simpler subproblems, have been studied extensively in the theory of consumers' behaviour. Many of the propositions established are relevant also in an economic planning context. For a survey of the theory, see for instance *C. Blackorby et al.*

The form of the structural model.   In general there are many interactions between the various parts of the overall model through the structure represented by (31) and (32). The instruments to be determined in one part of the problem influence the values of the variables belonging to the other part and vice versa. If there are strong interdependencies of this sort, then a partitioning of the problem would be unsatisfactory even if conditions should be favourable in other respects. As the equations stand in (31) and (32) they are, as observed under point (7) in Section 2.1, a "reduced form" of the full model, derived from an underlying system in implicit form. This means that each of the functions f_1 and f_2 depends on the whole model, not exclusively on any smaller part of it. Let us assume that the underlying model in its original form can be written as:

(39) $\phi_{11}(x_1, a_1, z_1) + \phi_{12}(x_2, a_2, z_2) = 0,$

(40) $\phi_{21}(x_1, a_1, z_1) + \phi_{22}(x_2, a_2, z_2) = 0.$

(The additive form is not essential; the following discussion could have been conducted from a more general starting point.) In (39) and (40) the equations of the model have been arranged in two groups so that the first group of equations represents behaviour, institutional relations, etc. related most directly to the variables in the first part, and the second group of equations refers most directly to variables belonging to Department 2. Thus in a rough sense x_1, a_1, and z_1 are (or include) the most important variables in (39), and similarly x_2, a_2 and z_2 are the most important variables in (40). ϕ_{11} and ϕ_{22} are therefore the most important parts, whereas ϕ_{12} and ϕ_{21} represent interactions between the two parts which are assumed to be of lesser importance. This means that, in working on the first subproblem one could concentrate on ϕ_{11} and try to make this as precise as possible, whereas ϕ_{12} could be treated in a more summary form, and similarly for (40). We assume that there are as many equations in (39) as there are variables in x_1, and similarly for (40). We could then think of (39) and (40) solved with respect to x_1 and x_2 so as to obtain:

(41) $x_1 = \psi_1(a_1, z_1, \phi_{12}),$

(42) $x_2 = \psi_2(a_2, z_2, \phi_{21}).$

This is not the same as (31) and (32). The functional forms ψ_1 and ψ_2 depend only on the corresponding parts of the full system, i.e., on ϕ_{11} and ϕ_{22} respectively, whereas f_1 and f_2 in (31) and (32), as already remarked, in principle depend on the whole system. Each set of equations (41) and (42) therefore represents more directly and transparently for each part of the problem only the equations representing the structure belonging to that sphere. We have however not got completely rid of the interactions, since ϕ_{12}, as a kernel function in (41), depends on variables belonging to part 2 of the problem, and ϕ_{21}

in (42) depends on variables belonging to part 1 of the problem. If the influences of these are small, in accordance with what was suggested in connection with (39) and (40), then we would not make too much of an error with regard to the decisions in each part of the problem by making rough assessments of these influences and not bothering too much about re-adjusting carefully in each department in response to all minor changes made in the other department. If the effects are too important to be treated in this very rough way, then the assumption about the smallness of the interaction effects represented by ϕ_{12} and ϕ_{21} would in any case help to speed up the convergence of an iteration process as described previously in this section.

The most obvious example of such a partitioning would be the division of the full set of production sectors of an economy into two groups with important interrelations (input–output deliveries) between sectors within the same group, but more or less insignificant deliveries between sectors belonging to different groups. (See for instance *A. Ghosh.*)

In the survey of conditions described above, we have not said much about z_1 and z_2, the exogenous elements. If all work is done in one institution, then the separation of these two groups is of course not of any great importance. If different institutions are involved, then a natural course is to divide z into two parts z_1 and z_2 in such a way that z_1 is of the greatest importance in ϕ_{11} and z_2 is of the greatest importance in ϕ_{22}. If this cannot be done, then some joint effort or pooling of information would be desirable. In any case, this does not create any great problems of principle.

Each of the conditions described above helps towards making partitioning of the problem workable and useful, but a complete partitioning with no need for iteration and exchange of information between the various subproblems or departments can only be achieved if all conditions are simultaneously fulfilled. Then the maximization (34) would be equivalent to solving two separate maximization problems, one problem maximizing W_1 subject to $a_1 \in A_1$ under a structure like (41) where ϕ_{12} is non-existent, and the other maximizing W_2 subject to $a_2 \in A_2$ under a structure like (42) where ϕ_{21} is non-existent. [In this case the set X_1 of possible x_1 could be generated from A_1, and the set X_2 of possible x_2 from A_2 independently of each other, and the set of possible states X could be written symbolically as a product $X = X_1 \times X_2$ similarly to (37). When ϕ_{12} and ϕ_{21} do not vanish, then this is not so even if (37) is fulfilled.

This is one way of seeing why important effects through ϕ_{12} and ϕ_{21} create difficulties for the partitioning.]

A special structure of some interest not covered by the conditions above occurs if $W_2 = 0$ identically, which means that the variables in Department 2 of the problem do not count in the preference function, and if furthermore the equations in (39) can be arranged so that $\phi_{12} = 0$. On the other hand, we do not require $\phi_{21} = 0$, nor do we require that ϕ_{21} represents minor influences. For convenience we rewrite the system as:

(43)
$$\text{Max } W = W_1(x_1),$$
$$\phi_{11}(x_1, a_1, z_1) = 0,$$
$$\phi_{21}(x_1, a_1, z_1) + \phi_{22}(x_2, a_2, z_2) = 0,$$
$$a_1 \in A_1, \qquad a_2 \in A_2.$$

In this case we may permit there to be more variables (x_1) than equations in the first part of the system (ϕ_{11}) so that there are some degrees of freedom left even when a_1 is specified. [Then the first part cannot be solved so as to give an expression like (41).] In the second part the number of equations will, correspondingly, exceed the number of variables in x_2, but we assume that there are sufficiently many instruments a_2 and such an extension of A_2 that the equations can be satisfied regardless of the values of x_1, a_1 and z_1 which enter through ϕ_{21}. In this case the optimization problem could be solved by first maximizing $W_1(x_1)$ subject to $\phi_{11}(x_1, a_1, z_1) = 0$ and $a_1 \in A_1$. The solution thus obtained is taken as a datum for part 2 of the problem, which is able to accommodate this solution from Department 1 since it is always possible, according to the assumption, to find values of a_2, with $a_2 \in A_2$, and x_2 which satisfy the equations of part 2 (for given z_2). In this case we might call part 2 an "*accommodating part*" of the problem, and the variables in this group "*accommodating variables*". It is not necessary to care about these variables in order to find the optimal values of the instruments a_1.

However, for actually implementing the solution, it is necessary to solve also the problem for the accommodating part so as to find the necessary values of the instrument variables a_2. If this is not solved in a correct way, and the instruments are set at incorrect values, then this will have consequences for x_1 and cause a departure from the optimal values. Furthermore, if we are not sure in advance about the possibility of finding a feasible a_2, then the second part of the model must be solved in order to check that the required a_2 really belongs to A_2.

An example of a sector which could perhaps be treated as such an accommodating part is the money and credit sector. The preference function will mainly contain real variables as arguments. The part of the full model characterizing the functioning of the money and credit system will in addition contain many other variables describing flows and stocks of various forms of money and credit, but which do not themselves count as arguments in the preference function. Furthermore it will contain a fairly large number of instrument variables. If the number of instruments is large enough, then the money and credit sector may be able to absorb and adapt to any constellation of variables determined in the main part of the model, i.e., it will imply no restrictions which must be taken into account in determining the constellation of the variables which enter the preference function. Nevertheless, for reaching an operational plan for economic policy also this accommodating part of the model must be solved in order to find out what values should be stipulated for the instrument variables belonging to the money and credit sector in order to support the constellation of variables in the main part of the model. This is more or less the philosophy of the endeavours in Norway, by a research team in the Central Bank of Norway to construct a special model for the money and credit sector which is intended to supplement the central national budgeting model.

The above discussion is rather intuitive and it does not exhaust all possibilities of partitioning a big problem into smaller parts. A very important case not covered by the discussion above is the separation from the rest of the system of some smaller problems which, taken together, do not make up the complete problem. In this case some elements of the complete model are retained as a sort of central model and the various smaller submodels considered as subordinate to, and mutually connected through this central model. A somewhat more precise discussion of such a situation will be given in a later chapter on centralization versus decentralization under the term "decomposition". This is a case which is very well elaborated in the theoretical literature and for which a large amount of practical experience now exists.

The main purpose of the discussion given above has been to give some suggestions as to what seems to be revelant criteria for trying to partition a problem which is too large for exact treatment in its entirety. As already suggested, such partitioning always takes place in practice. The criteria may then be useful for critical examinations of existing partitionings. Should planning of fiscal policy, monetary and credit policy, education, social policy, transportation policy, energy supply, etc. be partitioned in the way it is now done, or may rearrangement on some points be advantageous? The suggestions emerging from the discussion above may be summarized as follows:

(1) We should have a clear view of the instruments of policy belonging to the different parts and their ranges of feasible variation. The partitioning should preferably be such that condition (37) is satisfied, i.e., the set of feasible policies belonging to one department should be independent of the specification of policy in other departments; or, when this cannot be satisfied, the interactions should be simple and transparent, such as the condition that the sum of various items determined in one department should be equal to a total magnitude determined in another department.

(2) The preference function should be separable in the sense of (38), which means that the marginal rates of substitution in the preference structure between variables belonging to one department should be independent of the levels of variables belonging to other departments.

(3) The division between the departments should preferably be such that each department could manage its problems by concentrating on only a subset of the equations belonging to the full model, i.e., interactions between variables belonging to different departments should be less important than interactions between variables belonging to the same department.

(4) Sometimes it may be possible to separate what has been called an "accommodating part" from the rest of the system. In this case one part of the model contains all the variables which enter the preference function, in addition to other endogenous variables and some instrument variables. The remainder of the model, which is the "accommodating part", contains further endogenous variables and instruments, but the structure is such that it does not imply further

restrictions on the variables in the first part. The accommodating part can then be solved separately after the first part of the model has been solved. (It may also be necessary to check that the emerging values of the instrument variables in the second part are feasible.)

If we consider economic policy, educational policy, social policy, etc. in its entirety, then it is very unrealistic to imagine all these spheres planned by means of formalized methods. Administrative methods, based on rules of thumb, intuition, scattered pieces of more precise analysis, proposals and counterproposals, and exchange of information between departments will be the dominant methods for large spheres. Even then I think considerations along the lines suggested by the discussion in the present section will be of some relevance for judging whether the set-up as a whole could be expected to function reasonably satisfactorily.

References for Section 3.5

C. Blackorby, D. Primont, and R.R. Russell, "Budgeting, decentralization, and aggregation", *Annals of Economic and Social Measurement* (1975).
V.I. Danilov-Danilyan, "Some problems in social planning", *Economics of Planning* (1971).
A. Ghosh, "Input–output analysis with substantially independent groups of industries", *Econometrica* (1960). Also *Experiments with input–output models* (Cambridge University Press, Cambridge, 1964) Chapter 7.
W. Oberhofer and J. Kmenta, "A general procedure for obtaining maximum likelihood estimates in generalized regression models", *Econometrica* (1974).
J.D. Sargan, "Wages and prices in the United Kingdom: A study in econometric methodology", in *Econometric Analysis for National Economic Planning, Colston Papers* No. 16, edited by P.E. Hart, G. Mills and J.K. Whitaker (Butterworths, London, 1964). Especially Appendix A, "The method of iterative maximization".

3.6. Short-term, Medium-term and Long-term Plans

In Section 2.6 we considered a dynamic interpretation of the planning scheme used throughout most of the general discussion in these lectures. From this dynamic interpretation it is clear that what should be done in each time period cannot be determined in isolation from what happens and what is decided for other time periods. Nevertheless it has become customary in most countries, for practical reasons, to distinguish between short-term, medium-term, and long-term planning. The typical time spans for such plans are:

> Short-term plans: One year.
> Medium-term plans: Four to seven years.
> Long-term plans: Ten to thirty years.

Referring to the classification in Section 3.1 such a separation into plans for different horizons can be seen as an example of type 4 of simplification, i.e., splitting the overall problem into more manageable parts.

Depending on the historical background which formed the point of departure for the development in the direction of national economic planning, the emphasis has been placed differently on these three types of plans in different countries and in different historical periods. No country started with a well-developed planning system comprising short-, medium-, and long-term plans in a balanced and coherent fashion.

In the early period in the USSR the task of planning was seen mainly as the guidance of a process of structural change of the economy, and the first comprehensive plans, particularly the GO-ELRO plan mentioned in Section 1.1, were accordingly of a medium- or long-term nature. However, one was of course also faced with the problem of day-to-day management of the economy, and a system of short-term plans developed in the course of the 1920s. From 1928–29 there has been a fairly regular system of annual plans and medium-term plans covering five years. This system still prevails. The long-term plans have not been quite that regular, but in recent years increasing emphasis seems again to have been put on long-term plans. After World War II a similar system has prevailed also in the other East-European countries.

As to the importance of the various types of plans different sources give somewhat different impressions. Some Western authors (see for instance *M. Lavigne*) describe the annual plan as the operational and most important economic plan although the medium-term plan is important as an economic-political programme. On the other hand, Soviet sources (see for instance *The Soviet Planned Economy* and *Soviet Planning*) emphasize that the five-year plans represent "the basic type of national economic planning." They also describe the five-year plans as operational plans, pointing out that every enterprise have their own five-year plans with breakdown by years.

In most of the Western countries the recognized need for planning originated more from the desire to avoid serious depressions or trade cycles, and in some countries inflationary problems. With Keynesian ideas (and similar ideas coming up in other countries) as a main frame of orientation, planning naturally focused attention on demand management which is typically a short-term problem. An annual national budget (under this or other names) was the natural first step towards planning. In Norway medium-term plans, covering four years (and being officially called "Long-Term Programmes"), were also developed rather immediately after the war, but played a less important part than the national budgets. They have however been of growing importance. The more systematic efforts to look farther into the future started with the so-called "Perspective Analysis of the Norwegian Economy" which was presented in 1969. This document presented projections for the economic development up to 1990. Later the horizon has been extended up to 2000. This pattern of starting with annual plans and gradually putting more emphasis on the longer term seems to be typical for quite many Western countries. (In some countries medium-term planning was initiated for the reconstruction period after the war, but was considered to be planning for an emergency situation rather than part of a permanent system.) The overcoming of the most serious problems of economic depressions and a growing awareness of problems of regional development, scarcity of natural resources, pollution and other changes of environment, and the problems of long-term world development, particularly the comparisons between the industrialized countries and the developing countries, have all contributed to this relative shift of emphasis towards the longer term.

France seems to be somewhat of an exception from this general trend in that medium-term planning, represented by official four-year plans, seem to have played the most important part right from the beginning. (The first plan covered the years 1947–50.) Each plan has had some rather specific aims going beyond short-term demand management, such as reconstruction with priorities given to specified sectors, modernization of production equipment, structural change in the economy, improvements in the functioning of the markets, housing construction, education, social improvements of various sorts, etc.

The distinction between the three types of plans has evolved out of practice, and it is hard to say exactly what sorts of considerations have determined the distinctions. We could perhaps bring forward four, partly interrelated, groups of considerations.

(1) *Technology.* In planning for only one year ahead it is clear that most production activities will have to be carried out by means of plant and equipment existing at the beginning of the year. It will largely be a matter of utilization of existing production capacity. For a market economy this will take the form of regulation of total demand and its major components through budgetary policy and money and credit policy. In socialist countries with centralized management the coordinated planning of production and supply down to the individual enterprises with emphasis on utilization of existing capacity, available manpower, etc. will be a major task. In the medium term new production capacity will be a significant factor, i.e., the capacity-augmenting effects of investment will have to be given due consideration in planning in this perspective. However, very much of the new capacity will result from previous investment decisions, and most of the production activities will still take place on the basis of known and existing technology embodied more or less rigidly in fixed capital equipment. The structure of the economy will also not undergo dramatic changes. In the really long-term perspective these limitations no longer hold. Then a significant part of existing production equipment may be replaced by new equipment. Techniques of production existing only in embryonic form in the short run may take dominant positions, and the structure of the

economy may undergo drastic changes both with regard to sectoral and regional composition.

(2) *Balance and imbalance.*   At any moment of time an economy will probably experience "imbalances" of various sorts, such as unemployment or inflation (open/or repressed), deficit in the foreign trade, lack of proper proportions between production capacities and composition of demand, between regional distribution of demand for labour and regional availability of labour, between the skill compositions of labour in demand and supply, between the structure of export industries and international price structure, between private and public consumption (private cars vs. public roads), etc. Long-term planning will usually try to make a choice between possible growth paths which are not strikingly unbalanced in such respects. It is then left for planning for the shorter term to correct existing imbalances. Some of the imbalances (such as unemployment due to insufficient demand, inflation, trade deficit) can, at least to some extent, be corrected by demand management and prices and incomes policy in the short run, whereas others, including "structural unemployment" may require at least a medium-term span. These positions of balances and imbalances in the various time perspectives are often reflected in the different forms and contents of long-, medium- and short-term plans.

(3) *Operationality.*   As we have touched upon on several occasions before, some degree of operationality of the ensuing plans is necessary for national economic planning to be more than an exercise in analysis. It is however not necessary to determine "now" how all instruments of policy should be utilized and what instructions should be issued to the executing institutions in all future years covered by planning in one form or other. What is obligatory is that there should always emerge from the planning process operational decisions for the first short period. In the process, when new short-term plans are developed step-by-step, we will always have a plan basis for actions which have to be taken. This viewpoint is reflected in planning practice both in socialist countries and in market economies. Since medium- and longer-term plans do not necessarily have to be operational plans, they tend to be more highly aggregated than the short-term plans. The really long-term "plans" also tend to be pro-

jections, in the sense defined in Section 2.7, rather than plans in the stricter sense.

(4) *Informational aspects and preferences.*   It is an obvious fact that we know more about the conditions prevailing in the contemporary state and the near future than in the more distant future. In connection with economic planning this applies to such elements as e.g., technology, demographic development, and world market developments. To this we might add the problem of preferences. It may be hard enough to decide on choices for the near future. For the more distant future we may perhaps be able to specify *our* preferences to some degree, but we should be fully aware that these preferences are not binding or committing for future generations. Even if we should happen to make correct forecasts about technology, demographic development, etc., we would still "run the risk" that future generations might prefer to deviate from "plans" which we might elaborate now. In addition to the different requirements for operationality in the short and the long run this informational problem also suggests that long-term plans should have a more tentative or exploratory character than short-term plans.

There are thus good reasons for working with short-term, medium-term, and long-term plans with different forms and characteristics. We can however not neglect the fact that the long run consists of a series of short runs. In other words, the various plans can of course not be considered as independent. All the plans intend to govern or describe parts of the *same* development path. The division into three types of plans is made only for practical convenience. There is therefore a problem of coordination between the three types of plans. For instance, investments which are important in total demand management in the short run are at the same time generators of increased capacity which is important in the medium-term perspective and carriers of structural changes of the economy, both with regard to technology, sectoral composition, and regional development in the long run. If there is a deficit in the foreign trade in the short run, this must be compensated sooner or later if the medium- or long-term plans assume a balance in foreign trade, and so on. In practice in most countries the coordination between plans for different horizons is rather crude (and it has often happened that medium- or long-term plans have simply been abandoned or forgotten because they have been rendered obsolete under the pressure of events deviating too much from what was initially assumed and making short-term considerations gain the upper hand). Long-term plans often specify only the situation in some future target year rather than time paths, and then coordination is particularly crude and problematic. Medium-term plans also sometimes specify the situation only for one year, but more often give details for each year covered by the plan.

Some linear programming models, for instance as presented by *J. Sandee* for the Netherlands and several Hungarian models, cf. e.g., *Z. Daniel*, do however treat the longer run as a sequence of shorter runs in a interlinked fashion. The Hungarian models reflect particularly the differences in technological possibilities in the shorter and longer run as indicated under point 1 above. An interesting example of a rather sophisticated linking of a short-term and a medium- or long-term model is proposed in connection with the well-known *Cambridge Programme for Growth* directed by *R. Stone*. Here the balance vs. imbalance point of view suggested under point 2 above is applied. The long-term calculations aim at specifying a future situation on a balanced growth path, whereas a "transient model" is envisaged for calculating a path which during the first few years eliminates the current imbalances and sets the economy on the long-run growth path at the point specified by the calculations on the long-term ("steady-state") model. The full use of both models has however not been implemented in practice.

According to the discussion in Section 2.6, the ideal way to tackle the problems of operationality and lack of precise information about the future would be to develop a strategy, i.e., a set of decision rules which should generate operational instructions so to speak continuously as time passes and new information accrues. For a full-scale national planning this is beyond analytical possibilities, but a well-designed system of short-, medium-, and long-term plans with frequent revisions of the medium- and long-term plans may be conceived as a crude sort of strategy. With a clear understanding of the logics of the strategy approach to planning, one would not stick to plans to an undue degree because they are "plans", but treat them more like working hypotheses which are revised when new information indicates a change in the premises or conditions. Many countries have now initiated "rolling" or "sliding" plans which means that new medium- or long-term plans are worked out every year, always embracing the same number of future years. One would however come nearer to the idea of using a strategy if not only one medium-term and one long-term plan were developed at each stage, but several alternatives were elaborated and considered, depending on which external events would take place. The decisions implied by the operational short-term plan could then be judged in relation not only to one longer-term development, but on the basis of its effects in alternative future possibilities.

The use of "rolling" or "sliding" plans represents a valuable reform also from a more practical viewpoint. In the first place, a medium-term or long-term plan will be most reliable and relevant in the beginning of the period, but gradually get more irrelevant as actual events turn out to deviate more or less from prior expectations and effects of such deviations accumulate with time. In the second place, a strict division of time into periods of say four or five years may tend to generate cycles in investment starting and completion which are not efficient from an overall point of view. Both these tendencies have been observed in the socialist countries in Eastern Europe. There are however also dangers involved in the use of rolling plans. In connection with a proposal to introduce rolling in Ireland, *D. Norton* points out that one may object that "a drawback of such planning might be the absence of sufficient discipline in ensuring that serious effort is made to achieve the targets once they are initially set; with rolling plans there might be no day of reckoning when targets are compared with performance. It should be noted, in this context, that there is no reason why, with rolling plans, targets cannot be compared with performance. We are willing to concede, however, that frequent comparisons of targets and performance may in practice be less likely to occur when plans are revised from time to time (as with rolling plans) than would be the case with conventional fixed terminal date planning. The objection concerning the possible absence of sufficient discipline in ensuring that serious effort is made to achieve the targets once they are initially set is important, and underlines the need for periodic comparisons of past targets and performance, and assessment of that performance." Also *A. Qayum* points out dangers involved in rolling planning. The points made are however useful reminders rather than decisive arguments against rolling plans.

References for Section 3.6

Z. Daniel, "Planning and exploration: A dynamic multi-sectoral model of Hungary", *Economics of Planning* (1971).

J. Habr, "A contribution to the theory of sliding plans", in *Problems of Economic Dynamics and Planning*, Essays in honour of M. Kalecki (Pergamon Press, London and PWN, Warsaw, 1966).

M. Lavigne, *The socialist economies of the Soviet Union and Europe* (Martin Robertson, London, 1974). Translation from French.

D. Norton, *Problems in economic planning and policy formation in Ireland, 1958–1974* (The Economic and Social Research Institute, Dublin, 1975).

A. Qayum, *Techniques of national economic planning* (Indiana University Press, Bloomington, 1975). Especially pp. 9–12.

J. Sandee, "An experimental phased model for the Netherlands", in *Modelli econometrici per la programmazione*, edited by G. Parenti (Scuola di Statistica dell'Universita, Florence, 1965).

The Soviet planned economy (Progress Publishers, Moscow, 1974). Especially pp. 129–133.

Soviet planning, principles and techniques – See reference under Section 1.1. Especially pp. 186–89.

R. Stone, *A programme for growth, 5. The model in its environment* – See reference under Section 1.2.

United Nations Economic Commission for Europe, *Macro-economic models for planning and policy-making* (Geneva, 1967). Especially pp. 19–20.

United Nations *Multi-level planning and decision-making* – See reference under Section 3.4. Especially pp. 41–46.

3.7. Systems of Plans and Planning Models

This section draws a sort of general conclusion from what has been discussed in the three preceding sections. These sections suggest three directions for decomposing an unmanageably large planning problem into smaller and more manageable parts, perhaps with the implication that iterations through tentative solutions, exchange of information, and revisions of the tentative solutions and so on are necessary before a consistent set of plans for all parts can be arrived at. The three directions or dimensions of splitting the problem are a *"vertical" dimension* from the highly aggregated plans through intermediate stages down to plans for the smallest details; a *"horizontal" dimension*, i.e., a partitioning of one problem into smaller problems so to speak side by side, comprising different spheres of the economy; and finally, a *time dimension*, distinguishing short-term, medium-term, and long-term planning. All these methods of splitting up the overall planning problem can of course be used at the same time. One then ends up with a *system of plans*, and to the extent that models are used for elaborating the plans, also a more or less corresponding *system of models*. The system may for instance be as suggested in Figure 12. (Sometimes models may be used for purposes for which they are not directly constructed. Then the system of

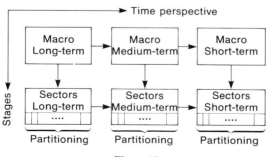

Figure 12

models will not necessarily correspond exactly with the system of plans; cf. the illustration for Norway below.)

In the figure there are two stages, a macro stage and a sector stage, and it is suggested that the sector stage may be further subdivided by horizontal partitioning. The arrows in the diagram indicate the direction of subordination in the following sense: Long-term sector plans should satisfy conditions determined in the macro long-term plan; the macro medium-term plan should be compatible with the macro long-term plan in the sense that the development described in the medium-term should appear reasonable as a first part of the development described in the long-term plan, and similarly for the other connections. The connections indicated by the arrows then also signify points of exchange of information and mutual adjustment through iterations. For instance, the medium-term sector plans should be compared with medium-term macro plans and long-term sector plans, while a direct comparison with the macro long-term plan would not appear very convenient or useful.

In addition to the plans comprised by the scheme in Figure 12 we may have regional plans, and for the centrally planned economies there are also more detailed enterprise plans. Including these in the figure would mean extending the figure in the "stages" dimension.

No country has ever had a fully developed system comprising all sorts of plans which could be placed in such a diagram. As already suggested the emphasis has shifted somewhat through time, and furthermore the economic-political system will of course be important for the structuring of the system of plans. For a market economy emphasis will naturally be placed on macro aspects, and sector plans will often only cover those sectors which are under more direct influence of the Central Authority. For a socialist economy with rather centralized management operationality requires that the lower stages are elaborated in details so as to end up as operational plans for individual enterprises, at least for the short run.

The types of connections between various plans and corresponding models are of many different sorts, the most typical perhaps being the following:

1. Time paths for a variable in a plan for a shorter term should not deviate too much from the trends in plans for the longer term, so as to avoid too abrupt changes.
2. The same variable may appear in several plans. This may apply

to forecasts of exogenous factor, and values of instruments as well as endogenous variables.

3. Sums of variables appearing in one plan, or in a series of partitioned plans, may be required to be equal to a total magnitude appearing in more aggregated plans; the same may apply to averages as in the example in Section 3.4.

4. "Shadow price" variables generated in one plan may be used as informational input in the calculations for other plans. Such variables typically reflect the marginal value of some resource or product, i.e., they measure to what extent one department could contribute to increasing the value of the preference function if it got more of the resource or the product for its disposal. Such variables are crucial in optimization based on decomposed systems. In such contexts subproblems may have their special objective functions to be maximized which draw information concerning the form of the function and the values of its parameters from the solution of problems higher up in the hierarchy of stages. (More on optimization in decomposed systems will be provided in a later chapter.)

To secure consistency with regard to all these kinds of links between plans and models is a major coordination aspect of economic planning.

The concepts used in characterizing the various types of plans and models above have no absolute and unambiguous meaning. For instance, a model constructed on the basis of an input–output description of the economy with a limited number of production sectors, might be called a macro model or a model for sector calculations. Norway is a case in point. Apart from a period in the 1950s models which are aggregated to such a degree that no input–output relations appear have not been used in connection with Norwegian economic planning. For the short-term planning (national budgetting) a model called MODIS (for MOdel of DISaggregated type), having some 150 sectors of production, has been used (in different versions with somewhat different numbers of sectors). This model has also been used in connection with the medium-term plans. Furthermore, a submodel related to this model (PRIM for PRice-Income Model) has been used in connection with income settlements, as touched upon towards the end of Section 2.3. Originally this model was more aggregated than the MODIS model itself, but has in recent years been more in conformity with MODIS, in fact constructed and used in the main as a block of relations from this model. For the long-term projections a model comprising near to 30 sectors of production has been used. This model is usually referred to as the MSG model (for Multi-Sectoral Growth). The models are not pure macro models and may be called multi-sector models, to emphasize the fact that they are not collections of disconnected sector models. Each model is solved as a complete system with no partitioning (with some reservation for MODIS where a "price block" of equations is first solved, and the results next used in the remainder of the model determining quantities).

In these models the disaggregation into many production sectors is introduced not primarily in order to work out plans for individual sectors, but rather in order to make the models more operational and make them able to absorb very much of detailed information. It is hoped that this feature of the models will help to make the calculations of the aggregates more precise and reliable than the use of models which are only able to absorb inputs in an already highly aggregated form. We might therefore say that the main aspects of the central planning are in fact the macro aspects of the development, but multi-sector models are used in order to make these plans (and projections) more reliable. This is however not the whole truth. Especially for the medium- and long-term projections some of the sectoral aspects are considered to be of interest and importance in themselves. For instance, the intersectoral transfers of labour, which can be analysed only on the basis of a multi-sectoral model, have many important economic-political and social implications.

In addition to these central models and plans some more specific models and plans are used. It was mentioned already in Section 3.5 that a special model (KRØSUS) is presently being developed for the money and credit sector, as an "accommodating part" according to the terminology in Section 3.5. Some long-term projections and more specific plans for the medium term exist for special sectors like energy production, transportation and road construction, education and health. Some elements of formal analysis have been used in connection with some of these plans and projections, but they are not well integrated with the central plans and projections. Also the long-term model and plans and the models and plans for the medium and short term are not quite well integrated. It is hoped that this aspect will be improved by relating the models to a common data basis through the new system of national accounts.

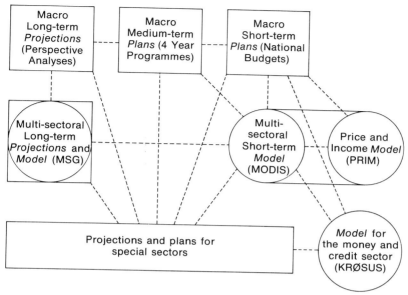

Figure 13

In Figure 13 we have tentatively indicated the Norwegian system as briefly described above. We have distinguished between multi-sectoral *models* and macro-economic *plans*. The system of models does not correspond strictly to the system of plans. We have therefore distinguished them in the figure by circles for models and rectangles for plans and projections. The dotted lines in this figure indicate flows of information.

The figure suggests very many links by flows of information between the various parts. As already suggested some of these are at present rather weak and a major task is to improve the overall system in this respect.

The development towards systems of interconnected models seems to be a rather general tendency observed in many countries. In France a system seems to be developing with emphasis on the medium term including a special money and credit model and a large regional model. (See for instance *R. Courbis.*) It is significant that a recent meeting of the Senior Economic Advisers to the governments in the countries of the United Nations Economic Commission for Europe (Moscow, 1974) was devoted to systems of economic models applied in economic planning and policy. Several earlier United Nations publications also contain material pointing in this direction. This development seems to be common to both market economies and socialist economies. One might perhaps say that the idea is more obligatory for socialist economies since operational planning there has to comprise a number of details far beyond that necessary for the form of economic planning in the market economies. The idea of interconnected systems of models seems to have been dominating for a long time already for instance in the research done at the Central Mathematical Economic Institute of the Academy of Sciences of the USSR, which is a leading research institute on planning methodology. This is witnessed for instance by books by *N.P. Fedorenko* and *V.S. Dadajan*, and in many other papers and books, and the relevance of this approach was pointed out quite early by *L. Kantorovich*. For practical use of some of the ideas developed there a large system of interconnected electronic computers at various levels in the hierarchy, exceeding that presently available, has been envisaged.

References for Section 3.7

G. Báger, "A system of models for medium-term planning in Hungary", *Acta Oeconomica* (1974).

J. Beck and V. Nachtigal, "Some problems of designing a system of macroeconomic models in Czechoslovakia", *Czechoslovak Economic Papers 16* (Prague, 1976).

R. Courbis, "Les méthodes de planification française: Évolution et perspectives", *Schweizerische Zeitschrift für Volkswirtschaft und Statistik* (1973).

V.S. Dadajan, *Ökonomische Gesetze des Sozialismus und optimale Entscheidungen* – See reference under Section 1.3. Translation from Russian.

Economic development and perspective planning, edited by N.P. Fedorenko (Progress Publishers, Moscow, 1975). Especially pp. 101–114.

N.P. Fedorenko, *Optimal functioning system for a socialist economy* – See reference under Section 3.4.

L.V. Kantorovich, "Further development of mathematical methods and the prospects of their application in economic planning", in *The use of mathematics in economics*, edited by V.S. Nemchinov, English edition edited by A. Nove (Oliver and Boyd, Edinburgh and London, 1964). Especially p. 321. Translation from Russian.

L.H. Klaassen and J.H.P. Paelinck, *Integration of socio-economic and physical planning* (Rotterdam University Press, Rotterdam, 1974).

3.8. Some Remarks on International Coordination of Plans and Planning Models

It is beyond the scope of these lectures to treat extensively the special problems related to international coordination of plans and planning models. However, in connection with the treatment of systems of plans and planning models in the previous section we may add some remarks on these problems since they represent a natural extension.

There will of course be plenty of links between what happens in one country and what happens in another. The most obvious connections are the necessary equalities between exports from one country and imports in other countries, capital outflows from one country and capital inflows in other countries, migration of labour, the relationships between exchange rates of one country and the corresponding exchange rates of other countries, interrelationships between prices through the "world market", etc.

In plan elaboration in most countries very much of what happens in other countries, or on the "world market", is taken as exogenously determined. From an overall point of view this is of course not the best representation of the actual mechanism. In the first place, some of the "exogenous" variables from the point of view of one country are *endogenous* from an overall point of view where the interactions are taken into account. This means that they are in principle also influenced by what happens in the first country itself. Secondly, some of the exogenous variables from the point of view of one country are economic-political *instruments* of other countries, or strongly influenced by such instruments. These are then more truly exogenous from the point of view of a country not in command of these instruments, but the most realistic representation would in many cases be to consider them as possible actions of other players in a *game*. In other words, referring to Section 2.2, and especially Figure 3, we might consider the possible actions of the own country as belonging to the set A whereas possible actions by other countries are represented as elements d_i in sets D_i as introduced in that section.

When plans are elaborated in different countries in an uncoordinated fashion, then there are possibilities of all sorts of inconsistencies concerning assumptions made and decisions taken in the various countries. If planning or forecasting models are used, it is an obvious idea to try to connect them into a system of models which takes care of such conditions as were mentioned above between exports from one country and imports in another country, etc. Since there are typically many more interrelationships between variables within one country than between variables in different countries, and since also many variables characterizing the state and the development of an economy are purely internal to the country, a full model comprising several countries will typically take the form of a system of interrelated models rather than a big model with no special structure.

If such a model system were available, it could be used for several purposes. We may perhaps distinguish between the following groups of problems and applications:

1. The complete system could be used for *forecasting*, in the hope that the recognition of the various consistency conditions pertaining to the connections between the countries will help to produce more precise forecasts than separate and isolated forecasting for each part of the system. The forecasts could be made available to the various countries as an aid in their national planning and policy-making.

2. The system could be *used by one country for its own planning activity*, with no further coordination with other countries. In this kind of use there would be several types of possible gains as compared with the situation of having only a "national model". Some of the variables which, in the national model, are considered as exogenously given, could be more precisely forecasted on the basis of the full model system. Some of the repercussions of the own decisions could be more completely elaborated on the basis of the overall system, including the feedbacks via foreign markets into the own country again. For instance, an expansionary policy in one country could have a secondary expansionary effect via the effects on the activity in countries with which the first country has a large foreign trade. For the Scandinavian countries, for instance, these effects would

not be quite negligible. Such an overall model would also give the planning authorities in one country a better view of the game situation as described by the reference to Section 2.2 above, which might help to clarify the situation and reach good decisions without necessarily trying to use more sophisticated game strategies. (Cf. the discussion in Section 2.4 of simplified ways of taking into account the game aspects of a planning situation.)

3. By the use of the model system just suggested, there would be nothing to prevent several countries from making mutually inconsistent assumptions about each other and about the "world market". By *exchange of information or joint use of the model*, the various countries might try to remove such inconsistencies and thereby reach more realistic plans and forecasts. Although it would not necessarily hold for each country, one would on average expect the assumptions made and the forecasts involved in the planning to become more precise when such adjustments and coordination are made. If we consider the international system as a game, then it is not obvious that each player would find it to his advantage to reveal unbiased information about the development under his direct or indirect influence, but it is at least conceivable that several countries might see a common interest in avoiding large discrepancies which might threaten the stability of the whole system.

4. The coordination under point 3 above was concerned only with exchange of information. One might go one step further in coordination by using the international model system jointly in analysing the effects for each country and for the group of countries as a whole of various possible *combinations of decisions*, with the intention to *reach agreements about decisions which improve the results for all participants as compared with the case of uncoordinated decisions.* If each country retains its own preferences and reserves for itself the power over its policy instruments in the sense that the consent of the country is necessary if the instruments shall be used as parts of a coor-dinated policy, then this type of coordination would mean turning the situation into a cooperative game as discussed in Sections 2.2 and 2.3.

If we should contrast cases 3 and 4 sharply we could say that the use of the model system under case 3 helps to improve the informational basis for reaching a *non-cooperative* equilibrium, whereas case 4 refers to the reaching of a *cooperative* equilibrium since the intention is to reach binding agreements about the use of the instruments. In comparing these cases it should be remembered that a non-cooperative solution is not necessarily an inferior solution, and an effective establishing of a non-cooperative equilibrium may in any case be much better than an an unstable, oscillatory movement generated by each country's lack of ability to forecast the behaviour of the other countries. But, in many cases there would of course be much to be gained by arranging for possibilities of agreements about the use of the instruments.

In actual life the distinction between cases 3 and 4 would not be as sharp as the theoretical definitions of cooperative and non-cooperative games suggest. If the countries get involved in joint undertakings to improve information and forecasts, then more wide-ranging cooperation may evolve, tacitly or explicitly. On the other hand, in cases which could be classified under case 4, coordination will usually be more or less partial, each country reserving some national instruments outside the coordination even if they have some effects also for other countries.

   5. The most far-reaching coordination is obtained if *an international authority is established and some power to take decisions is transferred to this authority.* Then the problem would again, from a formal and technical point of view, be more like planning for one country, with a search for the best policy according to a certain preference structure, now only posed for a larger system.

From this survey it appears that a system of models which represents the various links between the national economies in addition to the internal structure in each country will serve a useful purpose in many different contexts, ranging from pure forecasting to planning in the strictest sense, and from situations where each country is a completely sovereign national authority to situations where the countries have transferred more or less of decision-making power to a super-national or international authority. The form of the complete system, and the way of using it, will of course be different according to the type of situation.

In planning in some countries with highly open economies and large foreign trade some attempts have been made along the line suggested under point 2 above, i.e., constructing "world market models" to improve their own planning. Through such organizations as OECD there is a system of forecasting furnishing reasonably consistent forecasts for a group of countries (point 1 above), and also a system of exchange of information which might be considered as a step in the direction of point 3 above. The coordination of planning under the Eastern European organization CMEA (Council for Mutual Economic Assistance), could probably be referred to point 4 above, since there are attempts at coordination of plans for the various countries, but no overall authority to which the countries have transferred power to balance the interests of the various countries against each other and take decisions. In the EEC (European Economic Community) one will find elements of coordination of both type 4 and 5 in the list above.

These suggestions should not be taken too seriously. No actually existing international arrangement can be placed unambiguously in the categories indicated above, and it may perhaps be more confusing than revealing to discuss otherwise very different arrangements in relation to the same formal classification scheme. However, for a more thorough discussion both of the various types of international arrangements and of the uses to which systems of plans and models can be put under different arrangements, I think some sort of typology as suggested above may be a useful point of departure.

The most ambitious research project of combining national models into a system which takes into account the international linkages between the national economies is the *LINK project* (sponsored by the Social Science Research Council of the USA). This project comprises the USA, Japan, and some of the most important Western European countries. In most cases one uses national macroeconomic models, but for some countries where such models are missing the intention is also to construct new models for inclusion in the LINK project. The task of linking these models and solving the emerging complete system is of considerable size, there being ten or more national models, some of them having about 100 equations. The models are dynamic quarterly models, and the task is not only to solve for one quarter, but for several consecutive quarters.

The main task from the LINK point of view is to find solutions of these models which are consistent with regard to the international trade aspects. The model is solved by a sort of double iterative process. The national models are solved by "small iterations"; then the foreign trade magnitudes emerging from these solutions are compared and checked for consistency, first of all with regard to the export–import connections; to the extent that there are discrepancies some of the variables taken as given in the national models are adjusted, and the national models are again solved, by "small iterations". Altogether this requires an enormous amount of calculation. For each national model the number of solutions required is the product of three factors: the number of "large iterations", the number of iterations in the "small iterations" per solution of the national models, and the number of quarters covered. This runs into hundreds and perhaps thousands of solutions performed on each national model.

The representation of the linkages can be given in two different forms. The first form would seek to represent all flows between countries in a direct and detailed way, i.e., taking care of each flow of goods from each country to every other country. The number of flows would then be enormous, being of the order of magnitude of the number of commodities traded multiplied by the square of the number of countries. The second approach is to introduce "world market variables" such as total amounts traded internationally of each commodity. Then the export from each country of any commodity is supplied to a sort of anonymous world market, and imports into a country come from the same world market. One must then see to it that supply and demand are balanced, but one does not take care of the individual flows from any specified country to any other specified country. Then the number of variables will be much smaller than in the first approach. The complete system will then include the national models and their variables, a number of world market variables, and a number of equations representing balance requirements for the international trade.

In the LINK project this second approach has been chosen. Considering only constraints in the form of equations, the complete system can then be represented as follows:

$$\phi_1(x_1, a_1, z_1, y) = 0,$$

$$\phi_2(x_2, a_2, z_2, y) = 0,$$

(44)
.   .
.   .
.   .

$$\phi_n(x_n, a_n, z_n, y) = 0,$$

$$\Phi(x_1, \ldots, x_n, a_1, \ldots, a_n, z_1, \ldots, z_n, y) = 0.$$

The first ϕ_1 represents a set of equations of the national model for country no. 1. It includes national endogenous variables x_1, national instruments a_1, exogenous variables affecting country no. 1, z_1, and "world variables" y. In a limited national use of the model the variables included in y (or more precisely, those components of y which actually enter the model) would be considered as exogenous so that z_1 and the relevant components of y together now represent what would be the exogenous variables in the limited national use of the model. Similarly $\phi_2, \ldots, \phi_n$ represent the models for countries $2, \ldots, n$. The last set of equations in (44), symbolized by Φ, are linking or connecting equations. The most obvious form of such equations are balance equations for the world market. For instance, some equations define total exports of commodities in terms of exports from the various countries, and similarly for imports. Exports and imports for the various countries are included in $x_1, x_2, \ldots, x_n$, and total exports and imports are included in y. Other equations may define "world market prices" in terms of national prices and exchange rates, and so on. (For the truly exogenous variables some components may of course be common to $z_1, z_2, \ldots, z_n$, and it may be relevant to include in Φ some exogenous variables which are not included in the national submodels.)

The number of equations in each ϕ_i is equal to the number of components in x_i, so that each national model is determinate when the variables in y (and a_i and z_i) are given. However, for the system as a whole y is not given, but there are as many equations in Φ as there are components in y so that the system as a whole is again determinate when y is considered as endogenous.

As suggested above the procedure for solving the complete system when all a_i and z_i are specified might be as follows. First a tentative estimate of y is formed and inserted, together with a_i and z_i, in each national model. Next the national models are solved separately for $x_1, x_2, \ldots, x_n$, perhaps by iteration methods. Iterations may be required especially if the systems are non-linear. (These are the "small iterations" referred to above.) In the following step the resulting $x_1, x_2, \ldots, x_n$ are inserted into the equations represented by Φ, together with $a - s$ and $z - s$, and this system is solved for y. The resulting y will in general be different from the one originally assumed, and the new vector y may be inserted in the national models for a second round of calculations, and so on. (Such iterations between solutions of $\phi_1, \phi_2, \ldots, \phi_n$ and solutions of the linking equations represented by Φ are the "large iterations" referred to above.)

There may be many problems involved in such a procedure, referring to the more detailed formulations of the model and to problems about the convergence of the iteration procedure. The LINK project shows however that the mastering of such a system is a feasible task from a computational point of view.

The ambition of the LINK project has not been to go beyond the elaboration of consistent forecasts, i.e., applications of type 1 in the list above.

For the EEC countries there is a research project, called COMET, aiming at constructing a medium-term macroeconomic model for the European Economic Community. (See *A.P. Barten* et al.) This aims at taking care of the links between the countries in the elaboration of forecasts, but also goes some steps further in the direction of exploring the effects of the use of various instruments, particularly by tracing the effects of the use of the instruments through the linkages between the countries. For instance, the effects of changes in exchange rates have been explored by means of this system. (There also exist other model systems for the EEC countries. For brief descriptions and references, see *J. Waelbroeck.*) Another interesting system of interlinked models is elaborated by *S.A. Resnick.* His system includes 10 Western European countries, each represented by a national standardized econometric model comprising 23 equations. The model is dynamic and is used especially to elucidate the transmission of effects of fiscal policy in one country through the linking equations to other countries, and also the feed-back effects for the country from which the impulse originally started. Projects which combine models for the United States and the Canadian economy may also be mentioned. (For references, see *J. Waelbroeck.*)

For the socialist countries it has often been expressed that coordination of national economic plans is one of the main aspects of the economic integration in CMEA. It seems that this type of integration has been increasing in recent years, but that there are still difficulties in overcoming the exessive tendency towards bilateralism in the coordination and moving on to a more comprehensive multi-lateral coordination. Formalized systems of models have probably not yet played any important part for the decisions actually taken, but there appear to be several research projects in this field, partly emphasizing the elaboration of consistent trade plans, and partly elaborating more comprehensvie econometric model systems for groups of countries (especially the group consisting of Czechoslovakia, Hungary and Poland). There are also some attempts to apply optimization methods – expecially linear programming – to models representing the production possibilities of various countries in an interlinked fashion so as to investigate the efficient specialization and division of labour between the countries. (Reports on some of these projects have been presented at meetings in the United Nations Economic Commission for Europe.)

Finally it should be mentioned that there have also been constructed model systems for groups of developing countries. Some of these models are of the optimization type, using mainly linear programming. The planning of trade and coordination of instrument decisions are among the central problems elucidated in these studies. As examples, see *J. Mycielski, J.B. Nugent,* and *L.B.M. Mennes.*

References for Section 3.8

P. Alampiev et al., *A new approach to economic integration* (Progress Publishers, Moscow, 1974). Especially pp. 62–69, on joint planning activity in the CMEA.

A.P. Barten et al., "COMET; A medium-term macroeconomic model for the European Economic Community", *European Economic Review* (1976).

The international linkage of national economic models, edited by R.F. Ball (North-Holland, Amsterdam, 1973). Especially Chapter 4, "The methodology of linkage", by J. Waelbroeck, and Chapter 13, "Forecasting world trade within project Link", by L.R. Klein and A. van Peeterssen.

L.B.M. Mennes, *Planning economic integration among developing countries* (Rotterdam University Press, Rotterdam, 1973).

J. Mycielski, "A model for regional harmonization of national development plans", United Nations, *Economic Bulletin for Asia and the Far East,* No. 2 (September 1967).

J.B. Nugent, *Economic integration in Central America* (The Johns Hopkins University Press, Baltimore, 1974).

S.A. Resnick, "A macro model for Western Europe", and "Dynamic properties of the European macro model", in *European economic integration,* edited by B. Balassa (North-Holland, Amsterdam, 1975).

United Nations, Economic Commission for Europe, *Methods for international trade projections for a network of countries,* Vol. I and II (Geneva, 1971). Especially "The role of consistent trade-network models in foreign trade planning and projections of the socialist countries" by A. Nagy, "Report on the joint research project on the inter-country, inter-industry models for Czechoslovakia, Hungary and Poland" by a group of experts from the countries mentioned, and "A system of models for the optimization of foreign trade within a group of countries" by the Scientific Institute of Foreign Trade of Bulgaria.

J. Waelbroeck, "A survey of short-run model research outside the United States", in *The Brookings model: Perspective and recent developments* (North-Holland, Amsterdam, 1975). Especially Section 10.7, "International linkages".

3.9. Separation of Selection Analysis and Implementation

R. Frisch has argued on several occasions, see for instance his "Preface to the Oslo Channel Model", that it is useful for practical purposes to consider separately the selection problem and the steering or implementation problem which are involved in an overall planning problem. *The selection problem* is to select the "constellation of volume figures or figures in actual technical units which . . . one would like to see realized, provided one can find ways and means (institutional, administrative and financial) of bringing this constellation about." *The implementation problem* is to find out how to steer the economy (i.e., what institutional arrangements to make, which instruments of direct and indirect regulation of the economy to use, and how to use them) so as to achieve the real economic constellation selected as being the best one. In a very early paper ("Mathematical Appendix", 1949) where this distinction was perhaps explained for the first time, Frisch said that this splitting of the overall planning problem simply means "that we first ask what we want and next ask how to get it. That is to say the question of economic policy is decided upon only after consideration of the goals to achieve."

Frisch does of course not argue the case for a separation between selection analysis and implementation as a matter of principle, but only as a matter of practical experience and convenience. In his view precise quantitative analysis can be successfully applied to the selection problem, whereas intuition, political cleverness, ad hoc measures, etc. would have to play a greater part in implementation, where institutional arrangements and behaviour have to be taken into account to a larger degree. This argument is perhaps particularly convincing if we consider the game type of description of economic policy presented in Sections 2.2–2.4 where tactical moves and bargaining will replace some of the elements of permanent behavioural patterns assumed in simpler settings.

Let us try to make the idea of this distinction clear by first referring to the simpler planning scheme as represented in Figure 1 in Section 2.1. Let us disregard the effects of non-controlled factors in this connection, assuming that these are known by correct forecasts. The set X is now considered to be the set of possible states of the economy for the given and known constellation of these exogenous factors (corresponding to X_z for a given z in Figure 1.)

The admissibility of Frisch's distinction now hinges on the nature of this set of possible results. In order to see this clearly we may take a closer look at the delineation of this set. In general the set will be defined by a large number of constraints in the form of equations and inequalities. We may approach the complete delineation of this set by first imposing absolutely obligatory balance relationships which say that we cannot for each good use more for various purposes than what is available from all sources. Next we impose existing limitations on the supply from these various sources, such as availability of labour power, stocks of various goods, limitations on available flows of various natural resources, etc. In the third place we impose production restrictions in the form of production functions, input–output relationships and limitations on production capacity in various branches. By this we have now taken into account all purely physical constraints on the set of possible results. We designate by X^0 the set which has been delimited in this way. When we need a convenient term we shall call it the set of physically possible results.

Selection analysis in the strictest sense now means to find the solution x^* which maximizes the preference function $W(x)$ when x is permitted to vary over the set X^0, i.e., x^* is defined by:

$$(45) \qquad W(x^*) = \max_{x \in X^0} W(x).$$

Let us assume that x^* is uniquely determined.

When the most desirable solution x^* is thus determined, then the implementation problem is to find a constellation of instruments, say a^*, which produces the result x^* arrived at in the selection analysis. If the mechanism of the economy, relating results to instrument values, is given by $x = f(a, z)$ (where z is now given), then correct instrument values should satisfy:

$$(46) \qquad x^* = f(a^*, z).$$

If there exists such an a^* in the set A of possible policies, then the problem has been correctly solved.

Frisch's idea is that formalized and precise analysis can be used to solve the problem of determining x^* as indicated by (45). The types of constraints involved in the delineation of the set X^0 are balance relations, resource limitations, and production relationships, which are of a rather precise nature and amenable to formalized and quantitative analysis. On the other hand, in the determination of the policy a^* which should produce the desired result x^*, Frisch would leave more to intuition and practical judgement and experience because many additional elements are involved in the specification of f which cannot, at least at the present state of knowledge, be reliably represented in a formalized model.

Now whether the policy a^* is to be found by formalized analysis or by rougher methods, a condition for this two-step procedure to be successful is of course that there really exists a policy a^* which would satisfy (46). In general we have no guarantee that this condition is fulfilled. The set X^0 over which we have maximized W in order to find x^* is not necessarily the same as the set X of possible results which will be generated by the economic structure $x = f(a, z)$ when a varies over all possible policies in the set A. The latter set X must be included in the set X^0, i.e., $X \subset X^0$, since no policy can produce results which violate the physical constraints, but there may well be physically possible results which cannot be generated by any policy in A. This may be illustrated for instance by relations between total output and the distribution of output. Physically we may be able to utilize all productive resources maximally, and distribute the production result freely between members of the society. If the economy consists of free individuals and enterprises, subject only to indirect influences through tax rates, etc. by the Central Authority, then certain incentives are necessary in order to make people and enterprises exert the production activities necessary to secure the maximal results, and this may then not be compatible with any desirable distribution of the results. In order to achieve a desirable distribution we might then have to acquiesce with less than maximal output.

The situation in which the selectionally best result x^* cannot be produced by any permissible policy is illustrated in Figure 14. In the figure the selectionally optimal point x^* belongs to X^0, but not to X. There then exists another result x' which is the best result when all limitations are taken into account, i.e., x' maximizes $W(x)$ when it is taken into account that x has to be produced by $x = f(a, z)$ and a has to belong to the set A of possible policies. The result x' is generated by a policy a' where $a' \in A$.

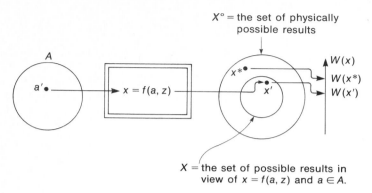

$X° =$ the set of physically possible results

$X =$ the set of possible results in view of $x = f(a, z)$ and $a \in A$.

Figure 14

Frisch was of course aware of the possibility that the result selected by the selection analysis might not be realizeable in practice. In "Preface to the Oslo Channel Model" he writes, "if on scrutiny one should find that practical difficulties of implementation under an existing institutional, administrative and financial set-up make it impossible to reach the high goals – for instance a rapid rise in national product – which have emerged as feasible from the selection viewpoint, two ways are open: Either to try to change the institutional, administrative and financial structure so as to make the high goals attainable, or to insist that this structure is not to be changed and that one will therefore have to acquiesce to the lower goals. In the latter case the computation of the difference between the two results will furnish a sound piece of information."

In explaining the distinction between the selection problem and the implementation problem above we defined the set X^0 as the set of physically possible results. In delimiting the set used in the selection analysis it is of course possible to take into account also other constraints than those originating from the consideration of physical possibilities. One might gradually introduce more and more constraints relating to behaviour and institutional aspects of the economy until one has narrowed down the set X^0 for the selection analysis to the set of really possible results X. The possibility of contradiction between selection analysis and implementation has then been eliminated. This means however that we have brought back into the analysis all the complicating factors which it was the intention of the distinction to avoid, at least for the time being.

A selection analysis separated from analysis of implementation will be most relevant and useful if the chances are not too large of selecting a result which deviates considerably from anything which it will prove possible to achieve in practice, i.e., if the set X is not too narrow as compared with X^0. This suggests that Frisch's proposal may be applicable particularly in the following cases:

(1) to planning in an economy which is very rich in instruments for direct and indirect steering of the economy, or which is prepared to introduce a large register of such instruments;

(2) to planning for the really long term since there is more scope for changing institutions and introducing new instruments in the longer than in the shorter run.

It is consistent with these observations that many of the planning models in socialist countries tend to be in the nature of selection models, and furthermore that models for the long run in most countries seem to be more free from institutional and behavioural constraints than models for the shorter run.

In the discussion above we have had as a background the simple planning scheme of Section 2.1. Let us briefly consider the matter on the basis of the game situation described in Section 2.2. In this case we have $x = f(a, d_1, \ldots, d_N z)$, and the set X is generated by letting a vary over A and d_i over D_i for $i = 1, \ldots, N$, where $i = 1, \ldots, N$ refer to important decision-makers other than the Central Authority. This case creates much more of uncertainty about the implementation aspect. Although any x in the set X so defined is in principle achieveable by joint actions, not all x in X may be achieveable by policies of the Central Authority when the Central Authority has no power to dictate the decisions about $d_1, \ldots, d_N$. Bargaining, pressure and counterpressure, more or less binding agreements, etc. will be parts of the implementation process. There is not much hope of clarifying all strategies and possible responses in advance. In this case it may, as suggested earlier in this section, be a practical and attractive procedure to carry out first a selection analysis which disregards these problems, and next to use the outcome of this as a sort of target in the more untidy implementation process. Any model which tries to include all elements and aspects of the implementation process might soon prove to be a misrepresentation of the real situation and a poor guide for decisions. A model which is incomplete and serves the planning process in a partial way, but which is reasonably correct as far as it goes, may be a more valuable tool than a more complete model which contains many incorrect elements and which is not able to represent the various possibilities or constraints that are gradually revealed and frequently changed during the process. When the complete, but partly incorrect model is used, it is not possible to say which aspects of the results are due to the incorrect elements of the model.

If we compare the selection/implementation distinction with the classification of types of simplifications listed in Section 3.1, it can be seen as a mixture of types 1, 3, and 4: The size of the problem is reduced by neglecting, or at least referring to non-formalized treatment, some elements of the total problem; the aspiration level is lowered somewhat with regard to optimization and accuracy since one can in general not hope to reach precisely the target x^* selected in the selection phase of the total process; and we split the overall problem into two parts, out of which at least one – the selection part – becomes somewhat simpler and more transparent.

In the introduction to this section I referred to *R. Frisch* as the first to introduce the selection/implementation distinction. He was certainly the first to discuss the distinction explicitly in relation to planning methodology, and he coined the terms, but there are other traces to be found in earlier literature.

In fact, the standard methodology and arguments in economic welfare theory could be seen in the light of these terms. Optimality is usually explored before behavioural assumptions are introduced ("selection"), and next it is explored what sorts of institutional arrangements – market mechanism, tax and subsidy schemes, etc. – are able to produce the optimal result ("implementation").

A clear exposition of this distinction is found in a remarkable paper from 1929 by *R. Remak*, a German mathematician who contributed to the discussion about the possibility of turning economics into an "exact science". Remak defines clearly the concepts of the set of possible states and optimal situations, distinguishing in the latter case between optimality in the sense of efficiency or Pareto optimality (without using this term), and optimality in the sense of "social optimum". He is explicit on the point that organization, financial considerations, etc. should not be taken into account in defining the optimal position; these are elements which should be brought in at a later stage in the analysis to see how the optimal situation could be brought about. A main point is that such arrangements should not preclude the achievement of an optimal state: "Behind every financial impossibility there should be a quantitative technical impossibility." Remak's exposition gives a more general and lucid formulation of the methodology of welfare economics than most economic authors from the same, or earlier periods, perhaps including Pareto himself, and displays clearly the kinship between this methodology and R. Frisch's distinction between selection analysis and implementation.

References for Section 3.9

R. Frisch, "Mathematical appendix to a memorandum on price–wage–tax–subsidy policies as instruments in maintaining optimal employment", *Memorandum* from the Institute of Economics at the University of Oslo (23 September 1949).
R. Frisch, "Preface to the Oslo channel model" – See reference under Section 3.2.
R. Remak, "Kann die Volkswirtschaftslehre eine exakte Wissenschaft werden", *Jahrbücher für Nationalökonomie und Statistik* (1929).

3.10. *The Approach of Fixed Targets*

Most of the discussion of quantitative economic policy in *J. Tinbergen's On the Theory of Economic Policy* is based on the approach of fixed targets. This means that certain endogenous variables are appointed to be "target variables", and the goal of policy is formulated by specifying directly certain values for these target variables. These are the "fixed targets". Next the policy model in the form of a system of equations involving instrument variables as well as endogenous variables is used to compute such values of the instrument variables as are necessary in order to reach the stipulated targets.

In principle Tinbergen is in favour of an optimization approach on the basis of a preference function. The approach of fixed targets is proposed for purely practical reasons: "The fixation of the function Ω (the preference function) is a difficult matter; generally it will not be considered consciously but intuitively by those responsible for the policy. In principle it must not only depend on the individual ophelimity functions, as estimated by the policy-makers, but on a certain measure of combining and hence the weighing of these individual interests as well. In practice the stage of fixing Ω and trying to maximize it will often be passed over and the targets y chosen directly." A similar "defence" is given in *J. Tinbergen's* and *H.C. Bos's Mathematical Models of Economic Growth*.

Let the equations of the model be written in general as

$$\phi_1(x_1, \ldots, x_n; \, t_1, \ldots, t_m) = 0,$$

(47)

$$\phi_n(x_1, \ldots, x_n; \, t_1, \ldots, t_m) = 0,$$

where now

(48) $\quad x = (x_1, \ldots, x_n), \qquad a = (t_1, \ldots, t_m).$

Thus x is the vector describing the results of the policy, and $t_1, \ldots, t_m$ are m instrument variables so that a policy, generally designated by a, is given by a vector of values for these instruments. There are as many equations in the system as there are endogenous variables. We assume the equations to be independent and not contradictory so that they imply a solution for x. This can be written as

$$(49) \quad \left. \begin{array}{l} x_1 = f_1(t_1, \ldots, t_m), \\ \quad \cdot \\ \quad \cdot \\ \quad \cdot \\ x_n = f_n(t_1, \ldots, t_m), \end{array} \right\} \quad \text{or} \quad x = f(a).$$

This corresponds to the general form $x = f(a, z)$ used previously, but we now omit the exogenous factors z from consideration.

Tinbergen's approach consists in selecting a certain number of variables from the vector x as target variables and imposing specified values on these. The policy problem then is to determine the instrument values $t_1, \ldots, t_m$. In the policy problem these are accordingly considered as variables to be determined. If we impose given values on m of the elements of x, then there remains $n - m$ free x-variables and m t-variables in the system of equations (47), i.e., altogether n unknowns. Provided that the equations are independent and not contradictory also as a system in this set of variables (a condition which can be made precise in terms of the Jacobian of the system), it can be solved to give

$$(50) \quad \begin{array}{l} t_1 = g_1(x_1^*, \ldots, x_m^*), \\ \quad \cdot \\ \quad \cdot \\ \quad \cdot \\ t_m = g_m(x_1^*, \ldots, x_m^*). \end{array}$$

We have here used $x_1^*, \ldots, x_m^*$ to designate the target values for the m endogenous values so appointed, and for convenience assumed that the variables are ordered in such a way that the m first variables are the target variables.

In addition to (50) we would also obtain the values of $x_{m+1}, \ldots, x_n$

as functions of $x_1^*, \ldots, x_m^*$:

$$x_{m+1} = g_{m+1}(x_1^*, \ldots, x_m^*),$$

(51)

$$x_n = g_n(x_1^*, \ldots, x_m^*).$$

These endogenous variables, which are not included among the target variables, are "irrelevant variables" in Tinbergen's terminology. They are however necessary elements of the analysis since the system in the original form (47) cannot be formulated without them.

If we had tried to impose target values on more than m endogenous variables, then the system would have had too many equations as compared with the number of variables and no solution could in general be found. On the other hand, if we had imposed target values on fewer than m endogenous variables, then not one unique constellation, but rather a set of different constellations of the instrument variables would satisfy the requirement. This is of course the logical background of Tinbergen's "normal case" where the number of targets is required to be equal to the number of instruments.

In addition to the equations of the system, we must in general take into account constraints on the ranges of variation of the instruments. This is what we have in general represented by the requirement that a should belong to a set A of possible policies, A in the present case being a set in the m-dimensional space. The specified set of targets $x_1^*, \ldots, x_m^*$ which satisfies the rule that the number of targets is equal to the number of instruments, is feasible only if it generates, via (50), a solution for the instruments $a = (t_1, \ldots, t_m) \in A$. In many parts of his discussion of economic policy problems Tinbergen recognizes this requirement in addition to the requirement concerning the number of targets and instruments.

In order to visualize the elements involved, Figure 15 gives a sample of cases. To the left is given the set of possible policies A, and to the right the set of possible results X. The arrow from A to X illustrates the function from A to X as given by (49). The relations in (50), instrument values expressed as functions of target values, are obtained by selecting $x_1^*, \ldots, x_m^*$ to the right and finding the point a in the $t_1, \ldots, t_m$-space which corresponds to the given $x_1^*, \ldots, x_m^*$-point.

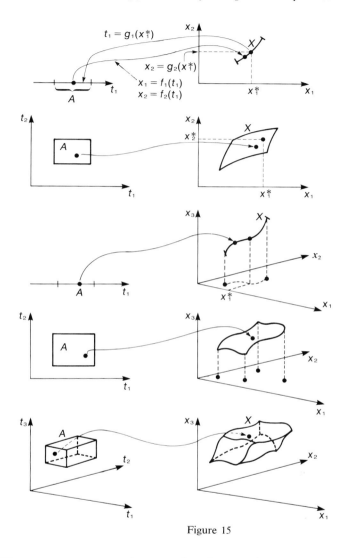

Figure 15

There are as many elements in $x_1^*, \ldots, x_m^*$ as corresponding to the dimensionality of A. If $m < n$, then $x_{m+1}, \ldots, x_n$ can be read off in the diagrams to the right corresponding to the form (51).

In the first case in Figure 15 there is one instrument, confined within an interval A, and two endogenous variables. In this case the set of possible results X is represented by a curve in the x_1, x_2-diagram. It is possible to specify the value of one target variable, as indicated by x_1^*. Then the value of x_2 follows corresponding to (51). Next there is the case of two instruments and two endogenous variables. In this case the set X is two-dimensional, and it is possible to specify two target variables as indicated by x_1^* and x_2^*. Below is a case of one instrument and three endogenous variables in which case X is a curve in the three-dimensional space. Here it is possible to specify one target variable as suggested by x_1^*; when this is specified the two other endogenous variables are determined. Next follow the case of two instruments and three endogenous variables with X as a flying carpet in the three-dimensional space, and the case of three instruments and three endogenous variables with X as a solid body.

In practice one will in most cases not be able to display the various sets of possibilities as we have done in Figure 15, because there are too many dimensions. However, a nice case is given in a paper by *P. de Wolff* and *J. Sandee* for the Netherlands in connection with a policy problem for 1959. Six policy instruments were considered: government expenditure, the wage rate, an indirect tax rate, a wage tax rate, a non-wage tax rate, and rents. (Wages and rents were under government control.) As target variables were considered the balance of payments, the change in the consumer price level, and the government budget surplus. The latter is an endogenous variable because tax revenues are endogenous, and it was considered a target variable in the short-term problem because an accumulation of deficits on the state budget would reduce the scope for possible policy variations in the future. For the six instrument variables upper and lower boundaries were stipulated on the basis of various practical and political considerations so that the set corresponding to A in our notations would be a box in the six-dimensional space. To this possibility set then corresponds a set in the three-dimensional space for the target variables. The authors calculated the boundaries of this set and displayed graphically its projections in the various planes for pairs of target variables. Alternative specifications of the boundaries of possible policies were given and the corresponding narrowing down of the set of possible results X exhibited. Within these sets some more specific solutions were calculated, and the information gained formed part of the basis for the final choice of policy. (P. de Wolff's and J. Sandee's paper has not been published in its original form, but a survey including the diagram described in the text is included in *J.G.*

Abert's book on *Economic Policy and Planning in the Netherlands, 1950–1965.* It is a good example of how a policy problem can be made transparent.)

In calculations according to the Tinbergen scheme one specifies values for target variables $x_1^*, \ldots, x_m^*$ and calculates the necessary instrument values $t_1, \ldots, t_m$. When the set of possible results is not nicely displayed in diagrams one does however not really know in advance whether the specified target vector $x_1^*, \ldots, x_m^*$ is feasible. An infeasible specification would reveal itself only when the instrument values have been calculated and possibly prove to be located outside the permissible set A. For such cases Tinbergen suggests a stepwise procedure. If, in a first trial, some instrument t_i proves to exceed an upper limit (or fall short of a lower limit), then this instrument should in the next trial be set equal to its limit. One variable originally on the list of target variables must be removed from this list so that the new set of target variables will contain the same number of variables as the reduced number of free instruments. A new calculation is then performed, and if all instruments are now inside their permissible limits, then the calculated solution should be accepted. It may however occur that this time another instrument gets outside its boundaries, and the procedure will have to be repeated with still another endogenous variable being abandoned as a target. Tinbergen asserts that "there is a great deal of chance that we shall obtain an acceptable solution" by this procedure, but he admits that "generally speaking the number of possibilities is large and it is, as a rule, difficult if not impossible to study them or detect them in a systematic way. It is by trial and error, albeit perhaps by a somewhat systematized trial and error method, that we have to proceed."

In practice the scheme proposed by Tinbergen, proceeding by first stipulating target values and then calculating the required instrument values, has not often been adhered to. The equation system of the policy models have usually been established in the form of (47) and used in the form of (49) instead of (50). That means that calculations have usually been performed by stipulating the values of the instrument variables and deriving the corresponding consequences for the endogenous variables. In most actual applications one has of course tried out several alternatives. In connection with the Norwegian national budgetting model the computational programme has for instance been arranged in such a way that many alternatives can be calculated simultaneously. This means that one can in an efficient

way make rather intensive search efforts towards finding a satisfactory solution. Usually two or three such collections of alternatives
have been calculated before one has settled for one definitive solution. (The possibilities for calculating several alternatives has been
utilized also for exploring several alternatives with regard to the
non-controlled exogenous factors, not only alternative policy specifications.)

The reasons why calculations from given instrument specifications
to resulting values of the endogenous variables have been more
widely used than the reverse procedure, are probably the following:

1. The set of possible alternatives in the policy space A will usually
   have a rather simple structure so that one can immediately check
   whether a proposed policy is feasible. On the other hand the set
   of possible results X is only implicitly defined by A and the
   equation system. A procedure which starts out from a stipulated
   target $x_1^*, \ldots, x_m^*$ can therefore easily run into infeasible alternatives as discussed above.

2. The policy for each year will not deviate dramatically from the
   policy in the preceding year. One will therefore usually have a
   good starting point for search and explorations by making
   moderate changes in last year's policy.

3. By starting from stipulated instrument values and calculating the
   resulting state x it is not necessary in advance to give priority to
   certain endogenous variables which should be appointed to the
   status of being target variables. If there are few instruments and
   many variables which count in the preferences, then this strict
   division of the endogenous variables into two groups may be felt
   to be rather artificial. By a search procedure through calculations
   for several alternatives from the instrument values to the resulting state x one is relieved of this artificial requirement and may
   evaluate the resulting states as one finds reasonable and convenient regardless of the number of instruments used.

Whether one calculates this way or that way should be considered
as a matter of convenience. Regardless of the practical procedure the
underlying idea is a planning scheme in which there is a preference

function to be maximized under various sorts of constraints. The simpler procedures are meant as rough methods of approaching what would have been the correct result if the preference function had been specified explicitly and correctly maximized under all constraints which apply in the problem. It appears from what is quoted above from Tinbergen and from many other pages of his book that this is his viewpoint. It would therefore be wrong to oppose his approach to policy analysis, as a matter of principle, against the method of maximizing a preference function.

Considering the method of fixed targets in relation to the classification given in Section 3.1, it should be referred to group 5 since it changes the form of the problem – from optimization to the solution of equations.

The fact that one will often prefer to carry out the calculations in a way different from that proposed by Tinbergen does not detract from the value of having a clear view of the relation between the number of instrument variables and the dimensionality of the set of possibilities which can be generated in the space of the endogenous variables. A clear understanding of this point helps to understand the choice situation in a policy problem, to design good search procedures for locating good, though not quite optimal solutions, and to understand when further search will be futile. It also helps in the qualitative policy choice as to whether the abandoning of some existing instruments or the introduction of new instruments would be desirable.

In addition to the exposition given by Tinbergen himself, the method of "fixed targets" is presented and discussed by *B. Hansen*, *L. Johansen*, and *M.H. Peston*. Critical viewpoints are found in a book by *W.A. Jöhr* and *H.W. Singer* previously referred to and in a paper by *J.M. Fleming*.

Recently some interesting extensions of the target–instrument approach of Tinbergen have appeared in the literature.

One extension attempts to give a more general treatment by using the theory of "generalized inverses" (or "pseudo-inverses") of a given, square or non-square matrix. By this device one can give a unified treatment of the cases where the number of instruments is smaller than, equal to, or larger than the number of targets. In the first case some approximation to the desired target values is achieved, in the second case the "classical" correct solution, and in the third case a range of solutions for the instrument values exhibiting the "superfluous" degrees of freedom. See e.g. *C.S. Russell* and *V.K. Smith.*

Another extension takes up dynamic aspects, using concepts and methods from control theory (especially the concept of "controllability"). First *A.J. Preston* showed that the number of instrument variables could be less than the number of target variables if the target is specified for some future period in a dynamic system. (One might perhaps explain this result intuitively by saying that the manipulation of a smaller number of instruments over a series of time periods may replace the use of a larger number of instruments in one period.) Next, however, *M. Aoki* pointed out that economic policy, in a dynamic setting, is rarely a question about reaching a target *in one period*, but rather a question about reaching a point on a specified development path *and continuing along the path.* Then a condition more like Tinbergen's requirement of a number of instruments equal to or exceeding the number of targets is again valid.

References for Section 3.10

J.G. Abert, *Economic policy and planning in the Netherlands, 1950–1965* (Yale University Press, New Haven and London, 1969). Especially Chapter 6.

M. Aoki, "On a generalization of Tinbergen's condition in the theory of policy to dynamic models", *Review of Economic Studies* (1975).

J.M. Fleming, "Targets and instruments", *International Monetary Fund Staff Papers* (1968).

B. Hansen, *The economic theory of fiscal policy* (Allen and Unwin, London, 1958). Especially Chapter 1.

L. Johansen, *Public economics* (North-Holland, Amsterdam, 1965). Especially Chapter 2.

W.A. Jöhr and H.W. Singer, *The rôle of the economist as official adviser* – See reference under Section 2.5. Especially the Appendix to Part One.

M.H. Peston, *Theory of macroeconomic policy* (Philip Allan Publishers, Oxford, 1974). Especially Chapters 4 and 5.

A.J. Preston, "A dynamic generalization of Tinbergen's theory of policy", *Review of Economic Studies* (1974).

C.S. Russell and V.K. Smith, "Targets, instruments and generalized inverses", *European Economic Review* (1975).

J. Tinbergen, *On the theory of economic policy* – See reference under Section 1.3.

J. Tinbergen and H.C. Bos, *Mathematical models of economic growth* – See reference under Section 3.4.

3.11. Some Further Observations on Selection Analysis versus the Target–instrument Approach – Preference Constraints

The selection analysis described in Section 3.9 and the target–instrument approach to the formulation of economic policy discussed in Section 3.10 emphasize formal and precise analysis of different parts of our general planning scheme. Selection analysis emphasizes the choice of an optimal result x from a set X of possible results on the basis of a preference function $W(x)$. The target–instrument approach emphasizes the relationships between instruments and endogenous variables, as represented by $x = f(a, z)$, and tries to find a policy which will produce desired results with respect to a number of target variables. The values of the target variables are chosen under observation of the dimensionality or number of degrees of freedom in the set of possible results, but without explicit use of any preference function. Figure 16 suggests the complementarity of these two approaches.

As already suggested R. *Frisch* would agree that the selection

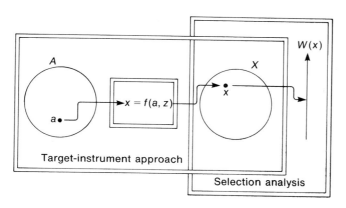

Figure 16

analysis is incomplete, and *J. Tinbergen* would agree that the target–instrument approach is incomplete. The interesting question is why they have chosen to emphasize the analysis of different parts of the complete scheme.

Before trying to review the possible reasons for this, it should be remembered that J. Tinbergen in many of his more theoretical works, i.e., in analyses not intended for direct empirical implementation, or analyses meant for drawing qualitative conclusions, has often used preference functions or welfare functions to be maximized. On the other hand, R. Frisch has also worked with economic policy models which belong to the target–instrument sphere. His memorandum on "Price–Wage–Tax Policies as Instruments in Maintaining Optimal Employment" from 1949 contained a policy model (by Frisch called a "decision model") with 50 equations between 64 variables, out of which quite many were instruments of policy such as tax and transfer parameters, and also some variables characterizing monetary policy. This memorandum and several other reports from the same period contain many exercises in analysing economic policy in terms of relations between target variables and instrument variables and careful considerations of the number of degrees of freedom within which the policy can be chosen. (Cf. the remarks at the beginning of Section 1.3 concerning the training of students in Oslo in this period.) Of special interest is a memorandum (in Norwegian) from 1950 which gives general rules for the use of a decision model with special emphasis on careful counting of degrees of freedom. According to these rules a certain number of variables are chosen as target variables and given specific values. To the extent that the number of target variables fail to exhaust the degrees of freedom permitted by the number of possible instruments in the model it is suggested that the remaining degrees of freedom should be disposed of by a requirement of maximization, for instance of the national product. It is pointed out that such a maximization will absorb all remaining degrees of freedom regardless of whether this is a small or large number. However, the fact remains that in his later writings Frisch emphasized more and more the selection aspect of economic planning, both by general arguments and in the construction of actual planning models.

Let us now try to survey the reasons for emphasizing either the target–instrument part or the selection part of a total planning scheme (partly repeating points suggested in Sections 3.9–3.10). Not all these reasons have been brought forward explicitly by Frisch and Tinbergen, but they may nevertheless underly their different attitudes.

(1) *The possibility of establishing a preference function.* It was suggested already in Section 3.10 that pessimism with regard to the possibility of establishing a preference function was one reason why J. Tinbergen, for practical application of planning models recommended the fixed target approach. On the other hand, R. Frisch was much more optimistic in this respect. In the first place he argued that systematic studies of feasible alternatives in economic policy will force upon the public and the authorities the fact that "the number of feasible alternatives is so great that it is impossible to keep track of them simply by listing them and looking at them. It will then be understood that one needs an analytical technique for picking that one – or those – alternatives that are in some sense of the word the *optimum* ones. This leads directly to the problem of *mathematical programming* applied to economics.... Any such programming technique must be based on a definition of the nature of the preference function to be applied in national – or even in international – economic policy." This line of argument implies optimism with regard to the possibility that "the public and the authorities" will recognize the *need* for using a preference function. Next Frisch declared, "I am convinced that the preference function problem for an economy at large can be solved when it is approached in an intelligent and cautious way," and referred to his own experiences with an interview technique for establishing preference functions. (See "Preface to the Oslo Channel Model".) (We shall return to the problem of establishing preference functions in a later chapter.)

(2) *The nature of the preferences.* Regardless of the problem of how to proceed in order to establish a preference function, the nature or form of the preferences may be of importance for the decision as to which aspect of the planning one will prefer to emphasize. Suppose that there is a result x^*, or perhaps a narrow neighbourhood around such a result, which defines so to speak minimum requirements for a successful policy. It may for instance be defined by full employment (according to some definition), balance in the foreign trade, a rate of inflation which is not higher than in other similar countries, and so on. Less than this might be considered devastating to the Central Au-

thority. On the other hand, it may not be considered very important if one does better than specified by x^* in some respects. Illustratively speaking we might say that the preference function has a sharp edge at x^* and remains almost flat in the preferred direction from x^*. If we now admit that no planning and steering of the economy can be perfect, then it seems that the reasonable strategy in a case like the one described here would be to allocate research and planning resources so as to increase the reliability of planning and steering so that we can be as sure as possible of reaching x^*. For this purpose it would be rather irrelevant to spend resources on trying to establish detailed and precise preferences concerning the choice between alternatives which are inferior to x^* and also for possible results which might be better than x^*. The important thing is to find out whether x^* is really feasible and to devise a policy which is as reliable as possible in reaching x^* (or the narrow neighbourhood around this point). In order to check whether the critical point x^* is really feasible it is necessary to delimit the set of possible actions A and work out the model connecting instrument variables and endogenous variables. The instrument–target model is also necessary in order to steer the economy correctly towards x^*. With a limited amount of resources and time for planning, it is clear that, under the conditions here described, it would be rational to devote most of the efforts to the target–instrument aspect of the overall planning. When the preference function has no such marked edge, then this argument cannot be brought to bear. There is no *general* answer to the question whether or not this is so in practice.

(3) *The nature of the economic system.* The nature of the economic system is reflected in the contents and extension of the set of feasible policies A and the structure of the economy as represented by $x = f(a, z)$. (The term economic system is here used in the sense defined in Section 3.2.) In an economy in which the majority of economic decisions are market determined and only indirectly influenced by decisions by the Central Authority through a limited number of instrument variables, very much of the restrictions on the set of feasible states or developments X will originate from the limitations on the set of feasible policies A, so that the set X will be much smaller than the set of physical possibilities X^0 as defined in Section 3.9 and illustrated in Figure 14. In this case a selection analysis isolated from the analysis of means of implementation would

be rather irrelevant. On the other hand, for an economy under a highly centralized direct planning each component of the description x of the state of the economy would be directly specified in orders issued by the Central Authority or by lower echelons which work out in more detail orders given by the Central Authority. In this case the main constraints defining the set of possible results would be physical constraints whereas the part of our planning scheme which falls under the target–instrument sphere would be absent or irrelevant. Selection analysis would accordingly remain as the main problem (with a reservation concerning the consistency problem to be discussed in the following section). From the examples of policy analysis provided by Tinbergen it is clear that he was mostly concerned with economies in which the target–instrument approach would be an important part of the overall planning problem, whereas Frisch, particularly in his later years, was very much concerned with methods of planning in which direct planning would take a dominant position.

This discussion could be related to the controversy between "geneticists" and "teleologists" in the early period of economic planning in the USSR. According to *P.R. Gregory* and *R.C. Stuart* this controversy "centered largely around the issue of whether planning was to be directed (and limited) by market forces or moulded by the will of the planners, unconstrained by market forces and limited only by the physical constraints of the economy." The geneticists "advocated a form of planning largely consistent with the precepts of NEP in view of the dominant role that market forces would be allowed to play in the planning process." On the other hand, the teleologists argued that "planning should seek to *overcome* market forces, rather than be directed by them." Furthermore, "The concept of equilibrium should be denounced as an unnecessarily severe constraint on the flexibility of planners." It is clear from this that the geneticists envisaged a very narrow set of possibilities X, being constrained by behaviour and equilibrium conditions, whereas the teleologists envisaged a set of possibilities X not much narrower than what we have symbolized above by X^0. It would seem that selection analysis would be a natural procedure to a teleologist, while on the other hand the philosophy of the geneticists did not leave room for much more than an indicative form of planning. (Indicative planning will be taken up in a later chapter of these lectures.)

(4) *The time perspective.* This just repeats a point mentioned

towards the end of Section 3.9, where it was pointed out that selection analysis in Frisch's sense would be more relevant to planning for the really long term whereas an analysis of the target–instrument relations would be obligatory for short-term plans which have to be operational. It is clear that many of the planning models used by Tinbergen and others to illustrate the target–instrument approach are short-term models whereas selection models are often models for the medium or longer term.

In view of the last point the system of medium- or long-term plans and short-term plans could be designed as suggested in Figure 17. In

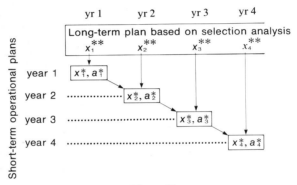

Figure 17

the figure years ordered horizontally indicate years covered by the plan, whereas years ordered vertically indicate years of working out the plans. Initially there is a long-term plan based on selection analysis which specifies selected states of the economy for the various years, indicated by $x_1^{**}, x_2^{**}, \ldots$. For the first year a short-term plan is worked out which borrows targets from x^{**}. However, in view of more recent information and facts, and limitations brought to light by the analysis of implementation possibilities, one may end up with targets for the first year, x_1^*, which are not necessarily identical with those contained in x_1^{**}. (Furthermore x_1^* may be more disaggregated as compared with x_1^{**}.) This plan then also specifies the intended use of the instruments a_1^*. Next, for the second year a target x_2^* is specified partly on the basis of the selection analysis in the long-term plan x_2^{**}, and partly influenced by experiences from the first year and dynamic conditions relating the possibilities in the second year to the achievements in the first year. This plan again specifies the intended use of instruments a_2^* which is deemed necessary for achieving x_2^*. In the same way one proceeds from year to year. (On the basis of such a scheme one would expect the correlation between x_1^* and x_1^{**} to be better than the correlations between x_2^* and x_2^{**} and so on, which is in accordance with experience in several countries.) By rolling or sliding planning one would work out a new long-term plan every year instead of keeping the same long-term plan through several years as suggested in Figure 17. This does however not change the relation between the selection analysis type of long-term planning and the target–instrument approach of short-term plans.

Before leaving the subject of comparison between selection analysis and the target–instrument approach it should be observed that in practical use of planning models one sometimes finds approaches which are, in a way, intermediate between full reliance on a preference function for performing the task of selection, and the use of fixed targets. The intermediate case consists in splitting the formal representation of preferences into two parts: Some elements of preferences are represented by constraints in the form of equations or inequalities (concerning one or more variables at a time), while other aspects are represented by a function to be maximized. The first type of representation, representation by *preference constraints*, may be considered as a simplified and approximate way of representing preferences which should ideally be expressed through the preference function.

This simplification will be particularly useful when the basic preference function, if it could be fully and correctly established, would exhibit some sharp edges, expressing the fact that for some variables there are critical levels or constellations which it is particularly important to reach. The balance of trade may represent one such variable. It may be particularly important not to incur a deficit on the balance of trade, but it may not be very important to achieve a surplus. Resources and possibilities which might be used for achieving a surplus had therefore rather been used for other goals. Non-negativity of the balance of trade might then be introduced as a preference constraint. This will secure the achievement of the required balance, but not introduce any inducement to earn a surplus at the cost of other goals.

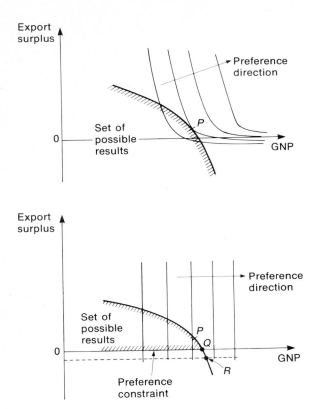

Figure 18

This case is illustrated in Figure 18. In the upper part is displayed the set of possible results described by GNP and the export surplus, and contour lines for the true preference function. It is assumed that the critical level for the export surplus is zero. When there is a considerable export surplus, then we are willing to give up very much of the surplus per unit of increase in GNP. But when we are close to the critical level, then we are willing to accept only very small further deteriorations in order to get an increase in GNP.

In the correctly represented case the optimal position is given by point *P*, showing a small export surplus.

The simplified case is displayed in the lower part of Figure 18. We have now introduced non-negativity of the export surplus as an additional constraint. The preference function is now simply the value of GNP. For this simplified situation the optimal position is given by point Q. Here the export surplus is zero and we have a slightly larger GNP than in the correct solution in the upper part of the figure, but the solution is very close to P.

This case was characterized by a sharp edge in the true preference function, representing a critical value for one of the arguments in the preference function. In other cases one may find it difficult to put down in numerical form the degree to which one is willing to trade off one variable against another, but one may nevertheless have some idea about permissible ranges. For instance, concerning the income distribution one may find it difficult to say to what degree one would accept a distortion of the distribution of income between wages and profits in order to achieve a higher rate of growth of national product, but one may be willing to put down figures for a permissible range of variation for the proportion between wages and profits. The limits to this range of permissible variation are the preference constraints.

When some preference considerations are taken care of by such preference constraints, then the preference function to be maximized can, as illustrated above, be simplified by omitting the corresponding variables from the list of arguments in the preference function. If a sufficient number of considerations are taken care of by preference constraints, one might for instance end up with a preference function which is simply identical with the national product. The more there are of preference constraints, the more limited will be the set of permissible results over which the preference function is to be maximized. In the limit the constraints may be so numerous and so tight that only one permissible state remains. In that case we have narrowed down the set of acceptable states to such a degree that this approach has become equivalent to the imposition of fixed targets. This illustrates the fact that the use of preference constraints as a device to simplify the preference function may be considered as intermediate between an optimization approach based on a full-scale use of a preference function, and the method of fixed targets. (As already suggested by the reference to R. Frisch's "Mathematical Appendix" above Frisch suggested the idea of a combination of preference constraints and a function to be maximized already in connection with some of his earliest expositions of economic decision models, and he returned to the same idea in many of his later papers, see for instance "An Implementation System . . .".)

When an optimization problem is to be simplified by relegating some variables to being taken care of by preference constraints, then it is sometimes argued that the most important variables should be retained in the preference function to be maximized while the less important ones should be left to the constraints. (For some suggestions in this direction, see e.g. *P.K. Rao* and *V.S. Rajamani.*) This is a rather ambiguous point of view, since the fact frequently is that the willingness to trade off one target against another depends upon the point of departure as illustrated in Figure 18. In the case of such non-linear preferences it is possible to speak precisely about the importance of various variables only in a local and marginal sense. In this sense we might say that the variables in the preference *constraints* should be the most important ones since we are not willing to accept any further deterioration in the values of these variables even if we could gain something in terms of the variables retained in the preference function. We might express the same point of view by saying that preferences which are expressed in the form of preference constraints are imposed as obligatory, i.e., given the highest priority, whereas preferences regarding variables in the preference function are flexible. For instance, if we have imposed a preference constraint requiring the export surplus to be non-negative, whereas the volume of the national product is included in the preference function, then we may arrive at a solution where the national product is of a modest volume, and this may be due to the preference constraint for the balance of trade. In other words, it may be that if we had been willing to give way a little bit concerning the balance of trade we might have achieved a much larger national produce.

This inflexibility concerning preferences that are taken care of by preference constraints can be controlled by *sensitivity analysis*, i.e., by calculating the solution by maximizing the preference function for alternative constellations of the preference constraints. If the calculations are performed by some of the standard methods of mathematical programming, then "shadow prices" will automatically emerge from the calculations which show numerically by how much the value of the preference function can be increased by relaxing each preference constraint by one unit. For instance, if there is a preference constraint concerning the balance of trade, and the maximand of the planning problem is the national product, then the shadow price (dual variable) related to the balance of trade requirement will tell by how much the national product can be increased if we are willing to accept an increase in the deficit on the balance of trade by one unit (for instance one mill. *kroner*). This is illustrated in the lower part of Figure 18. The dotted horizontal line represents a more liberal balance of trade constraint. The new optimal solution is given by point R. The increase in GNP per unit of decrease in the export surplus by moving from Q to R is the "shadow price" of the balance of trade requirement. If we are uncertain as to whether the preference constraints are reasonably formulated the knowledge about such shadow prices will be very useful. Even if we have not formulated precisely the true trade-off rate in the complete, underlying preference function we may be able to say whether or not a calculated shadow price indicates that the preference constraint should be liberalized.

The use of preference constraints instead of including in the preference function everything concerning which the authorities have preferences has a few years ago been subject to a controversy in the journal *Co-Existence*, with contributions by *J. Tinbergen, J. Drewnowski* and *M.J. Chossudovsky* (followed by an exchange between *J. Kornai, J. Tinbergen* and *G. Adler Karlson* on the relevance of welfare theory for development planning). The point of departure of the controversy was partly viewpoints presented by *J. Kornai* in his book *Mathematical Planning of Structural Decisions.* Kornai recognizes the fact that the preference function and the constraints of a model "on the abstract theoretical level" can be logically separated as serving different purposes. Nevertheless he believes that it will be impossible to uphold this distinction clearly in practical planning: "There is no self-evident and natural criterion for separating in each case the relationships which are to be enforced within the system of constraints ('necessary') from those coming under the objective function ('the more the better').... The more normal and natural must be considered the procedure to present certain numerical targets which express the most general economic policy in *absolute terms* instead of relative proportions.... This train of thought leads to a certain degradation of the objective function from its rank occupied in the 'pure' model described above. It is not the objective function itself, but the latter *together* with the requirements of economic policy figuring in the system of constraints, which will express the aims of higher economic administration." Kornai then describes a planning process where the targets may be set tentatively at certain levels, and next modified during the process.

J. Tinbergen has no objection to raise against these viewpoints. J. Drewnowski, on the other hand, considers them as tending to create confusion. He argues that what one avoids by transferring some variables from the preference function into the form of constraints is not the relative weighting of the variables, but simply "clarity in the presentation of the problem." He holds on to the view that "the constraints should reflect objective conditions and the limitations which these objective conditions put in the way of achieving plan objectives. If value judgements are included in the constraints the situation is falsified."

To me it seems that there is no reason to be dogmatic about this issue. If the constraints are properly explained, then the use of preference constraints does not "falsify" the situation. But if they are set on the basis of value judgements there is always a need to explore what it would entail of gains or costs in terms of other variables to relax or strengthen the preference constraints. As pointed out above this can be done by means of sensitivity analysis and shadow prices.

Above we have considered the introduction of preference constraints as an analytical substitute for elements of the preference function, for the purpose of simplification. Another trend of literature argues for preference constraints rather than preference functions to be maximized, for more fundamental reasons. I have in mind the theory of "satisficing" and "bounded rationality", associated with the names of *H. Simon, R. Radner* and others. This line of thought considers the assumption of maximizing behaviour, which permeates almost all branches of economics, as unrealistic, and introduces instead aspiration levels and "satisficing" as determinants of decisions. The approach of fixed targets in economic planning might be said to be nearer to the spirit of this trend of theory, whereas the use of preference functions to be maximized is in line with the classical assumption of maximizing behaviour in economics.

References for Section 3.11

M.J. Chossudovsky, "The social welfare function: A note", *Co-Existence* (1969).
J. Drewnowski, "Valuations systems implied in planning decisions: Shall we try to reveal them?", *Co-Existence* (1969).
R. Frisch, "Price–wage–tax policies as instruments in maintaining optimal employment" – See reference under Section 1.3. Also "Mathematical Appendix" – See reference under Section 3.9.

R. Frisch, "Determineringsskjemaet som hjelpemiddel under spesifiseringen av desisjonsmodellen", *Memorandum* from the Institute of Economics at the University of Oslo (23 January 1950).

R. Frisch, "Preface to the Oslo Channel Model" – See reference under Section 3.2.

R. Frisch, "An implementation system for optimal national economic planning without detailed quantity fixation from a central authority", *Proceedings of the 3rd International Conference on Operational Research*, Oslo, 1963 (English Universities Press, London, and Dunod, Paris, 1964).

P.R. Gregory and R.C. Stuart, *Soviet economic structure and performance* (Harper and Row, New York, 1974). Especially pp. 96–97.

B. Hansen, *Lectures in economic theory, Part II* (Studentlitteratur, Lund, 1967). Lectures 1–6.

L. Johansen, "Ragnar Frisch's contributions to economics", *The Swedish Journal of Economics* (1969).

J. Kornai, *Mathematical planning of structural decisions* – See reference under Section 1.3.

P.K. Rao and V.S. Rajamani, "A new approach to public investment", *Socio-Economic Planning Sciences* (1975).

J. Tinbergen, "Optimization – of what?", *Co-Existence* (1968).

3.12. Some Remarks on Consistency of Plans

The term consistency in connection with economic planning generally means that the various parts of a plan are not contradictory. In relation to our general planning scheme this would simply mean that the state of the economy aimed at, and the planned values of the instruments should be compatible with the structure of the economy as represented by the relations $x = f(a, z)$, with due account for the expected values of non-controlled exogenous factors z, and the constraints on the set of permissible instrument values given by A. A plan which is not consistent in this sense is bound to fail. In this sense consistency is a prime requirement, more basic than the requirement of optimality.

This general interpretation corresponds to the sense in which R. *Stone* uses the term when he discusses "consistency in an altogether wider sense, to include consistency with everything we know, everything we expect, and everything we desire to achieve." The term consistency is used in a similar, but perhaps somewhat narrower sense in the literature from the socialist countries. A representative definition, given by the Hungarian economist, B. *Csikós-Nagy*, reads as follows: "A plan is consistent if it can be implemented in keeping with the actual economic conditions and if the programming targets are in harmony with each other. In other words: a plan is consistent if it is in conformity with the law of input–output balances of production."

The reason why I take up this point here, in a chapter which treats "various ways of simplifying the planning problem and the planning scheme in practice," is that it has often been asserted, in connection with descriptions of planning practice in the socialist countries, that the problem of achieving consistent plans is so overwhelmingly difficult in those countries that all efforts have to be exerted in this direction to the neglect of optimization. There is definitely something to this; the question is why this problem should be more paramount in socialist countries than in private enterprise, market-oriented economies.

The most obvious reason is of course that planning in the socialist countries has to concern itself with many more details. Concretely speaking it will involve a mass of figures of an entirely different order of magnitude. Then the task of achieving internal consistency will of course be much bigger. *B. Csikós-Nagy*, quoted above, asserts that in the period of the most highly centralized planning and management in Hungary "the main problems of planning and of the breakdown of the plan were – in this period – the internal contradictions among the various plan indicators."

In addition to this comes the different consequences of lack of consistency in the case of direct and indirect planning (in the sense given in Section 2.7). Under indirect planning there will be a set of instruments in the hands of the Central Authority which are used to influence the endogenous variables only indirectly. There is then a consistency problem concerning the complete set of actions to be taken as symbolized by a. Particularly if the planning problem is partitioned among departments as discussed in Section 3.5 there may be problems on this point. However, let us disregard this problem for the moment. Then inconsistency may prevail if the non-controlled exogenous factors have been wrongly forecasted, or if the structure of the economy is not correctly known, or if the knowledge about this has not been correctly used in working out the plan. We may then have a plan containing specified values of the endogenous variables aimed at, x^*, and specified values of the instruments, a^*, which are erroneously expected to produce x^*. What will be the consequences of this?

If the specified values of the instruments are consistent with the constraints defining A, then the planned actions a^* can be carried out. The administrative bodies executing the economic policy know what they have to do, and the various other agents in the economy behave according to their objectives and the constraints they are subjected to. The fact that all this taken together fails to produce the expected result x^* does not prevent the economy from functioning. There will be no deadlock or breakdown; one will "only" fail to achieve the targets of the plan.

In an economy under direct planning, where all enterprises are subject to instructions coming from higher echelons in the planning and administrative hierarchy, this will be entirely different. Suppose that inputs and outputs for individual enterprises are specified in the plan. Suppose furthermore that the supply system, giving instructions about which commodities should be delivered in what amounts from each enterprise to other named enterprises, is also included in all details in the plan. That means, all these magnitudes are given as plan instructions to the enterprises – they are not determined by the enterprises and only indirectly influenced by instruments of the Central Authority as in a market economy. If the plan then fails to be consistent, then we may run into a deadlock or breakdown. Enterprises may be unable to produce what they are requested to because of deficient input plans, the planned deliveries from enterprises may fail to be consistent with plans for receiving enterprises, and so on. If this happens, then the whole mode of functioning of the system may be interrupted.

Now this is of course a matter of degree. It is not the case that any inconsistency, however small, will gear the economy into a stalemate. In practice problems of smaller dimension of this sort have been solved by various kinds of inofficial contacts between enterprises, i.e., contacts which are established directly instead of via the higher echelons in the hierarchy, by individual enterprises starting producing some spare parts etc. themselves instead of relying on deliveries from other enterprises, by running down stocks in critical periods, and so on. It has also been observed in the socialist countries that the economy, consisting of enterprises which should in principle act on the basis of detailed plan instructions, continue to function rather smoothly even when plans are delayed so that there, for some interval, does not exist any plan. An interesting "experiment" was the introduction of the economic reforms in Hungary on the 1st January 1968. By this reform the system of detailed plan instructions to the individual enterprises was abolished. Instead of these were introduced a new price system and various material and financial incentives while the plans of the Central Authority were formulated in more aggregated terms than before. There was then in practice an interregnum in which the old system had been abolished while the new system had not yet asserted itself in all respects. *J. Kornai*, who (in *Anti-Equilibrium*) discusses the experiences from this period, reports that "no vacuum ensued; economic life continued to function smoothly." He ascribes this partly to what he calls "autonomous functions of organizations" which characterize most sorts of organizations, including enterprises and other economic entities. The nature of autonomous functions is described in the following way: "Autonomous function is based on the average diligence, conditioning, routine, identification with one's job of the people working within the system. Beyond that, it also relies on the fact that, as in every material system, a certain inertia prevails also in economic systems. Until some force disturbs the system, it will repeat itself. One might lament the fact that it conserves the old, or one might rejoice that it promotes stability. But however one feels about it inertia exists and acts, and one of its effects is evident in the autonomous functions of the system." The economic system does of course not consist *only* of autonomous functions, but Kornai considers the existence of autonomous functions as one of the important stabilizers of the functioning of an economic system and considers the experiences from the introduction of the reforms in Hungary as a case in point. Another experience from Hungary, also reported by Kornai (in *Overcentralization in Economic Administration*), is the fact that, even in the period under highly centralized management, and in which central plan figures for the various branches were fulfilled with a high degree of accuracy, plan fulfilments for individual enterprises in the various branches were very different, ranging from gross underfulfilment to considerable overfulfilment. That means that, even if branches did approximately as indicated in the plan, individual enterprises did not adhere in any way strictly to their plans. A large measure of adjustment and discretion apparently take place at the enterprise level in spite of the principle of working on the basis of enterprise plans sanctioned by central authorities.

This degree of autonomous functioning and flexibility even under centralized management suggests that plans which are somewhat inconsistent would not necessarily create very bad results. Nevertheless, it is clear that both the magnitude and detailedness of plans, and the role of plans as direct instructions, make consistency a more important consideration in socialist economies with centralized management than in economies more characterized by free enterprise and market system. Since the working out of even one plan which is approximately consistent in all details is a tremendous task, it is understandable that optimization, which requires comparison in one form or other between many alternatives, has drifted somewhat into the background.

Consistency is of course particularly important for operational short-term plans. In the literature from the USSR on economic planning it is often stressed that the planning process for annual plans starts with plan proposals submitted by the individual enterprises.

This way of starting the planning procedure probably helps to achieve approximate consistency rather early in the process when the economy is moving along a reasonably smooth development path.

In spite of this emphasis on consistency it would be wrong to think that the plan arrived at is an arbitrary plan among the possible consistent plans. The annual plans are formulated on the background of medium-term and perhaps long-term plans which are worked out by the central planning authorities, and these are often marked by clear priorities, i.e., they reflect preferences rather than for instance automatic trend extrapolations or arbitrary decisions. To the extent that the short-term operational plans use these medium- and long-term plans as guidelines they cannot be considered as arbitrary plans emerging from administrative procedures with no trace of optimization. Also the process of plan proposals and counter-proposals may tend to push the economy towards the "efficiency frontier". However, whether the achievements in the direction of optimality have been modest or considerable, present trends in planning methodology in the socialist countries in any case tend to bring optimization more consciously and explicitly into planning procedures at various stages and in various time perspectives.

Historically it is of some interest, in connection with the issue of consistency versus optimization, to refer to the previously mentioned GOELRO plan (see Section 1.1) in the USSR. The GOELRO plan was obviously not formally and explicitly an optimized plan. But neither were the considerations underlying the plan limited to consistency. This is clearly illustrated for instance by a letter from *V.I. Lenin* to *G.M. Krzhizhanovsky* of March 1920. In this letter Lenin requested an exposition of the plan which should illustrate the "tremendous advantage" of electrification. He suggested the style of presentation in the following way:

"Transport: To restore in the old way –

we need α millions (at pre-war prices)
or α fuel $+ \beta$ working days.

But to restore it on the basis of electrification

α minus x million rubles
or α minus y fuel $+ (\beta$ minus $z)$ working days,"

and similarly for other branches. Here is clearly a choice between alternatives with a concern for the saving of resources, i.e., not only concern for consistency.

References for Section 3.12

A. Barrère, "Internal consistency in the public economy: The plan and the market", in *Public economics*, edited by J. Margolis and H. Guitton (MacMillan, London, 1969).

B. Csikós-Nagy, *Socialist price theory and price policy* (Akadémiai Kiadó, Budapest, 1975). Especially p. 91 and pp. 101–102.

J. Kornai, *Overcentralization in economic administration* (Oxford University Press, Oxford, 1959). Especially Chapter I. Translation from Hungarian.

J. Kornai, *Anti-equilibrium* (North-Holland, Amsterdam, 1971). Especially Chapter 13.

V.I. Lenin, *On the development of heavy industry and electrification* (Progress Publishers, Moscow, 1972). Letter to M.G. Krzhizhanovsky, pp. 61–62.

R. Stone, "Consistent projections in multi-sector models" – See reference under Section 2.7.

T. Watanabe, "Quantitative foundations and implications of planning processes", in *Economy-wide models and development planning*, edited by C.R. Blitzer, P.B. Clark, and L. Taylor, published for the World Bank (Oxford University Press, London, 1975).

Chapter 4

GENERAL OBSERVATIONS ON THE USE OF MATHEMATICALLY FORMULATED MODELS IN ECONOMIC PLANNING

4.1. Brief Remarks on the History and Present State

Section 1.3 offered a brief review of theoretical developments which are relevant to economic planning. Some observations were also made on the actual use of mathematical models in planning contexts. Some scattered references have also been made in other sections. As an introduction to the present chapter I shall give a very brief review of *actual applications* of mathematically formulated models up to the present state. I concentrate attention on a few countries which seem to have been early starters in this field.

The earliest application of mathematical models seems to be the application of *G.A. Feldman's* growth models in connection with medium- and long-term planning in the *USSR* in the late 1920s. This was however not followed up in the 1930s and 1940s. *L.V. Kantorovich* developed linear programming in the late 1930s and the 1940s, but there seem to have been only some limited applications at the micro level. However, mathematical methods moved into the foreground again in the USSR from the late 1950s, and through the 1960s increasing use seems to have been made of input–output types of models, both in connection with short-, medium-, and long-term planning. First static models were used, but later also dynamic models of increasing complexity. The importance of the increasing use of mathematical methods has been emphasized in several statements from the highest political authorities, and the leading economist *N.P. Fedorenko* has even advanced the view that "economics is now becoming the main sphere in which mathematical methods and electronic computers are being used." However, mathematical methods have not replaced traditional administrative planning methods. They rather seem to play a supplementary part. Explicit optimization only seems to be at the experimental stage in connection with central macroeconomic planning. On the other hand mathematical methods, including optimization methods, seem to be rather widely used at the sector level. It has been reported that the USSR State Planning Commission, jointly with ministries and research organizations, has planned the development and location of production for more than 70 sectors with the help of mathematical-economic methods. In most cases the models used are optimization models, usually in the form of linear programming. (This information is taken from a Soviet publication from 1972.)

As described in Section 1.3, *J. Tinbergen* was instrumental in giving *the Netherlands* an early start in the application of mathematical models. Continuing his work from the 1930s the Central Planning Bureau (founded in 1945 with Tinbergen as its first director) immediately started constructing macroeconomic models for practical applications, first in connection with short-term planning, and later also for medium- and long-term planning. The Central Planning Bureau is not directly subordinate to the Government or any ministry, but rather plays a role as an advisory institution. The use of the models is therefore not fully integrated into the planning and policy decision process in the politically responsible bodies. The Central Planning Bureau takes the premises and assumptions from what is known about Government intentions and works out forecasts rather than plans. It is hard to say to what extent these forecasts again influence actual decisions in the regular policy process. But there have been several cases in which the Government has raised more specific questions about economic policy with the Central Planning Bureau and used results of calculations on the basis of the mathematical models as guidance in the actual decisions.

The first planning and policy models constructed by *R. Frisch* in *Norway* were never used in practice in connection with the formulation of economic policy. They did however inspire later developments. In connection with national budgetting some tentative applications of input–output analysis were made in the 1950s. The first version of the national budgetting model, MODIS, which was based on an input–output framework extended by relations for income generation, taxation, and private consumption demand, was used for the first time in the preparation of the National Budget for 1961. This model has been improved and extended through several stages since then and is now a large model with thousands of entries for inputs into and outputs from the computations. Later a special model was designed as a tool for elucidating quantitatively problems in connection with income settlements. More recently this model, which emphasizes price formation, taxation and income generation, has become an integral part of MODIS. In connection with the four-year programme for 1970–73 long-term projections were worked out on the basis of a multi-sectoral model (the MSG model) which is a sort of disaggregated neo-classical growth model with some 30 sectors of production. This model has also been used in several connections in later years. (Compare Figure 13 in Section 3.7 and the comments given there.)

The remarkable fact in connection with the Norwegian planning models is that they are programmed for, and used in the regular administrative planning process by the Ministry of Finance. They seem to be more fully integrated into the process of policy formation than in any other country.

France seems to have used elements of macroeconomic models, input–output analysis and mathematical programming in connection with various aspects of medium-term planning for quite many years. This seems however to have been on an ad hoc basis. In recent years more systematic efforts have been made to establish large mathematical models which are now, or are expected to become, regularly used tools for economic planning. Interesting members of the family of models are FIFI, which integrates financial and "physical" aspects in an original and interesting way, and REGINA, which is a large scale model with emphasis on the regional break-down of the economy.

At the sectoral level the electricity sector of France has long traditions in applying advanced methods of planning, including linear programming and mathematical decision theory.

In *England* the most innovative and interesting project has been *A Programme for Growth* under the direction of *R. Stone* in the Department of Applied Economics at the University of Cambridge. This project has established a large model (mentioned in Section 3.6), or perhaps rather a system of models, based on input–output relationships for the production sectors, income generation, private consumption demand, and various other types of relationships, somewhat different at different stages of the project and in different applications. This is primarily a research programme and has not been used directly for economic planning and policy. However, in recent years a modified and simplified version of this system has been used by the ministries responsible for the elaboration of economic policy. Various macroeconomic models of the more traditional type, including quite many aspects of behaviour, have also been used.

In the *USA* econometrically estimated macroeconomic models have been used regularly by various institutions for working out forecasts, mainly on a short-term basis, since the publication of the

Klein–Goldberger model in 1955. There are now several very large models, i.e., models containing several hundreds of equations and endogenous variables, in regular use for forecasting. They are not only very large in terms of number of equations and variables, but they are also dynamic and to a large extent non-linear. They are therefore very demanding from a computational point of view, but great progress has been made in this field in recent years. There are also some models based on input–output relationships supplemented with various other types of relations in use for forecasting for the longer run. Some of the models are run by research institutions, and some by institutions which play some part as advisory or consultative institutions for the Government. None of them are however (as far as I am aware) integrated into the regular process of formulating economic policy. When the forecasts from several models tend to be in agreement they do probably influence policy decisions to some extent.

At least with some of the forecasters the intention to help in the formulation of economic policy has been conscious and explicit right from the beginning. *L.R. Klein* made this point clear in a paper on "The Use of Econometric Models as a Guide to Economic Policy" already in 1947. He referred to the discussion on the Full Employment Bill and the fact that the Bill in the original draft called for periodic forecasts of the deflationary or inflationary gap. These forecasts should then form the basis for policy decisions for fulfilling the intentions of the Bill. Klein saw the advantage of mathematical (or rather econometric) models partly in their ability to produce more accurate forecasts than earlier methods, and partly in their objectivity: "It is desirable to provide tools of analysis suited for public economic policy that are, as much as possible, independent of the personal judgements of a particular investigator. Econometric models are put forth in this scientific spirit, because these models, if fully developed and properly used, eventually should lead all investigators to the same conclusions, independent of their personal whims. The usual experience in the field of economic policy is that there are about as many types of advice as there are advisors (sometimes even more!)." (In fact the econometric forecasts for the first post-war years in the USA were not successful; they predicted much more of a depression than actually occurred. The reasons for this were discussed at length by econometricians in the following years.)

Altogether the use of mathematical and econometric methods has been more forecast-oriented in the USA than in most other countries.

However, some planning models in the stricter sense have been constructed for emergency situations, especially for planning reconstruction and recovery in a centralized fashion after a possible nuclear war – see for instance *M.K. Wood's* and *C. Almon's* descriptions of the PARM model. Fortunately these models have remained unused in practice.

To return to the *socialist countries in Eastern Europe*, the development in the other countries has been somewhat parallel to that of the USSR. Input–output models, static and dynamic, seem to be the most widely applied tool at the central macroeconomic level of planning, whereas linear programming is more used for sectoral or partial planning. Linear programming also seems to play a part in the planning of foreign trade in some of these countries, i.e., Hungary, Poland and GDR, where foreign trade is relatively much more important than in the USSR. Hungary is a particularly interesting case. Here linear programming has played a more prominent part also in the formulation of plans for the whole economy, or at least for major parts of the economy. Special methods of decomposition (which will be taken up for further consideration in a later chapter) have been used. Up to now Hungary seems to provide the best example of application of optimization methods for central economic planning.

In the *developing countries* the first interesting application of a mathematical model to economic planning was *P.C. Mahalanobis'* growth model which was used to elaborate India's second five-year plan as mentioned in Section 1.3. This model is especially designed to elucidate the relationship between the investment goods sector and the consumption goods sector in a growth process and is akin to Feldman's earlier model. Since then many planning models have been constructed and partly implemented numerically for developing countries, many of them based on some form of dynamic input–output analysis. Most of them seem to have been constructed by foreign experts and by groups working for the United Nations or other organizations concerned with economic development. Very few, if any, of the models seem to be integrated into the regular political decision process. In most cases they miss the necessary prerequisites for elaborating *operational* plans. They therefore remain as methodological experiments and research efforts rather than models actually used in planning practice.

What is said here does apparantly not apply to *Japan* (which is also a "developed" rather than "developing" country). A rather simple macroeconomic model was used in connection with the elaboration of the "Ten Year Plan for Doubling the National Income" (1961–70). Later more extensive and systematic efforts were made. In 1964 a "Committee on Econometric Methods" was set up by the Japanese Planning Commission with the primary objectives of "the construction of models and the examination of consistency of target values" – target values referring to targets in various official economic plans. A series of models, or rather a system of models in the sense discussed in Section 3.7, has been constructed which comprises both input–output relations as well as many types of behavioural relations. Some of the models included in the system also contain variables which represent many aspects of economic policy such as fiscal policy and monetary policy. This is an effort sponsored by the Government, and it seems that the formalized models are to some extent integrated in the process of policy formulation. One observer (*Y. Yasuba*) remarks in connection with one of the Japanese models that it "has proved reasonably accurate in overall performances and helped make econometric models a part of everyday life."

What has been mentioned in this very brief survey is intended to represent more or less leading cases. At the present time mathematically formulated models are developed in almost all European countries and in many other countries as well, but it is hard to say to what extent they have become parts of the regular routines of the planning agencies and to what extent they actually influence officially adopted plans and decisions. There is however no doubt about the direction of the trend.

References for Section 4.1

Many of the references under Section 1.3 are relevant to this section as well. United Nations publications mentioned in several sections contain much of material on the use of mathematical models in various countries. Further references will be given in a later chapter in connection with the more detailed discussion of a sample of planning models. The references given below refer only to some specific points in the text above.

C. Almon, "Mathematical methods and the use of computers for planning in the United States", in *Planning and markets*, edited by J.T. Dunlop and N.P. Fedorenko (McGraw-Hill, New York, 1969).

P.J. Bjerve, "Trends in quantitative economic planning in Norway" – See reference under Section 1.1.

S. Chakravarty, "The mathematical framework of the third five year plan", in *Capital formation and economic development*, edited by P.N. Rosenstein-Rodan (London, 1964).

R. Courbis, "Les méthodes de planification Française" – See reference under Section 3.7.

Econometric models for medium-term economic plan (Economic Planning Agency, Government of Japan, Tokyo, 1965).

N.P. Fedorenko, *Optimal functioning system for a socialist economy* – See reference under Section 3.7. Especially p. 184.

A. Ghosh, "The evolution of planning techniques and organization in India", *Economics of Planning* (1964). Also as Chapter 1 in *Planning, programming and input–output models* (Cambridge University Press, Cambridge, 1968).

L.R. Klein, "The use of econometric models as a guide to economic policy", *Econometrica* (1947).

Modelling the economy, edited by G.A. Renton, published on behalf of the Social Science Research Council (Heinemann Educational Books, London, 1975). Especially Part I, "Econometric models of the UK economy".

Quantitative planning of economic policy – See reference under Section 1.1. Especially papers by C.A. van den Beld on "Short-term planning experience in the Netherlands" and by S. Shishido on "Japanese experience with long-term planning".

S. Shishido and A. Oshizaka, "Econometric planning models in Japan," in *Economic planning and macroeconomic policy*, Vol. I (The Japan Economic Research Center, Tokyo, 1971). Also other papers in the volume are of relevance.

Soviet economic reform: Progress and problems (Progress Publishers, Moscow, 1972). Especially p. 124.

W. von Urff, *Zur Programmierung von Entwicklungsplänen* (Duncker & Humblot, Berlin, 1973). Especially Chapter 5, "Modelle zur indischen Entwicklungsplanung".

P. de Wolff, "Central economic planning in the Netherlands", *Weltwirtschaftliches Archiv* (1964).

M.K. Wood, "PARM – An economic programming model", *Management Science* (1965).

Y. Yasuba, "Modern economists' views on the Japanese economy", *Japanese Economic Studies* (1972–73).

4.2. Planning with or without Models?
– Contacts with Traditional Methods

A model is generally a simplified representation of the underlying reality. If the question is asked as to whether planning without models is possible, then the answer is *no* if the term "model" is used in this general sense. It will never be possible to grasp and process information concerning all details of economic development. Nevertheless, purposeful planning must be based on some ideas about the relationships between policy decisions and the resulting states or developments of the economy and also about desirability of various possible alternatives. There is then no way round basing planning explicitly or implicitly on some approximate, simplified representation of the reality, i.e., a "model". On the other hand, these ideas need not be shaped in the form of a mathematical model. If the question is asked as to whether planning can be performed without a *mathematical* model, then the answer is definitely *yes*. Considering the actual history of planning there is also no doubt that more planning has been done without than with mathematical models, although the present trend is in the direction of using mathematical models to a larger extent.

P.J. Bjerve has conducted an interesting experiment which throws some light upon the problem of planning with or without mathematically formulated models. In Norway national budgets have been worked out annually for all years since World War II, but not until around 1960 were mathematically formulated models used more systematically (as mentioned in the preceding section). However, a macroeconomic model has been estimated for the Norwegian economy for a period including these "non-model" years of planning. This model (elaborated and estimated by A. Amundsen) was of a simple Keynesian type with a macroeconomic consumption function and an import function as the central behavioural equations. Investment and exports were taken to be exogenously determined. The main instruments were government expenditure and the level of taxation. It was well-known that, in national budgetting in Norway in this period, ideas prevailed which corresponded more or less with such a model although they were not formalized mathematically. Now Bjerve used the estimated model in two different ways:

1. In the first place the model was used to forecast (ex post) the actual development of gross national product, imports, and total consumption for the years 1947–58, using *observed* values of the exogenous variables and the instruments in the calculation of the forecasts. These forecasts were then confronted with the *observed* development of the endogenous variables. This represents a test of the model as against the underlying realities.

2. Next Bjerve inserted the *national budget estimates* for the exogenous variables and planned values of the instruments into the model and calculated again the values of gross national product, imports, and total consumption. The resulting figures were now compared with the *corresponding figures in the National Budget*, i.e., not with observed development. This represents a confrontation between the model and the thinking of planners and politicians.

The interesting observation now is that the model performed better in the second confrontation than in the first. Bjerve concludes that "Amundsen's model explains the projections of the national budget somewhat better than it explains reality." For this reason he also refers to the model as representing "the implicit national budget model." (He also concludes that for most of the years the accuracy of the national budget figures for gross national product and its major components could hardly have been improved by a mechanical application of a model like the one used in this experiment. However, a flexible use of the model, including adjustments of the parameters for each year so as to exploit the most up-to-date information, might have given better results than the administrative methods actually used.)

In Section 1.1 we mentioned the GOELRO plan of the USSR as the first serious attempt at national economic planning in practice. Although it is well-known (as pointed out in Section 1.3) that some of the economists engaged in planning in the early period in the USSR were aware of the potential usefulness of mathematics in this context, no documents exist which provide evidence that the planners behind the GOELRO plan actually used formalized mathematical models.

However, an experiment somewhat reminiscent of Bjerve's for the early period of national budgetting in Norway has been performed for the GOELRO plan by the Polish economist *V.I. Pshelyaskovskiy* by trying to adapt a mathematically formulated growth model to the figures of the GOELRO plan. He concludes that the confrontation is successful and that the model used later on by G.A. Feldman was "a mathematization of the GOELRO plan."

These studies support the conclusion that even if mathematically formulated models are not used, planning is performed on the basis of certain ideas about regularities so that it appears, at least with some degree of approximation, *as if* there is an underlying or implicit model in the planning process.

The question then is whether an explicit mathematical formalization of these underlying ideas is useful.

The advantages of formalization are of course by now well-known:

 (i)   Formalization provides a means of securing logical consistency between assumptions made at various points.
 (ii) It provides a framework for efficient use of various sorts of information, through estimation of structural relations and utilization of forecasts for various exogenous elements.
 (iii) Through the development of modern computational equipment formalization provides the basis for large-scale computations which take into account a tremendous amount of information and constraints of various sorts, but can nevertheless elaborate many alternatives.
 (iv) To the extent that one aims at optimization this can hardly be achieved with any degree of accuracy without formalization.
 (v)   Formalized methods can be taught and learnt more systematically than good intuition and judgment.
 (vi) Formalization may help to clarify issues with regard to the division of tasks and responsibilities between experts and politicians.

Because of these advantages a *need* for formalization evolves out of practice in many quarters where planning is attempted. A very interesting example of such an evolving need, or rather growing awareness of the need for formalization, is described by *W. Tims* in connection with planning in Pakistan. He describes how planning first started by disconnected efforts for various sectors of the economy, and how awareness about inconsistency between what was done by the various agencies gradually developed. It became clear that "increasing difficulties were being met in coordinating the work on the Third Plan within the Planning Commission itself. The International Economics Section would make certain changes in its balance of payments projections, the estimates of domestic resources would be revised in the Fiscal and Monetary Section and, at the same time, some of the sectoral growth targets and investment requirements would be altered in discussions with the Provincial Governments. As a result the Plan could rapidly become distressingly inconsistent. Some means for keeping track of these changes and their consequences was a necessity and therefore the Perspective Planning Section developed a set of interrelated tables in which changes at any place in the Plan could be traced to their consequences elsewhere. With the exception of a small set of equations, relating the balance of payments to the domestic resources, this group of tables in fact represented the recursive solution of a macroeconomic model." This method was however still rather cumbersome, and the fact that it represented a recursive solution also implied some undesirable limitations. Many of the planners involved "continued to feel that this approach was like tackling steak with a fruit knife." There was too little of sectoral details, and the approach was not sufficiently flexible to tackle the problem of whether to substitute domestic production in various branches for imports, which is a very important question for developing countries. It was also too cumbersome to work out and compare a sufficient number of alternative solutions by this method. In the end it was decided to construct a fairly large mathematically formulated model. W. Tims' account describes very interestingly how the awareness of the need for formalization grew out of practice. It is probably representative of many of the more successful cases of developing planning models for practical applications. Many of the planning models which have failed to be used in practice, have apparently been constructed by "theoreticians" in environments where the need has not yet asserted itself among the "practitioners". (Many of these "unsuccessful" models are of course valuable from the viewpoint of methodological and theoretical development.)

One should however not conclude that there are *only* advantages by formalization. Authors like *J. Tinbergen* and *J. Kornai*, who are of course not opposed to formalization, have on several occasions emphasized the need for communication between planning experts on the one side and politicians and other authorities on the other side, and pointed out that this need should be reflected in the way of formalizing the planning procedure. Formalization should be kept within some limits, and transparency should be a major consideration. Several of the simplifications of planning methods discussed in the preceding chapter, such as aggregation, planning in stages, and partitioning, gain additional support from this viewpoint.

The Polish economist *J. Pajestka* (referred to in Section 2.5), who has held high positions in actual planning in Poland, has emphasized the dangers of a lack of communication between policy-makers and experts particularly strongly and has urged the need for active participation of the policy-makers in the planning process itself. From this he draws the following conclusion: "The planning techniques and procedures should be so devised as to make it possible for the policy-makers to take an active part in the planning process." This implies inter alia that "the methods of plan elaboration should be as simple as possible and never unnecessarily sophisticated. It should be possible for the educated non-experts to follow all the argumentation behind the major solutions of the plan." He warns that "particular caution should be taken in introducing the mathematical programming models. Mathematical models which produce the final solution of a plan in an ununderstandable way (even to experts) can never be taken as a basis for a dialogue between experts and the policy-makers. . . . A plan should never be produced like a *deus ex machina*, but should be worked out in a way which is fully understandable." On this basis he advocates, inter alia, "planning in stages".

In France communication problems have been felt in connection with the planning model FIFI. To many of the participants in the planning process the model appears to be rather "esoteric". According to *D. Liggins* "several participants said they felt dominated by the model, and overwhelmed by the masses of information it produced. Consequently, they said, imagination and innovation were effectively paralysed, and the initiative passed from the hands of the decision-makers to the technicians."

Also the French economists *A. Aglietta* and *C. Seibel*, who have been engaged in economic planning in France, have warned against excessive formalization. They mention three groups of reservations against formalization, the first stemming from computational difficulties, and the second from inadequate knowledge of economic realities. The third group is perhaps the most interesting. I quote from Aglietta and Seibel: "The third reason which restricts the usefulness of formalized models bears on the actual nature of the process of preparation of the Plan. Formalization presupposes that the problems to be solved shall be clearly and explicitly defined from the outset. Now, the preparation of the Plan is a process of gradual elucidation of the problems to be solved by a two-way exchange of information. During this exchange, the information content of the programming studies gradually increases in quantity; the constraints are gradually revealed, the policy-making bodies formulate their objectives (in the light of their growing knowledge of the problems to be solved and of the constraints). Thus the necessary dialogue between the economists and policy-making authorities implies the preparation of a sequence of sketches for the end year of the Plan. The progressive integration of the information of all kinds also presupposes that this iterative method shall be used in the actual technical study. To fit all these projection studies into a formalized model, it would be necessary to alter the structure of the model in the course of the preparation of the Plan."

This quotation partly points to similar arguments as those reviewed above. However, in addition it points to a serious problem by emphasizing that "formalization presupposes that the problems to be solved shall be clearly and explicitly defined from the outset." Literally interpreted this statement is too strong since *one* model will generally be helpful in solving a *class* of problems. But, clearly, when a model has been constructed it is a somewhat rigid framework. This has to do particularly with limitation to treating quantitative aspects of planning, although some steps could be taken in the direction of including also qualitative choices as suggested in Section 3.2. In actual economic planning and policy, circumstances and problems and problems will often be rapidly changing, and there is then always a danger that the model will either be useless or provide only a distorted and artificial framework for analysing the problems which the actual development imposes upon planning. A similar consideration applies to the ability of the model to absorb information. A formalized model must have a finite register of input points which can absorb information. We must therefore know in advance what *types* of information we are going to use in the future. However, in actual developments new types of information will continuously appear. There is therefore always the possibility that some important relevant information will have no place on the list of inputs into the calculations on the basis of a formalized model.

These observations would carry no weight if the construction of models for economic planning were a costless affair and required no time. However, with the large-scale types of models now being used, the construction of a model should be considered as an investment, and often a costly investment, rather than as current expenses in the planning process. In addition to the intellectual efforts in constructing the model itself comes the quantitative estimation of relationships, the establishing of links between the model and various branches of statistical reporting, and the construction of computational programmes. There is not much evidence available on the actual costs of construction and operation of models. The Norwegian models have been constructed by great efforts by a very modest number of economists and computational experts; on the other hand, *J. Kornai* reports that "several hundred economists, practical planners, engineers and mathematicians" participated in the elaboration of a mathematical planning model in Hungary. For the USA *O.P. Hall* refers to an estimated figure of $4 million being spent on forecasting models in 1965, but, writing in 1975 he suggests that, "considering the tremendous proliferation of social models since that date, the figure today probably is more in the range of $50 to $100 million annually."

In spite of this we are, in my opinion, far from the optimum amount of investment and operational expenses on mathematical and quantitative planning and policy models. It is useful to recall *T. Haavelmo's* vision in the concluding section of *The Probability Approach in Econometrics*: "In other quantitative sciences the discovery of 'laws', even in highly specialized fields, has moved from the private study into huge scientific laboratories where scores of experts are engaged, not only in carrying out actual measurements, but also in working out, with painstaking precision, the formulae to be tested and the plans for the crucial experiments to be made. Should we expect less in economic research, if its results are to be the basis for the economic policy upon which might depend billions of dollars of national income and the general economic welfare of millions of people?"

For the present discussion the main point is not that the cost of model building is a heavy burden on society, but rather that the size of the task creates rigidities, strains on qualified labour power, etc., and that models of the required size cannot be instantaneously adapted to changing circumstances and problems. Updating of estimates, etc., can often be made as a matter of routine when the computational programmes are good, but major revisions of the whole structure of the model cannot be done every year. There is therefore always the danger that a formalized model with all the accompanying programmes and procedures will become a straightjacket on the form of policy problems which can be posed and the types of information which can be used in plan elaboration. If the model should be redesigned so as to fit the problems and circumstances and be able to absorb all relevant information every time a decision is to be taken, one might get into a position similar to that of a meteorologist who needs 48 hours to work out, by means of the most advanced methods, a weather forecast for the next 24 hours (a metaphor used by "teleologists" in arguments against some methods proposed by the "geneticists" in the planning debate in the 1920s in the USSR).

Such considerations sometimes seem to be neglected by mathematically inclined economists who argue in favour of formalized models. For instance, *J. Marschak* argues that "mathematics does not suppress any information available for other methods," and *G.C. Chow*, after having pointed out that decision-makers at least implicitly use some sorts of models, goes on to assert that "the use of a mathematical model *merely* (my emphasis, L.J.) forces a decision-maker to state explicitly, and in quantitative form, the dynamic reactions of the economy he is assuming in making decisions." If such considerations contained the whole truth, it would be hard to explain why it is so difficult to construct a computerized chess-player programme which beats the best (human) chess champions. In an economic planning and policy context the considerations cited seem to me to be valid only if either

(1) models were always of a size which permits economists to write them down on their favourite place, i.e., on the back of an envelope; or
(2) the structural relations of the economy, the types of problems encountered, and the types of information available were the same through time.

Neither of these conditions is realistic.

These viewpoints do of course not decide the case against the use of formalized methods, but they should be born in mind in the formulation and presentation of the models, and in connection with the way of using them.

For the reasons given here, and perhaps also for other reasons, it would be unrealistic to expect formalized models to replace more traditional planning procedures completely. Formalized models will play the role of a tool which is used parallel with and supplementary to more traditional administrative methods.

An interesting and important question is, on the background of the discussion and conclusion reached above, whether one can give guidelines for how to establish fruitful connections between plan elaboration by traditional methods and by formalized methods. Exchange of information, "administrative iteration" and intuition will always be important in this connection, but some more specific methods are also suggested in the literature.

The first approach is to *check the consistency of official plans by means of a formalized model.* The intention then is not to work out an alternative plan by means of the formalized model, but simply to perform a test which the official plan ought to pass. If the official plan is detailed enough in presenting assumptions and figures concerning all types of variables which are relevant, then the test may be performed as a purely logical check of *internal* consistency. If the plan does not provide all necessary information, which is the more likely case, then there will be some open ends so that a definitive answer cannot be given concerning internal consistency, at least not for all parts of the plan. More information must be established or brought in from other sources, and the test will then be conditioned by the conformity between this external information and the assumptions which the planners explicitly or implicitly intend to make. Such consistency tests do not necessarily require the computation of complete solutions of the model in the mathematical sense of the word, but can be performed by checking whether given figures satisfy all equations and constraints of the model. It can therefore be done by means of models which are too large or complicated for other kinds of applications. If the test is successful, then the feasibility of the plan is corroborated; if not, then the test may be useful in directing attention towards critical points and may either call forth a revision of the plan or at least sounder expectations concerning the possible fulfilment of the plan. Such checking can be performed by persons or institutions not necessarily subordinate to the Central Planning Authority. Several examples of checking of official plans for consistency are available in the literature. Interesting cases referring to developing countries are reviewed by *P.B. Clark*. The models used are in most cases dynamic input–output models with several constraints added. Some studies have revealed rather convincingly existing inconsistencies in official plans and presented several calculations which have shown what the bottlenecks and critical points were.

A related, but somewhat more ambitious approach is to *introduce the targets from the official plan as constraints in the formalized planning model*. Constraints in this connection means inequalities, so that for instance a target with respect to gross national product will be represented by a constraint saying that GNP should be equal to or greater than the official target figure, and similarly for all other official targets. These constraints then play a part as preference constraints in the sense discussed in Section 3.11. Next a preference *function* may be introduced which should be maximized under these constraints as well as all other constraints of the model. Or perhaps several different preference functions may be used in order to work out alternative solutions. There are then two possibilities: in the first place, the result of the experiment may be that there appears to be no feasible region left after the constraints based on the official plan targets have been introduced. In that case the situation is as under the first approach when the consistency check reveals lack of consistency. In the second place, there may exist a feasible region, and then the formalized calculations will indicate a plan, or several alternative plans if different preference functions are used, which are all definitely preferable to the official plan since they are constrained by *all* plan figures for target variables. As a special intermediate case there may remain only one feasible plan, in which case the official plan is both feasible and efficient. This approach to using formalized methods as a supplement to traditional planning methods has been proposed by *J. Kornai* in connection with economic planning in Hungary.

A third avenue is to accept the draft plan worked out by traditional methods as a sort of reference point or reference path and *use mathematical methods to explore possible alternatives in the neighbourhood of this reference point or path*. It may then be necessary to adjust some of the parameters of the mathematically formulated model in such a way that the official plan appears as a feasible solution of the mathematical model. If the official plan contains inconsistencies which violate balance or accounting relationships, then this can of course not be done. Otherwise there will be plenty of parameters about which only imperfect and uncertain knowledge is available, such as parameters describing the development of labour productivity, technological change, export possibilities, etc., which can be used for this adaptation of the mathematical model to the official plan, if the mathematical model does not already in its original version confirm the feasibility of the official plan. Next the model is used to explore alternative possibilities in the neighbourhood of the official plan, i.e., alternatives which do not deviate very much numerically from the official plan. If the model is formulated as a mathematical programming model several techniques are available for such calculations. So-called "parametric programming" will be particularly useful. By this technique one can spell out how the solution to a programming problem changes with the values of various parameters in the model. In the present context it will be particularly valuable to see how the solution changes when parameters of the preference function change. This will then generate alternative efficient plans. Shadow prices are of course also useful since they indicate how important the various constraints are in restricting the set of feasible plans. Explorations along these lines have been carried out in connection with the elaboration of the 1965–70 plan in France, see *J. Raiman* and *A. Moustacchi.* This method is particularly attractive if one can argue that the most obvious consistency requirements are taken care of by traditional methods and furthermore intuition and practical experience accumulated in the traditional planning apparatus are as good as or better than formalized mathematical and econometric methods in assessing some crucial elements for consistency in a wider sense such as labour productivity, technical change, export possibilities, etc. The main advantage of formalized methods is then that they are superior to traditional methods in generating systematically alternative possibilities, since they can take advantage of modern computational methods.

Some questions related to the discussion above are elucidated in a broad perspective by *J. Kornai* in a paper from 1969 concerning the experiences gained in introducing a mathematically formulated multi-level programming model into the planning practice in Hungary. It is worthwhile quoting the conclusion: "Certain economic models may be worked out in the quiet rooms of a research institute, quantified on the basis of printed statistics, and published together with their results in periodicals without research workers ever being in contact with practitioners. The multi-level planning model is not one of these. It is linked by a thousand threads to the living machinery of planning, from the data requirements and the practical advice needed for its concrete construction to the utilization of the results. *The model will either succeed in fitting organically into the living work of planning or be eliminated.*"

Before concluding this section it should be pointed out that what we have called *mathematically* formulated models do no longer necessarily exist in the form of mathematical formulas written out in traditional mathematical notations. In its operational form the model may be much too large for this kind of presentation. It will rather exist in the form of computer instructions and programmes, data files in the form of punch cards, magnetic tapes, etc., suitably arranged tables to be filled in with stipulated figures for exogenous variables and instrument variables, and standard instructions for how to interpret the output from the computer. Formulation of a model in terms of standard mathematical symbolism will be used mainly at explorative stages of the elaboration of the model where many details are still neglected, and for expository purposes where transparency is particularly important and again many details can be neglected.

Since there is now also a tendency in all branches of administration to transfer administrative routine work concerned with figures to computers, the borderline between what has been called "traditional administrative methods" and "mathematical models" may no longer be so clear as the discussion above tends to imply. Some of the computational programmes in connection with large planning models are in fact not much more than a translation and a transfer of administrative routines to a computer. This may in itself produce large savings of time and labour and may be justified even if, in substance, no more sophistication is involved than what was involved in the traditional administrative methods. However, there is no doubt that planning models now used in practice also involve elements which go beyond such translations and transfers of administrative routines to computers. They involve more sharply formulated hypotheses about technology and behaviour, they take into account many more factors simultaneously, and they provide more powerful checks of consistency than can be achieved by administrative routines. They provide means of speedy and efficient elaboration of many alternative plans, and to the extent that they are optimization models they perform a task which has never been performed by administrative routines. Although the tendencies mentioned above to some extent blur the borderline between "administrative methods" and "mathematical methods", it is therefore still meaningful to uphold the distinction.

References for Section 4.2

M. Aglietta and C. Seibel, "The national accounting system and the preparation of the fifth French plan", *The Review of Income and Wealth* (1969).
P.J. Bjerve, *Planning in Norway 1947–1956* – See reference under Section 1.1. Sections III-D and X-D.
G.C. Chow, *Analysis and control of dynamic economic systems* (Wiley, New York, 1975).
P.B. Clark, "Intersectoral consistency and macroeconomic planning", in *Economy-wide models and development planning*, edited by C.R. Blitzer, P.B. Clark, and L. Taylor, published for the World Bank (Oxford University Press, London, 1975).
T. Haavelmo, *The probability approach in econometrics*, Supplement to *Econometrica* (1944).
O.P. Hall, "A policy model appraisal paradigm", *Policy Sciences* (1975).
J. Kornai, *Mathematical planning of structural decisions* – See reference under Section 1.3. Section 27.9.
J. Kornai, "Mathematical programming as a tool of socialist economic planning", Paper presented at the First World Congress of the Econometric Society, Rome, 1965. Published in *Socialist economics*, edited by A. Nove and D.M. Nuti (Penguin Modern Economics Readings, Harmondsworth, Middlesex, 1972).
J. Kornai, "Multi-level programming – A first report on the model and on the experimental computations", *European Economic Review* (1969). Especially Part II of the paper.
J. Kornai, "Models and policy: The dialogue between model builder and planner", in *Economy-wide models and development planning*, edited by C.R. Blitzer, P.B. Clark, and L. Taylor, published for the World Bank (Oxford University Press, London, 1975).
D. Liggins, *National economic planning in France* – See reference under Section 1.1. Especially pp. 19 and 153.
J. Marschak, "Economic measurement for policy and prediction" – See reference under Section 3.2.
A. Moustacchi, "The interpretation of shadow prices in a parametric linear economic programme", in *Econometric analysis for national economic planning*, edited by P.E. Hart, G. Mills, and J.K. Whitaker, Colston Papers No. 16 (Butterworths, London, 1964).
G. Myrdal, *Asian drama, Vol. III* (Pantheon, Random House, 1968). Appendix 3 on "Economic models and their usefulness for planning in South Asia", contributed by P.P. Streeten.
A. Nataf, "Éssais de formalisation de la planification", *Économie Appliquée* (1963).
A.M. Okun, "Uses of models for policy formulation", in *The Brookings model: Perspective and recent development*, edited by G. Fromm and L.R. Klein (North-Holland, Amsterdam, 1975).

J. Pajestka, "Dialogue between planning experts and policy makers in the process of plan formulation" – See reference under Section 2.5.

V.I. Pshelyaskovskiy, "Elements of the theory of growth in Lenin's plan for the electrification of Russia", *MATEKON* (Autumn 1969). Translation from Russian. With an epilogue by A.L. Vainshtein.

J. Raiman, "A study of prices in a planning model", in *Price formation in various economies*, edited by D.C. Hague (MacMillan, London, 1967).

W. Tims, "A growth model and its application – Pakistan", in *Development policy – Theory and practice*, edited by G.F. Papanek (Harvard University Press, Cambridge, 1968).

4.3. Types of Relationships and Constraints in Planning Models

Most of the time in the preceding chapters and sections we have been representing the elements of a planning model in a very condensed and abstract form, but it has of course been pointed out or implied on several occasions that an actual planning model will be a very complex structure with a large number of relationships and constraints of various sorts. In this section we shall give a systematic and rather complete review of the types of relationships and constraints involved. We shall however only give brief comments concerning the various types in this section. Some problems concerning central and more or less obligatory types of relationships for planning models (referring to balance relationships, production and consumption demand) will be taken up for more detailed treatment in later chapters, and some points will also be taken up in connection with the discussion of a sample of planning models towards the end of these lectures. The aim of the present section is to get a bird's eye-view of the *types* of relationships and constraints involved, not to go into the more detailed formulations. *R. Frisch* has given an overview in his paper on "An Implementation System . . .", and the United Nations publication *Macroeconomic Models for National Economic Planning* also provides a survey. Classifications of relations according to types are of course also suggested many other places in the literature on planning or forecasting models. The following classification is somewhat more detailed than the usual classification schemes.

It is not implied that all planning models ought to contain all these types of relationships, regardless of the type of economic system and regardless of what are the most pressing problems. Some considerations as to what parts of the list would be the more relevant under different circumstances will however be postponed until the following sections.

(1) *Definitional relationships, balance relationships, circulation relationships.* The relationships included in this group are rela-

tionships which have to hold as a consequence of the definitions of the concepts involved. One might perhaps also refer to the conservation of matter. The three different terms mentioned here are not meant as indicating different subclasses. They may be more or less appropriate for different types of relationships included in this group, but there will be no clear border-lines between them. Some subclasses are the following:

(1a) *Balance relationships in physical terms or in terms of volume indexes.* For all items these balances say that the sum of available quantities from various sources is equal to the sum of the uses in various directions. To "uses" one may sometimes add disposal and undesirable emmissions in the form of pollution, etc. Such relationships may apply to stocks and/or flows of commodities and resources of all sorts.

(1b) *Similar balance relationships for values,* i.e., balances between incomings and expenses in monetary terms for various entities. This group includes equations which define income and disposable income after taxes for various income earners. This special group may be called *income generation* relations.

(1c) *Definitional relationships which express the fact that values are equal to volumes multiplied by prices.* (It is of course not necessary to put these down as independent relations if value terms which can be defined in this way have already been introduced in this form in equations under group 1b.)

(1d) *Definitions of various indexes.* This is particularly relevant for price indexes. In many models with a rather detailed structure many individual prices are included while at the same time price indexes are important as explicit variables, partly in some behavioural relations (group 3 below), and partly as target variables.

(1e) *Financial circulation relations.* Such relations are of course particularly important when financial institutions and their behaviour are included in the model.

Many planning models fail to include prices as endogenous variables, i.e., they are constructed as if prices remain constant, or, if they change, as if they have no "feed-back" effect upon volume variables. To the extent that the variables entering relations of type (1a) are expressed in terms of volume indexes, these will often be given as "values in constant prices." Many of the relations under (1a) and (1b) would then collapse into expressing the same thing, and equations like (1c) and (1d) could be omitted.

Many variables in an economic model are restricted to taking only *non-negative values*. Furthermore, if proportions are involved, some variables may be restricted to the interval between 0 and 1. Such constraints follow from the definitions of the concepts and might therefore also be classified under the present group. It is particularly important to introduce them explicitly in optimization models.

Relationships belonging to group (1) must be present in any planning model. Even the most extreme selection type of models as defined in Section 3.8 must at least include relations of type (1a) and non-negativity constraints.

(2) *Technical relationships of production.* These are intended to describe the possible outputs from production processes as conditioned by inputs into the processes, i.e., they describe the technology of production. We may perhaps subdivide them into two classes:

(2a) *Relations describing the production possibilities in the short run*, i.e., on the basis of existing fixed capital equipment. They may take the form of *input–output relationships* which assume fixed production coefficients, or they may take the form of more flexible relationships which admit some degree of *substitutability* between inputs. *Capacity constraints*, which indicate the production capacity embodied in the existing fixed production equipment, should also be included in this group.

(2b) *Relationships which describe how investment in new capital equipment changes production capacities*, or more generally changes the various types of short-run relations mentioned under (2a). This description may take many different forms. *Time profiles of investment activities* intended to expand production capacity in the future may be involved, perhaps expressed in terms of *gestation lags*. "Negative investment", to the extent that it is technologically determined, for instance in the form of *depreciation* coefficients, *average life time* for production equipment, or *survival curves* may also be classified under this point.

Since there are so many different ways of describing technical production possibilities we have not subdivided these groups further. For some production models it may not even be very meaningful to classify the relations under (2a) and (2b) separately. We have however done this because short-term models on the one side, and medium- and long-term models on the other side will be typically different, relationships of type (2b) being included only in the latter type of models.

Besides traditional inputs and outputs technical relationships may also include or refer to pollution of environment, the use of non-marketed resources or various sorts, etc.

Technical relationships will, in the same way as balance relationships for volumes, be obligatory to all planning models, including the most extreme selection models.

(3) *Behavioural relationships.* These relationships describe the behaviour of the various agents (enterprises, persons, institutions) which are not directly subordinate to the Central Authority, i.e., they have some scope for choice and decisions according to their own motivations. There are of course many groups of such relations, most obviously subclassified according to the types of agents.

(3a) *Producers' behaviour*, which could perhaps again be divided into two groups:
   (i) *Short-run adaptations*, i.e., choice of input combination and scale of output on the basis of existing production equipment. These adaptations may be expressed in different forms. Explicitly or implicitly they may imply *factor demand and product supply functions*, but the further elaboration of these equations will of course depend upon the strategic situation in which the producers find themselves. Many models in actual use assume that short-run adaptation is characterized by *mark-up relations for price setting* and by production being adapted to demand at the prices thus determined (subject to a capacity constraint) rather than by adaptation according to the profit maximization conditions of ordinary micro theory.
   (ii) *Relations describing producers' investment behaviour*, as influenced by interest rates, pressure on existing production capacities, expectations about future market conditions, finan-

cial constraints, etc. This is a weak and uncertain point in many models as one would expect on the basis of the current state of the theory of investment behaviour.

(3b)   *The behaviour of consumers/workers*, perhaps subdivided in the following way:

(i) *The consumption/saving decision.*

(ii) *Demand functions for individual goods* (or groups of goods) which together make up the total consumption determined under (i).

(iii) *Relations for labour supply.* In the most highly aggregated models there is no need for the relations under (ii). If the model is somewhat disaggregated, then the relations under (i) and (ii) could be described as the result of *one* decision concerning saving and consumption, but it is often found convenient to describe the behaviour as if there is a two-step procedure: first the consumer decides on consumption versus saving, and next his demand for individual goods is explained in terms of prices and the total consumption expenditure determined under the first step. Labour supply is often treated as a given magnitude, but in some models efforts are made to estimate the behaviour on this point as influenced by various economic variables. Changes in labour supply will then often be split in changes which refer to changes in *labour force participation* and changes in *hours worked*.

(3c)   *Financial behaviour.* This group includes the behaviour of financial institutions, as well as aspects of producers' and consumers' (income earners') financial dispositions. The latter might have been included under (3a) and (3b) above.

(3d)   *Foreign trade relations.* These are relations referring to exports and imports. *Export relations* might be split into demand relations explaining the demand in foreign markets towards "our" country's export, and relations describing the behaviour of "our" exporters. However, very often relations are used which represent some sort of mixture of both these aspects. For *imports* it may be relevant to introduce supply relations describing the behaviour of exporters in foreign countries. Import demand may already have been included at various places under (3a) and (3b).

The groups of behavioural relationships classified above under

(3a)–(3b) are the ones most often included in planning models. However, there is almost no limit to the list of behavioural relations that might be included. The *determination of wages* may be taken out from the standard treatment of supply and demand and given a special behavioural pattern, for instance in the form of *Phillips curves*. For producers it may often be of interest to try to include relations describing *changes in inventories*. In connection with labour supply one may broaden the *demographic aspects* of the model [bordering on group (5) below] and include also relations for *education and training*, and perhaps relate this also to productivity. In connection with foreign trade it may also be relevant to introduce relations in the form of *equations or constraints describing the terms for capital exports* or the *terms of and limitations on possible capital imports*. In some of the behavioural relations listed above expectations about the future (expectations held by the decision-makers in question) may enter. In order to make the model determinate it may then be necessary to introduce *relations describing how expectations are formed* on the basis of information from the current and earlier periods.

(4) *Institutional relations.* These are relations which describe the organizational or institutional arrangements in the economy and the rules and regulations under which the various entities operate. They may express fundamental aspects of the economic system, or reflect laws and regulations passed by some central authority as parts of its qualitative policy in the sense given in Section 3.2. In contrast to technical and behavioural relations, institutional relations should be *exact* relations which could in principle be established with absolute accuracy by studying the laws and regulations and finding out about administrative practices and so on. However, in their exact form they may often contain too many inessential details for purposes of macroeconomic planning, and they are therefore in practice often introduced in simpler forms with the result that these equations also involve "error terms" or "disturbances" like technical and behavioural relations, but in most cases of a rather small magnitude. Major groups of institutional relations are the following:

(4a)   Relations describing the various aspects of the system of *direct and indirect taxation*.

(4b)   Relations describing *the social security system*. In many countries this stands for a very considerable redistribution of incomes, and in a country like Norway changes in the rules and rates characterizing the social insurance system sometimes represent the most important instrument changes from one year to another as measured by the impact upon disposable income and consumption demand.

(4c)   Some relations describing the *connections between different levels of the government sector in the broader sense,* e.g., the State, counties, municipalities, etc. This may overlap with (4a) and (4b).

(4d)   Relations describing *the rules under which the financial institutions in the economy operate.* Some of these will take the form of inequalities, such as for instance reserve requirements for banks.

(4e)   Relations referring to *price formation.* If there are rules of price regulation, for instance obliging enterprises to change prices only in response to changes in costs, then these are institutional relations. For socialist countries very much of the description of price formation should probably be done by means of relations which are properly classified as institutional relations. Rules of price calculations and also the values of parameters involved, such as interest rates or capital charges, are centrally determined and imposed on the branches and enterprises.

(4f)   Rules referring to *the formation of incentive funds, profit sharing funds,* and limitations on the uses of such funds, etc. are also institutional relations. There will be more of these in a socialist economy than in a private enterprise economy, but there is a tendency for more such relationships to be established also in several countries in the latter group.

(4g)   Relationships and constraints describing the working of *rationing and licencing systems.*

(4h)   *Relations of market clearing.* This point is only tentatively entered here. The idea is that equality between demand and supply is not an obligatory requirement in a planning model where several types of instruments interfering with the markets may be included. If, in a market, no such interferences exist so that prices are free to adapt so as to make supply equal demand, then the latter equality may be interpreted as an institutional relation (but this is not the only possible interpretation). In many models such relations are of course present only in an implicit or disguised form, by failure to distinguish notationally between supply and demand and actually traded volumes. In a more general model in which there is some scope for qualitative policy by switching on and off various kinds of interferences with the markets, for instance in the way suggested by formulas (6)–(9) in Section 3.2, the restrictions on the switch parameters as given by (6) and the last line of (9) are probably most correctly classified as institutional relations.

(5) *Demographic, biological and ecological relationships.* While classes (1)–(4) represent rather "traditional" types of relationships in economic models, the class here suggested is less frequently found. However, the tendency is for such relationships to become more and more frequently represented in the models, especially in models for developing countries and models which reflect the increasing concern for population problems, environmental problems, and the limitation of natural resources. Such relationships are often relevant also in connection with social indicators [see (7c) below]. Examples of the introduction of such "non-economic" relationships (and further references) are found in the works of *F.L. Golladay* and *I. Adelman, S.I. Cohen* and *H. Correa.* [The failures of economic models to take into account the effects of nutrition on health and labour productivity was, in 1955, criticized by the leading biologist *J.B.S. Haldane* in a brief note on the *Mahalanobis* model for Indian planning (see Section 1.3). He suggested that the economists' models would lead to a too high quota of physical investment in GNP in the early stages of a development plan, and proposed as a remedy a separate treatment of "consumer goods industries where the goods produced substantially increase the efficiency of industrial workers."]

(6) *Forecasts of non-controlled exogenous variables.* It is perhaps somewhat artificial to classify such forecasts among the various types of relations. As relations they take the very trivial form of saying that a variable in the model is equal to a forecast value, a statement which is of course not necessarily written down as an equation in the model. However, it is convenient to introduce such forecasts as a special entry in the classification since there is often a choice between introducing an equation explaining a variable in terms of other variables and treating the variable as a non-controlled exogenous variable. If the introduction of such a forecast does not in

itself represent a "relation", it does at least often *replace* a relation in the truer sense of the word.

(7)   *Preference relations.*   As explained in Section 3.11 we may here have two types of relations, represented by (7a) and (7b):

(7a)   *A preference function* which is to be maximized or minimized.

(7b)   *Preference constraints* which, in a simplified form, represent preferences which are not taken into account under (7a).

(7c)   In addition to these two types of relations we may perhaps also introduce here relations defining so-called *social indicators*. These are indicators of aspects like the health situation in a population, the quality of environment, the level of education and cultural activities, etc. They could be classified under definitional equations, but they will usually reflect preferences, partly in the selection of variables from which the indicators are constructed and partly in the weights attached to these variables. In principle such social indicators should again be entered as arguments in the preference function. The use of social indicators is however at a very tentative stage in connection with economic planning, and the first steps to be taken should probably be to try to establish links between social indicators and more traditional economic variables and try to calculate the consequences for the development of the social indicators of various plan alternatives. The links between "traditional economic variables" and social indicators would partly be technical and partly behavioural relationships. For an extensive survey of the construction and uses of social indicators, see *K.A. Fox*. Attempts to include social indicators or "social variables" in planning models and economic plans have been made particularly in France and Japan, see *G. Martin*. For Italy, see *F. Archibugi*. For Hungary very interesting ideas of how to combine traditional economic planning with the concerns intended to be covered by social indicators have been suggested by *G. Báger* and *A. Hajnal*. The attempts to construct and measure a *"National Economic Welfare"* – see particularly *W. Nordhaus* and *J. Tobin* – could be considered as an attempt to construct a sort of aggregate social indicator, a quantified indicator more relevant than the traditional GNP concept for a social preference function.

We should nourish no illusions about the purity of the classes defined above, perhaps apart from class (1) which includes definitional, balance and circulation relationships. For instance, as soon as some aggregation is introduced, which can hardly be avoided, production relationships must rely on some behavioural assumptions which restrict the domain of variation. (Cf. the discussion in Section 3.3.) They are then no longer *purely* technical. Behavioural relationships are in almost all cases conditioned by other types of relations; for instance, producers' factor demand and product supply relations are conditioned by income generation or income balance relations. This is however not disturbing in relation to our classification system if we define a behavioural relation as a relation which depends more or less on choices made by some decision-maker. The fact that the scope for choice is restricted by other types of conditions does then not exclude the relations mentioned from the class of behavioural relations, as long as the scope for choice is not completely eliminated. For institutional relationships simplification and aggregation may again be achieved by relying on some behavioural aspects, and to the extent that they represent not only explicit rules and regulations, but also administrative *practices*, the borderline vis-à-vis behavioural relationships may not be entirely clear. Relationships in class (5), demographic, biological and ecological relationships, will often border on technical and behavioural relationships. Finally preference relations will in practice never express pure and clear preferences and nothing more. In an analysis which for practical reasons has to be of limited size and scope, "preferences" will be attached to some variables, not because there are preferences *directly* concerned with them, but because one knows or feels that they will have some effects in addition to or beyond what is formally represented in the model (for instance beyond the horizon of the formalized plan calculations). "Preferences" attached to such variables are then mixtures of pure preferences and assumptions, beliefs or intuition about effects which are of a technical and/or behavioural nature. (Some further remarks on this point are given in Section 4.5.)

In spite of such considerations I think it is still meaningful and useful to classify relations for instance according to the scheme given above by basing the classification on the *essence* of the equations and the *intentions* of introducing them. Formally we could save some of the clarity and unambiguity of the classification by adopting the rule that an aggregate relationship should be referred to the class of relations defined by the basic (non-aggregated) relationships which it is intended to represent in a simplified fashion.

Next we might raise the question if the list given above is complete in the sense that any conceivable relationship of relevance to an economic planning problem would find its place under one of the seven classes. My tentative answer is yes, but this might perhaps reflect lack of imagination. As it stands the classification – but the subclassifications more than the main classification – reflects conditions and experiences from the economic systems in countries which have attempted to use formalized models. Other systems, existing or hypothetical, may give rise to types of relations which fall outside the classification, although I do not now see how. I must however make one exception to this statement. In Chapter 2, particularly in Section 2.2, it was pointed out that the situation in which a planning authority has to make its decisions can often be more appropriately described as a game situation than as a pure planning situation. It was suggested in Section 2.4 that a simplified treatment of the game aspects by means of a planning model could be achieved by inter alia referring some aspects to the class of exogenous variables, by introducing some behavioural relationships, and by introducing restrictions on the use of some instruments. This means that we would use classes (6), (3) and (4) above. By a more satisfactory treatment of the game aspects one might need types of conditions which could not be suitably classified under our seven main classes.

Most types of relationships classified above might be included in any type of economic model whether or not the purpose of constructing the model is to use it for planning. Planning models are therefore not entirely different from for instance models designed for forecasting. However, there are some differences, partly qualitative and partly as matters of emphasis and degree.

(A)   The first and most obvious point is that preference functions and preference constraints are requisites of a planning model, but not of models constructed for other purposes.
(B)   A planning model intended for the elaboration of operational plans should preferably contain a large number of instrument variables and relationships relating other variables to these instrument variables. To some extent the same types of variables and relations

will be present also in a forecasting model, but being free from the concern for operationality in the planning sense one may, in a forecasting context, use more aggregated and simplified representations of this aspect of the economic mechanism.

(C) A forecasting model which aims at yielding unconditional forecasts should contain behavioural relations for the Central Authority and its subdivisions. This is not meaningful in a planning model.

(D) Generalizing on the preceding point a good maxim for the construction of planning models is to try to keep open as many and diverse alternatives as possible. In a planning context we are interested in exploring and choosing from among a wide set of possibilities, and we should therefore take great care not to introduce into the model types and forms of relationships which reduce the ability of the model to span the full set X of possible states or developments of the economy. For a forecasting model this is not an essential requirement. It was partly for this reason that market clearing conditions were entered explicitly as a special group of relations under point (4h) above. One should be conscious about their role and interpretation in order not to introduce unintentionally too many of such relations.

R. Frisch was particularly clear on this last point already in his early writing on models for economic planning and policy. In the "Mathematical Appendix" referred to in Section 3.9, he wrote that "the class of institutional and political systems which form the constant set of assumptions on which the model is built, must at least be large enough to include as special cases the more important of the institutions and types of economic policy that are currently debated in a present-day economic democracy. This means for instance that we set an all too special model by imposing from the beginning the sort of equilibrium assumptions which are usual in classical theories (quantity demanded equals quantity supplied, etc.). The model should be general enough to be able to generate the classical equilibrium theories by suitable specialisations, but it should also be able to generate a much larger range of theories. . . . Each condition imposed constitutes a new limitation on the range of possibilities that may be considered."

In practice the differences between planning models and forecasting models may be less striking than suggested by points (A), (B), (C) and (D) above because the models rarely reflect the full consequences of the purpose of the model. A planning model may fail to involve preference relations. It may be less consequent in trying to keep many possibilities open than indicated under point (D) above. And it may be less perfect in its concern for operationality than indicated under point (B). On the other hand a forecasting model may be more modest than indicated under point (C) and aim only at establishing conditional forecasts. Nevertheless, for the progress of the use of formalized models it is important to keep the purpose in mind, and we might therefore expect models in the future to differ more than they do at present according to the purposes they are intended to serve.

References for Section 4.3

F. Archibugi, "A progress report: The 'quality of life' in a method of integrated planning", *Socio-Economic Planning Sciences* (1974).

G. Báger and A. Hajnal, "Organisational aspects of social planning" – See reference under Section 2.5.

S.I. Cohen, *Production, manpower and social planning: With applications to Korea* (Rotterdam University Press, Rotterdam, 1975).

H. Correa, *Population, health, nutrition and development* (Lexington Books, D.C. Heath, Lexington, MA, 1975).

K.A. Fox, *Social indicators and social theory* (Wiley, New York, 1974).

R. Frisch, "Mathematical appendix ..." (1949) – See reference under Section 3.9.

R. Frisch, "An implementation system ..." (1964) – See reference under Section 3.11. Especially pp. 34–41.

F.L. Golladay and I. Adelman, "Socio-economic policy alternatives", *Behavioral Science* (1972).

J.B.S. Haldane, "The maximization of national income", *Sankhya* (1955).

G. Martin, "The French experience of social planning", *International Social Science Journal* (1975).

W. Nordhaus and J. Tobin, "Is growth obsolete?", in *Economic growth* (National Bureau of Economic Research, Columbia University Press, New York, 1972).

H.M. Peskin, "National accounting and the environment", *Artikler* No. 50 (The Central Bureau of Statistics of Norway, Oslo, 1972).

United Nations Economic Commission for Europe, *Macro-economic models for planning and policy-making* – See reference under Section 3.4. Especially pp. 23–26.

4.4. The Nature of Economic Systems and the Forms of Planning Models and their Relationships

In Section 3.2 we introduced the term "economic system" for the basic rules, institutional arrangements and other qualitative aspects of the economic organization of a country which are not subject to planned changes by one and the same authority, but rather change when a new set of preferences ascends to power and replaces the old one consequent upon major changes in the power structure in a country. It is accordingly not meaningful, in my opinion, to think of some sort of general planning model which could cover all sorts of systems and changes between systems. A planning model must take the basic aspects of the economic system as given premises, and the form of the model and its relationships must accordingly be conditioned by, and bear the marks of the economic system in which the model is intended to be used. This is not always born out in practice, and the Polish economist *J. Pajestka* has complained with some justification that "formal planning models are very much similar all around the world," while at the same time "the actual situation and economic conditions are very diversified." This is a weakness in the present state of development of planning methodology. As time passes and models get more complete and better adapted to the conditions in the various countries, more striking differences, reflecting differences in the underlying systems, will probably become more prevalent.

For instance, one often sees models constructed for developing countries which borrow most of their characteristics from Keynesian theory and/or growth theory developed in the Western industrialized countries and which hardly represent the conditions in the developing countries very well. One also occasionally sees econometric models constructed for the socialist countries which, at least in my opinion, seem to neglect too much of the differences between the economic systems in the East and the West. One explanation of this may be that the advanced and complicated methodology of estimating relationships in simultaneous systems can be more easily applied if a model is patterned after models where this methodology has been used before than if completely new types of models are constructed.

There is however a contrary tendency which should also be observed. With regard to types of relationships emphasized it will be suggested below that models in market economies often emphasize behavioural relationships on the demand side to the neglect of production and supply relationships, whereas models in socialist countries emphasize production relations to the neglect of behaviour and demand. To the extent that this is true the models appear more different than they "should be".

In order to elucidate some points concerning the influence of the system on the form of the planning model and its relationships we shall in most cases contrast against each other a socialist economy and a private enterprise economy and try to see in which ways the models should differ if they should take proper account of the differences in the economic systems. This is only meant as an example. A similar confrontation could be made between models for industrialized countries and developing countries, and also for countries which represent different shades within such groups rather than having basicly different economic systems.

We proceed by commenting on the various groups of relationships set out in the preceding section.

Many of the relationships under group (1), *definitional relationships, balance relationships and circulation relationships*, would be similar under different systems. This applies particularly to (1a), balance relationships in physical terms or in terms of volume indexes. Some of the relationships pertaining to the definition of values and circulation relationships in value terms would of course also be similar under different systems. However, income generation relationships would have different contents under different systems of ownership. Financial circulation relationships would clearly be different as between socialist and private enterprise economies, but even within each of these groups there would be many special features in various countries. The system of relationships for financial circulation in for instance the USA or England could not be automatically taken over and used in a country like Norway because the financial institutions are rather different.

Traditionally there have been some considerable differences in *national accounting systems* in socialist countries and private enterprise countries. These differences have their roots in the predominance of Marxian theory in the socialist countries and Keynesian type of macroeconomic theory in the private enterprise economies. Marxian theory emphasizes the value of material product, gross production in the most "gross" sense, and the distinction between the production of means of production and means of consumption, while Keynesian and related macroeconomic theories emphasize categories of total demand and a national income concept which is not limited to material production. Through the international cooperation through the United Nations on standardizing systems of national accounts there is now a tendency to overcome these differences. Furthermore, as the national accounting systems become more disaggregated and detailed, the importance of the differences also tend to diminish. If an accounting system involves all relevant details, then it is no longer a pressing question to decide what are *in general* the most interesting and relevant aggregate indicators. Aggregates can then be formed differently for different purposes and in different contexts.

Group (2), *technical relationships of production*, should contain relationships which are in principle independent of the type of economic system. This means that one could in principle study inputs into, and outputs from production processes and establish correct formalized representations of the relationships and constraints involved without knowing in what type of economic system the processes take place. It does *not* mean that the mathematical forms and the values of the coefficients involved, etc., would necessarily appear to be the same for the production of the same kind of output in different systems. Production is a process organized by human beings on the basis of technical and organizational knowledge, and many coefficients in a system of relationships describing a production process would depend upon the physical and mental strength, education and competence, moral and material incentives of the labour force. There are of course many reasons why such elements may vary from one system to another. One might perhaps expect some basic qualitative features to be the same, such as the lists of relevant inputs and outputs, the possibilities of substitution between inputs, the existence of increasing or decreasing returns to scale, etc., while on the other hand the elements just mentioned might influence the values of parameters and coefficients which describe the production system more precisely in quantitative terms.

For *aggregated relationships* there are some further elements which might create differences as between different systems. For instance, macroeconomic production functions may look quite different according to whether the individual enterprises are technologically similar or different. There are perhaps reasons to expect the enterprises in a socialist economy to be more similar than in a private enterprise economy. The system of diffusion of inventions and technological knowledge, the incentives (or perhaps disincentives) to try out new and uncertain technologies, more standardized systems of decision-making, and perhaps more similar expectations about the future prevailing in a socialist economy may tend to create a more homogeneous set of enterprises than is common in a private enterprise economy. Some tendencies in this direction have been observed. For instance, within the same branch the enterprises in the USSR seem to be of a more similar size than in the corresponding branch in Western economies. However, there are also tendencies in the opposite direction. The forces of competition, which squeeze inefficient enterprises out of the market, is an element which operates with greater strength in a private enterprise market economy than in a socialist economy where enterprises can survive for a very long time even if they are not able to recover production costs.

With the reservations mentioned here, the production system in equally advanced economies under different systems could be described by the same type of relationships and constraints. It may however not be equally relevant to formalize the various aspects of the production system to the same degree of detail and with the same emphasis under different systems. In the history up to now, and under present circumstances, the socialist economies have largely been run under a high pressure of demand and taut plans so that production constraints have set the effective limits to what has been achieved, while demand conditions, producers' *behaviour*, particularly with regard to investment, the concern of the policy-makers for the balance of trade and the rate of inflation have in many periods caused production to remain well below capacity in private enterprise economies. Accordingly, if a model is to be of a limited size, we would expect the formalization of the production relationships and constraints to be relatively more strongly emphasized in a planning model for a socialist economy than in the case of a private enterprise economy.

Coming to group (3), *behavioural relationships*, there are striking differences. This refers mainly to the extension of centralized versus decentralized decision-making under different systems. From the viewpoint of a central planning authority the general principle is that *behavioural relationships are required in the planning model corresponding to each type of decision which is left to decentralized decision-makers.*

Moving down the subgroups of behavioural relationships in the list in the preceding section, we first come to *producers' behaviour.* Many aspects of producers' decisions which are made in a decentralized way in a private enterprise economy are in a socialist economy parts of the direct planning and decision-making of the Central Authority. This applies particularly to the most important investment decisions, but also to important short-run adaptations concerning inputs and outputs (to a varying degree as between countries and over time). But, to the extent that material incentives, various success indicators, profit-sharing schemes, etc. are used to stimulate and influence the direction of production activities, a complete planning model should contain behavioural relationships which describe the responses to these arrangements.

In the case of the *behaviour of consumers* there would probably be more similarities since the general rule under all prevailing systems is that consumers, under normal conditions, are free to adapt the composition of their consumption to given prices. But the quantitative description of the structure of consumers' behaviour might of course exhibit some systematic differences. Savings behaviour and labour supply would be different for reasons which refer to the social security system, the child care and education system, types of incentives and moral obligations felt under different systems, etc., and the more detailed demand structure might be influenced by the environment in different ways in different systems. Cultural trends and marketing methods are cases in point. As a more specific example concerning the form and numerical characterization of demand functions it has been suggested that more equal incomes and more homogeneous tastes in a socialist economy may create some difficulties for the market mechanism for durable consumers' goods because more people with more similar tastes simultaneously reach the critical income level where they start demanding a certain type of consumers' durables. This may be one aspect of the well-known queuing phenomenon or waiting lists for certain consumers' durables in socialist countries.

Financial behaviour would of course be very different under different systems, and *foreign trade relations* in the case of a market

economy would often be replaced by direct decisions by a central
authority in the case of a socialist economy (but subject to constraints
determined by the conditions in other countries).

In a market economy *price formation* would be determined partly
by behavioural relations, group (3), and partly by institutional relations, group (4), especially if "relations of market clearing" are
interpreted as institutional relations as suggested under point (4h). In
a socialist economy many more prices would be directly determined
by the Central Authority or calculated on the basis of rules laid down
by the Central Authority so that the corresponding relationships in
the model should be classified as institutional relationships, as suggested under point (4e).

Group (4) consists of *institutional relations.* Looking down the list
from (4a) through (4h) in the preceding section one will probably find
that the relationships will differ between different economic systems
on almost all points. Since enterprises, market organizations and
financial institutions are circumscribed by stricter rules and regulations in a socialist economy than in a private enterprise economy,
implying that groups (4d) through (4g) would carry heavier weight,
one would probably expect a larger number of institutional relationships in a socialist than in a private enterprise economy. The
balance is however not quite obvious without further empirical explorations and stock-taking since some institutional arrangements
may become very complicated and diversified when the State tries to
regulate and control privately owned enterprises and financial institutions as it does to some degree in most countries. Furthermore,
many aspects of taxation, social security and other types of income
transfers are more diversified and complicated in a private ownership
system than under socialist ownership.

Group (5), *demographic, biological and ecological relationships,*
would depend more on climate and geographical conditions, the
density of population and so on than on the economic system *per se.*
The level of economic development may influence the degree of
relevance of such relationships or the degree to which one will
emphasize such relations in the formulation of planning models.

For group (6), *forecasts of non-controlled exogenous variables,*
there should perhaps be no difference in principle. However, in an
actual planning model not only truly non-controlled exogenous
variables are placed under this category (cf. the following section).
Then for some variables which are treated as non-controlled ex-

ogenous variables in the case of a market economy, for instance relating to foreign trade or investment behaviour, the corresponding variables in a model for a socialist economy might be determined directly by the Central Authority.

For *preference relations* it is hard to point out any definite trends. On the *theory* side the idea of preference functions has a longer history in some market economy countries, but this may be a rather incidental fact. There is hardly any reason, based on the nature of the economic system, which should tend to make the idea of preference functions and optimization less natural and important in a socialist economy than in a private enterprise economy. Perhaps the opposite case would be the more plausible. After all, the economic system prevailing in a private enterprise economy defines rather directly social classes and interest groups with partly conflicting interests, and the corresponding ideologies and codes of conduct also tend to promote and emphasize the confrontation of diverse interests. Although we think of the preference function as an expression of the preference of a well-defined decision-maker rather than some sort of aggregate representation of the welfare of the total population, these factors should tend to complicate the establishing of a preference function both on principle and in practice. (Some of the viewpoints mentioned in the discussion of the concept of planning in Section 1.4, particularly with reference to *L. Rychetnik, O. Kyn* and *J. Kornai,* are also of some relevance for the use of preference functions under different systems.)

The general conclusion to be drawn from the considerations given above is that we would expect relatively more of behavioral relationships and of variables treated as non-controlled and exogenous in a market economy, and on the other hand probably (but not necessarily) more of institutional relationships, and definitely more variables treated as directly determined by the Central Authority in a socialist economy. Furthermore, we would expect the production structure to be elaborated more in detail in the planning model for a socialist economy. For balance relationships and demographic, biological and ecological relationships there is no a priori reason to expect a deviation in any particular direction.

These conclusions are exhibited in Figure 19. The figure is intended to represent the "profile" of planning models. We may think of the model as a system of equations and an assignment of variables to the categories endogenous variables, non-controlled exogenous variables

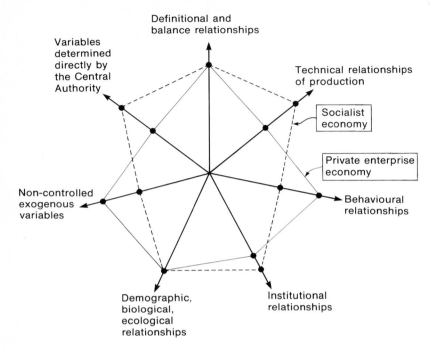

Figure 19

and variables determined directly by the Central Authority. Then, for models at the same level of aggregation so that the total number of variables of all sorts is approximately the same, we must have approximate equality between the following sum for each model:

> The number of variables determined directly by the Central Authority
> + The number of non-controlled exogenous variables
> + The number of relationships (including all types of relationships classified above apart from preference relations).

The "Model profile" is then given by the relative composition of this total sum. The illustration in Figure 19 is meant to represent the conclusions drawn in the discussion above. It is of course only suggestive, but the approach may be pursued in a more precise way in comparing specific models and will then perhaps reveal interesting patterns.

I think some of the conclusions suggested above are born out in practice, perhaps even to an excessive degree. Some models for market economies have very little of interest to say about the production structure, and some planning models in socialist countries contain almost nothing but production relationships in addition to balances for resources and products (and perhaps lower limits for private consumption of various goods). When the models in both "camps" get more complete, their profiles will probably to some extent become more similar in these respects, but the discussion above also indicates that some distinctive differences will nevertheless still remain.

The statement just made implies that studies of behavioural relationships have been lagging somewhat behind in the socialist countries. The importance of studying such relationships has however become more widely recognized in recent years. This fact is partly related to the trends of economic reforms which furnish decentralized units in the economy with wider scopes for free decisions. In a broad discussion on *The Scientific Management of Society* the Soviet philosopher and sociologist *V.G. Afanasyef* makes the following observations on the nature of a socialist society: "Socialist society is a complex aggregate of self-controlling subsystems at different levels. Each of them has its specific features, conditions of functioning and development, its particular objectives and ways and means of achieving them. Each has a scope of its own, a specific set of 'inputs' or orders coming from corresponding subjects of control, and of 'outputs' or results of its operation." This description implies that a planning model intended to be used in "the scientific management of society" must, in our terminology, contain a large number of behavioural relationships. *A.I. Katsenelinboigen* has also pointed out that increasing attention has in the USSR in recent years been directed to the representation of the socialist economy by models which are "characterized by the presence of many participants, each of whom seeks the optimal value of his own target function on the constrained set of possibilities." By now studies of consumers' behaviour constitute a well-established branch of economic research in the USSR. Studies of producers' behaviour seem to be developing faster in some of the other socialist countries, particularly in Hungary. A forerunner at the theoretical level is provided by *J. Kornai* and *T. Liptak* (1962), and a more recent example is given by *M. Tardos* (1969). Both are concerned with the behavioural responses to profit-sharing systems.

In this connection it may be pointed out that there has for a considerable time already existed a special branch of economic theory in Western countries which tries to establish theories for the behaviour of socialist enterprises, labour-managed enterprises and collective farms, with contributions by *E. Ames, E. Domar, S. Gindin, M. Keren, J.E. Meade, R.D. Portes, A.K. Sen, J.Vanek, B. Ward*, and others. These models have not been tested and confirmed empirically (see however the interesting report by *B. Balassa* on "The Firm in the New Economic Mechanism in Hungary" for some relevant descriptive material), and it would take us too far to do more than to point out the possible relevance this branch of theory may gain for planning models in the future. (An overview and further analysis of some of these models are provided by *H.G. Nutzinger*.)

The discussion above has been concerned mainly with comparisons between the profiles of planning models in socialist economies and private enterprise economies. As suggested in the introduction to this section the intention has however been to use this as an example in order to get an impression of where and how premises from the basic economic system enter and take part in shaping the profile of the planning model. If the models are well adapted to prevailing conditions one would obviously also find characteristic differences between countries which represent shades or subgroups within the basic types discussed here. Also for developing countries versus industrialized countries there ought to be some basic differences in the profiles of the models (i.e., not only in values of parameters and in the initial situation for the development), partly due to the level of development of the various branches of production, and partly due to differences in systems, organization and behaviour. Some viewpoints in this connection are given in papers by *L. Klein* and *R. Vernon*.

References for Section 4.4

V.G. Afanasyef, *The scientific management of society* (Progress Publishers, Moscow, 1971). Especially Chapter 5, Section 1.
B. Balassa, "The firm in the new economic mechanism in Hungary", in *Plan and market, economic reforms in Eastern Europe*, edited by M. Bornstein (Yale University Press, New Haven and London, 1973).

A.I. Katsenelinboigen, "On the various methods of describing the socialist economy", *Matekon* (Winter 1973–74). Translation from Russian.

L.R. Klein, "What kind of macroeconomic model for developing economies", *The econometric annual of the Indian Economic Journal* (1965). Also published in *Readings in economic statistics and econometrics,* edited by A. Zellner (Little, Brown and Company, Boston, 1968).

L.R. Klein, "The role of econometrics in socialist economies", in *Problems of economic dynamics and planning,* Essays in honour of M. Kalecki (Pergamon Press, London, and P.W.N., Warsaw, 1966).

J. Kornai and T. Liptak, "A mathematical investigation of some economic effects of profit sharing in socialist firms", *Econometrica* (1962).

H.G. Nutzinger, *Die Stellung des Betriebes in der sozialistischen Wirtschaft* (Herder & Herder, Frankfurt, 1974).

J. Pajestka, "Dialogue between planning experts and policy makers . . ." – See reference under Section 4.2.

M. Šestokova, "The firm in the Czechoslovak economy", *Journal of Industrial Economics* (1967).

M. Tardos, "A model of the behaviour of central agencies and enterprises", *Acta Oeconomica* (Budapest, 1969).

R. Vernon, "Comprehensive model-building in the planning process: the case of the less developed economies", *The Economic Journal* (1966).

4.5. Other Considerations which Influence the Profiles of Planning Models

The considerations given in the preceding section are the most basic points which influence the profile of a planning model. This means that they would tend to give different profiles even to complete and ideal planning models. Other differences in model profiles emanate from the needs to simplify procedures and to limit the size of planning models. In this connection all the considerations discussed in Chapter 3 ("Various Ways of Simplifying the Planning Problem and the Planning Scheme in Practice") may be more or less relevant.

The most decisive choice will be whether to concentrate on *selection analysis*, as defined in Section 3.9, or to emphasize the *target-instrument approach*, as set out in Section 3.10 (and further discussed in Section 3.11). An extreme selection model which concentrates on the choice of an optimal solution from among the physically possible solutions would contain mainly definitional and balance relationships, technical relationships of production, and demographic, biological and ecological relationships. Within the first group balance relationships in physical terms or in terms of volume indexes would again be the main subgroup. Furthermore, the selection model would contain preference relations. Taking some steps away from the most extreme type of selection model, relations describing the behaviour of consumers might perhaps be the first candidates to be introduced.

A model designed according to the target–instrument approach should in principle contain relationships of all kinds apart from preference relations; the latter are replaced by the stipulation of fixed targets. Since many of the instruments used to regulate the development of the economy operate by influencing the conditions under which the decentralized units make their choices, the behavioural pattern of all decentralized units must in principle be described in the model if it shall be possible to trace the effects from changes in instruments to changes in target variables, or the other way round: to find the instrument values necessary to achieve stipulated values for the target variables. A model for the target–instrument approach would also have to contain institutional relationships since these so to speak define the meaning of the instrument variables and the transmission mechanisms through which these influence the other spheres of the economy. Altogether the two approaches mentioned here therefore require radically different model profiles. (One might vizualize this in a similar diagram as Figure 19.)

Since short- and long-term aspects of economic planning are not usually taken care of in one and the same model (cf. Section 3.6) *the time perspective* will also be of great importance for the profile of the model. In the first place, a long-term model will usually not be required to provide the basis for operational plans and will often be used for selection analysis rather than careful analysis of how to use the various instruments in order to achieve the desirable development. Some of the same tendencies as those just discussed for selection models will therefore to some extent be valid also for long-term models. Accordingly there will be less of institutional and behavioural relationships. (Because of this long-term models may be more similar as between countries with different systems than short-term models.) On the other hand, concerning technical relationships a long-term model must contain relationships in group (2b) in Section 4.3, relationships describing how investment in new capital equipment changes production capacities. These are not necessarily present in a short-run model. Relationships in group (2a), which describe the production possibilities in the short run on the basis of existing fixed capital equipment, should in principle be present in short-term models, but particularly in market economies there is often more concentration on demand relationships than on production relationships in the short run.

Demographic, biological and ecological relationships are of course in most cases concerned with effects which operate in the long run, and such relationships will accordingly be more explicit and more carefully elaborated in long-term models than in models for the shorter run. (But they should of course influence decisions for the short run. This is a question of coordinating short- and long-term planning – see Sections 3.6 and 3.7 and the comments in connection with Figure 17 in Section 3.11.)

In addition to the fact that the selection of relationships to be included will be different for short-term and long-term models, the *form* given to the various relationships will often be different for practical reasons. This applies particularly to dynamic aspects. For short-term purposes it may be very important to include a detailed lag structure in order to determine the phasing of various effects, whereas this is not necessary to the same extent for long-term purposes. The dynamic elements will therefore often be simpler in long-term models than in short-term models, particularly when the latter are formulated for instance as quarterly models.

Finally we will always have to limit the size of a model somewhat artificially by *treating some aspects as exogenously given which should in principle be treated as endogenously determined*. There are several considerations which determine how to do this.

Some variables are transferred to the group of non-controlled exogenous variables because there is doubt about the theoretical foundation for treating them as endogenous. Common examples are private investment and various variables referring to foreign trade. No doubt there are (in a market economy) endogenous factors operating concerning such variables, but at the same time there are many effects which are not understood and which it is not possible to predict reasonably well on the basis of present knowledge. In such cases one might perhaps argue that one ought to introduce rela- tionships explaining such variables even if they are unstable because doing otherwise would mean wasting some information which we do have. However, there is another aspect which should be opposed against this consideration. As mentioned towards the end of Section 4.2 a model, once constructed, is a somewhat rigid framework and it is designed so as to be able to absorb and utilize types of information which it is known in advance that we will get. However, concerning private investment and some variables referring to foreign trade the situation will often be that we get some new information every moment, but we do not know in advance exactly what *type* of information this will be. If we have introduced relationships making the relevant variables endogenous, then only a priori known types of information can be utilized systematically, whereas the method of treating them as if they were non-controlled and exogenous permits an intuitive and discretionary use of all sorts of information, re- gardless of whether or not we knew in advance that these types of information should become available. In practice the latter method may not necessarily be inferior to the former one.

When variables that are in fact endogenous are treated as if they were exogenous, it is necessary, after the calculations have been performed, to subject the total picture obtained to a critical examination in order to judge whether the constellation arrived at contradicts the more intuitive notions we have about the determinants of the quasi-exogenous variables, and perhaps make another round of calculations based on revised values for these variables.

A model may be limited in size also by *transferring into the class of target variables some variables which should properly not belong there*, either by introducing them as arguments in a preference function, by subjecting them to preference constraints, or by introducing target values for them if we pursue the instrument–target approach. This is often done particularly in order to limit the time horizon of the model. Investments in a certain period or capital stocks at the end of the planning period are often treated in this way. In principle they should not be target variables; we attach preferences to them not for their own sake, but because they are of importance for the possibilities beyond the horizon.

Similar treatment is sometimes also given to for instance the development of foreign debt. Here again we should in principle, if we were to construct a complete model, take into account relationships which describe how the development of foreign debt influences the set of future possibilities by the requirements for servicing the debt or by influencing the possibilities of raising new loans in the future. These relationships are however rather uncertain, and in practice one will cut the chain of relationships by simply imposing a preference constraint or setting up a target for the debt position, either for every year in a plan period, or at least for the terminal year.

As a final example may be mentioned the rate of inflation. In principle one might say that the rate of increase of the price level is in itself not something to which we should attach preferences. The change in the price level is of importance only because of the effects it has upon income distribution, competitiveness in foreign markets, the problems and uncertainties it creates for investment calculations, and so on. If all these effects were taken care of as endogenous in the model by suitable relationships, then it would be unnecessary to attach preferences to the rate of inflation itself. If inflation is harmful, then this would reveal itself through the effects mentioned on the basis of the preferences we attach to the things which are of importance in themselves. However, the relationships in these fields are again vague and uncertain, and we simplify matters by limiting the

chain of effects formally represented in the model and introducing
instead a preference constraint for the rate of inflation, or by
introducing it in a preference function.

Further details concerning this way of limiting the size of a model
is given in notes by *T. Lindholt.*

Reference for Section 4.5

T. Lindholt, "Om kvasi-mål i økonomisk mål-middel-analyse", *Memorandum* from the
Institute of Economics at the University of Oslo (2 January 1966). Based on lectures
by L. Johansen.

4.6. The Importance of Having Autonomous Relationships

The term *autonomy* of relationships in economic models was introduced into the discussion on econometric methodology by *R. Frisch* in the late 1930s. It was further discussed and defined in more precise terms by *T. Haavelmo* in his *Probability Approach in Econometrics*. Since then it has, in my opinion, received too little attention in econometrics. For the construction and use of mathematically formulated models in connection with economic planning I consider the idea underlying the concept of autonomy of relationships to be even more important than in econometrics in general. From the following discussion it will appear that the requirement of autonomy is more important the larger is the set of possible policies A taken into account.

Roughly the term autonomy of relationships refers to how basic a relationship is, or to the degree of generality of its validity. A relationship is more autonomous the wider is the range of circumstances under which the relationship is valid. A relationship is valid under a wide range of different circumstances if it is derived from one or very few simple and generally valid principles; on the other hand, its validity may easily be impaired if it is dependent upon the simultaneous validity of a large set of principles or hypotheses with less than perfect generality.

In order to give more precise content to the term autonomy of relationships Haavelmo introduces a set Ω of *structures* such that one member or another of this set would describe (approximately) economic reality in *any practically conceivable situation*. Furthermore he supposes that one could define some non-negative measure of the "size" (or "importance" or "credibility") of any subset ω of Ω. If one subset ω_1 is contained in another subset ω_2, then the measure of ω_2 is larger than or at least equal to the measure of ω_1. If we now explore the range of circumstances under which a certain relationship – symbolized by R – is valid, then this is tantamount to searching through the full set of structures Ω and "marking off" those elements (structures) for which R is valid. Let the subset consisting of these elements be ω_R. According to Haavelmo's terminology the relationship R is then *autonomous with respect to the subset of structures* ω_R. For two relationships R_1 and R_2 we have that R_1 is more autonomous (possesses a higher degree of autonomy) than R_2 if the subset with respect to which R_1 is autonomous is larger than the subset with respect to which R_2 is autonomous, i.e., if ω_{R_1} is larger than ω_{R_2}, and vice versa.

This is the abstract definition. In practice one would of course find it difficult to settle for a specific measure of the size of the relevant sets, but for discussions of specific relationships it is often the case that the subset corresponding to one relationship is contained in the subset corresponding to another relationship, and then the *ranking* of these relationships with respect to the degree of autonomy is independent of the specific measure chosen for the "size" of the subsets of Ω.

Any relationship which is derived by combining in some way two or more "original" relationships is called a *confluent* relationship. Such a relationship will, according to Haavelmo, usually have a lower (and never a higher) degree of autonomy than each of the relationships from which it is derived. (Thus the individual relationships in our reduced form model $x = f(a, z)$ are confluent to the utmost degree, each one of them being dependent in general on the whole set of "original" relationship.)

In this connection Haavelmo takes up for consideration how we can actually distinguish between an "original" system and a derived system of confluent relationships. He points out that this is not a problem of mathematics or logics, but a problem of actually knowing something about real phenomena and of making realistic assumptions about them. "In trying to establish relations with a high degree of autonomy we take into consideration various *changes* in the economic structure which might upset our relations, we try to dig down to such relationships as actually might be expected to have a high degree of invariance with respect to certain changes in structure that are 'reasonable'. . . . The construction of systems of autonomous relations is, therefore, a matter of intuition and factual knowledge; it is an art."

A sort of "test" for autonomy may perhaps be the following hypothetical experiment. Consider a certain relationship R in a model. If this relationship could be established by an expert in a limited field of knowledge without need for consultation with people elaborating other parts of the model, then the relationship R must be expected to have a high degree of autonomy. Another way of thinking of the same "test" is to ask if we would retain the relationship R in unchanged form even if other parts of the model in which we use it should undergo some changes.

Haavelmo also discusses the similarities and differences between, on the one side, the concept of autonomy of relationships, and, on the other side, the permanence of relationships under actually observed developments. Approximate fulfilment of the relationships under consideration in the observed situations or developments is a necessary indicator of its autonomy, but not a sufficient criterion. Autonomy refers to the validity of the relationship "in any practically *conceivable* situation", i.e., for the discussion of the autonomy of the relationship we refer to a set of *hypothetical* variations that may be much wider than the set of variations actually observed.

It is Haavelmo's view that "the principle task of economic theory is to establish such relations as might be expected to possess as high a degree of autonomy as possible," and accordingly of econometrics to establish such relationships quantitatively.

In connection with economic planning we are interested in revealing and exploring a set of alternative states or developments which is as wide as possible. We may be interested in constructing models conditioned by qualitative policies which have not been tried before and models which are valid under external disturbances which have not been experienced before, and we may be interested in exploring consequences of varying instruments outside the ranges of previous variations. In the terminology above we may be interested in exploring "structures" which do not correspond to observed situations, but they will of course have to belong to the set Ω of structures which correspond to the set of all "practically conceivable" situations. From this it is clear that the establishing of autonomous relationships, which is important in general, is *particularly* important in connection with the use of models for economic planning. The use of models for historical explanation, or for forecasting, or the elaboration of projections under assumptions of "unchanged policy" would be less demanding in this respect.

This is the conclusion stressed in somewhat different terms by *J. Marschak* in a discussion of "Economic Measurements for Policy and Prediction". In Marschak's discussion "theory" refers to relationships established on the basis of postulates about "plausible

human behaviour, under given institutional and technological conditions," in contrast to relationships which merely reflect observed
correlations or regularities. Marschak concludes that "theory may
appear unnecessary (i.e., observed correlations and regularities may
suffice, L.J.) for policy decisions until a certain structural change is
expected or intended. It becomes necessary then. Since it is difficult
to specify in advance what structural changes may be vizualized later,
it is almost certain that a broad analysis of economic structure, later
to be filled out in detail according to needs, is not a wasted effort.
Thus, practice requires theory." This "broad analysis" which should
yield robust results in the case of structural changes, is an analysis
aiming at establishing autonomous relationships.

Let us try to elucidate the discussion above a little bit further by
considering an almost trivial example. Let us assume that total private
consumption in an economy C depends upon total income Y less
taxes T, the rate of interest r and a vector of parameters α characterizing the distribution of income:

(1) $C = f(Y - T, r, \alpha)$.

For the present purpose we assume that this relationship will hold
under all "practically conceivable circumstances," i.e., this relationship is valid in all structures contained in Ω. In other words, (1)
is – for the purpose of the argument – an absolutely autonomous
relationship.

Within the set Ω we may distinguish the following subsets:

Ω_1 = a set of structures which is such that the income distribution is
constant and the same, expressed by $\bar{\alpha}$, for all structures in this
set.
Ω_2 = a set of structures which is such that the rate of interest is
constant and the same, equal to $\bar{r}$, for all structures in this set.
Ω_3 = a set of structures for which total tax revenue depends on total
income and the distribution of income in a way characterized by
a specific function $T = T(Y, \alpha)$.

The structures contained in Ω_1 may be structures where behavioural relationships together with technical relationships combine
in such a way as to create a particular stable relative income distribution, and furthermore economic policies are not used to interfere

with this distribution (or does so in an unchangeable way). In the same way the structures in Ω_2 may be structures which are such that market forces tend to give the same interest rate r, or structures where economic policy enters actively so as to keep r constant. Ω_3 contains structures where a specific tax function holds, but is not constrained in any other way. Now consider a consumption function which is simplified so as to let total consumption depend only on total income Y, i.e., a consumption function F which is such that:

$$(2) \qquad C = F(Y) \equiv f(Y - T(Y, \bar{\alpha}), \bar{r}, \bar{\alpha}).$$

Then this consumption function is valid only for structures contained in the intersection of the subsets Ω_1, Ω_2 and Ω_3 because changes in the income distribution, the rate of interest or the tax function would disturb the relation $C = F(Y)$. In other words, if $C = F(Y)$ is our relationship R as used in the definition of autonomy given above, then the set ω_R, with respect to which the relation R is autonomous, is given by:

$$(3) \qquad \omega_R = \Omega_1 \cap \Omega_2 \cap \Omega_3.$$

To be strictly correct there is possibly an extension of the set outside that defined by (3) where $C = F(Y)$ would also hold good, namely structures where the income distribution, the interest rate and the tax function are changed in exactly compensating manners, but this is likely to be a set of negligible measure.

Intermediate cases could be given in the same way. For instance, a consumption function, given by:

$$(4) \qquad C = F_1(Y - T, r) \equiv f(Y - T, r, \bar{\alpha}),$$

would be autonomous with respect to Ω_1 and so on.

For certain forecasting purposes or for understanding the development in a specific historical period a simple relationship like $C = F(Y)$ may be useful, but in a planning context more autonomous relationships are required.

In the quotation from T. Haavelmo given above it was suggested that the construction of systems of autonomous relations is a matter of intuition and factual knowledge, or "an art". It may nevertheless be possible to give some more practical guidelines (in addition to the "test" suggested above, referring to "experts in limited fields of knowledge"). It may be useful to do this on the background of the classification of types of relationships in planning models given in Section 4.3.

First concerning *definitional relationships* and *balance relationships*. In principle these should be perfectly autonomous: there would be no conceivable circumstance under which they do not hold. The main question would here be about *relevance* rather than autonomy. However, there is a question about *completeness* which may have something to do with autonomy. Consider for example the balance relationship for labour. If it has not been customary with import of labour, then one may have inherited from the past a labour balance equation where such a term is absent. This equation is then not perfectly autonomous since import of labour belongs to the set of conceivable circumstances. It is of course easy to amend the equation so as to take care of this possibility and thereby increase its degree of autonomy. Similar considerations apply to many balance equations. One should be careful to see to it that no relevant te.ms have been omitted for historical reasons or for convenience. Changes in stocks are variables which are often omitted in theoretical models, but which may be important in planning models for practical purposes. In balances describing financial circulation changes that would alter habitual structures and necessitate the introduction of new terms, may often occur, or at least be conceivable. Only if balance and circulation equations contain terms like "unspecified", "various items", "residual", etc., can one be sure that they are formally complete, but in that case it is of course important to find out whether any important items are hidden behind these unspecified entries.

For *technical relationships* a main consideration would be the degree of aggregation. As we have seen before aggregate relationships may hold with sufficiently good approximation only if we rely upon some other relationships, for instance relationships derived from profit maximization. There is therefore a tendency for technical relationships to become less autonomous the higher is the level of aggregation. Other "dangers" lie in the convenience of adopting the assumption of fixed proportions between inputs, or perhaps more general forms of limited substitution possibilities, when these are not contradicted by observations from the past. History may however have failed to reveal the actual substitution possibilities, perhaps because some input prices have remained in almost constant proportions. What has been observed is then a stable expansion path which looks as if there were no substitution possibilities. Relationships derived on the basis of this appearance may then be autonomous only with respect to structures where the relevant input prices remain in the same proportions, which may be too narrow an assumption to make for planning purposes.

For the set X of possible results depicted by the planning model the consequence of introducing the non-autonomous fixed proportions relationships will be that the set appears smaller than it actually is. In other cases the introduction of non-autonomous relationships may work in the opposite direction. Consider for instance the case of labour inputs in production. For certain operations in a production process the skill or education composition of the labour force may be important. If all empirical evidence used in establishing the production relations stems from periods in which there has been balance in the markets for the various categories of labour, then a model which treats all labour as homogeneous (perhaps with weight factors corresponding to relative wages) may fit the historical facts very well. However, this type of relationship may have little autonomy for situations in which the balance in the labour market may be disturbed. In actual fact there may then appear bottlenecks which effectively limit production possibilities much more than the production model with homogeneous labour tends to indicate. A set of possible results X spanned by means of a model containing the non-autonomous production relationship which treats labour as homogeneous will then exaggerate the set of actual possibilities.

In addition to these points the considerations mentioned in Section 4.4 concerning technical relationships are also relevant for the degree of autonomy of such relationships.

Coming to *behavioural relationships* it is much more difficult to say what would constitute autonomous relationships. However, some guidelines can be given.

In Section 4.4, I put forward the rule that there should be "behavioural relationships in the planning model corresponding to each type of decision which is left to decentralized decision-makers." This principle suggests that a behavioural relationship is more autonomous if it describes the behaviour of one well-defined decision-maker than if it expresses in a joint fashion the results of decisions by several decision-makers. Now some aggregation is always necessary, and then this rule cannot be applied literally as it stands, but the natural extension is that a behavioural relationship is more autonomous if it represents the aggregate result of similar types of decisions taken by well-defined and similar decision-makers in similar situations. (This is almost the definition of autonomy given by *C.F. Christ* in one of the very few textbooks of econometrics which take up the concept. Christ's definition is that the property of "being affected only by changes in the behaviour of one group or sector in the economy, is referred to as autonomy.") Consumer demand functions would perhaps be the best case in point. It is however easy to find examples of relationships in planning and policy models which violate this principle. For instance, many relationships which purport to explain price formation do this in a form which must be understood as a resultant of decisions by both sellers and buyers. Many relationships referring to the foreign trade part of planning models often summarize effects which stem from decisions taken by both domestic and foreign decision-makers. The most striking example would perhaps be the Phillips curve type of relationship, relating the rate of change of the wage level (or sometimes the price level) to the level of unemployment, previous price changes, and often also some other variables. This will represent the total or net result of decisions taken by individual wage earners and employers as well as trade unions and employers unions, and perhaps also sometimes some sort of interference from the Central Authority.

In the terminology of Frisch and Haavelmo such relationships are confluent relationships, and they possess a lower degree of autonomy than relationships which would reflect the pattern of decision-making by one well-defined group of rather similar decision-makers.

Next consider behavioural relationships which satisfy the requirement that they should express the behaviour of a well-defined group of similar decision-makers. Can anything be said about the degree of autonomy of such relationships? If the relationships are derived on the basis of an assumption about some sort of maximizing behaviour [an assumption which has been subjected to criticism, see particularly *J. Kornai* (1971)], then I think this problem can be divided into two parts, referring to the objective function which the decision-maker wants to maximize (or minimize), and the set of constraints under which this is done. Changes in the structure in other parts of the system would interfere with the behavioural pattern under investigation only if they change the one or the other of these two elements.

Concerning the first element, the objective function, questions which come up are for instance whether the function which consumers try to maximize represents innate preferences of the consumers, or whether consumers' preferences are influenced by the decisions and activities taken by producers, and to what extent preferences in a certain period will be influenced by experiences in the preceding periods.

On the constraint side an important question is whether the behavioural pattern is derived under all sorts of constraints which may become relevant in situations to be explored. For instance, consumer demand functions are usually derived under the assumption of free adaptation in the markets subject only to a budget constraint. If there is in addition rationing for some commodities, then the demand relationships so derived will break down, and this applies in general to *all* demand functions even if only *one* commodity should be rationed. A demand function which should be completely autonomous vis-à-vis the possibilities of rationing should be a function of the quantities assigned through the rationing system as well as the traditional variables disposable income and prices.

In many cases constraints on decisions by consumers and producers contain variables, e.g., prices and income components, which refer to future periods. In this case the decision-makers must substitute expectations for actual variables (or perhaps behave in more sophisticated manners in the face of uncertainty). If so the set of perceived constraints may be more volatile than the actual constraints. However, decisions have to be taken on the basis of the set of perceived constraints. Then everything which may influence the expectations of the decision-makers may influence the resulting behaviour. In some forecasting models, particularly in the USA, one has attempted to remedy the behavioural relationships to some extent on this account by introducing variables which indicate the state of expectations or intentions of consumers taken from statistical surveys based on interviews. This may be useful for short-term purposes when such indicators can be considered as non-controlled exogenous variables for which forecasts can be made on the basis of the most recent surveys. In models for the slightly longer run this method becomes less useful since the basis for forecasting these variables will then be much weaker, and it may be hard to find reliable relationships which relate the expectations to observed facts for the preceding periods.

In Section 2.4 [under point (2)] we suggested that cases which should properly be treated as game situations are in practice often represented by means of ordinary behavioural relationships in the model. Such relationships must be expected to be less autonomous than behavioural relationships stemming from non-game situations. A decision-maker who sees himself as a player in a game, will be influenced in his own decisions by his evaluation of the situation of other players and his estimates of their preferences. Any relationship which tries to capture the behaviour of *one* player will have a tendency therefore to be dependent upon elements which are associated with other players, at least to the extent that there is some correlation between one player's estimates of the situation and preferences of another player and the actual situation and preferences of the latter. The most typical example would perhaps be relationships describing the behaviour of an oligopolist. His behaviour would be influenced by his estimates of cost conditions and other relevant facts pertaining to his competitors as well as his estimate of the behaviour of his customers. It will therefore be a mixture of elements and effects which have their origins with many different decision-makers.

Turning to *institutional relationships* we are again in a less problematic field. There is of course here the question about aggregate relationships which are in practice often used instead of the absolutely correct more detailed relationships. For instance, an aggregate relationship describing the functional relation between tax revenue and total income may not be autonomous with respect to changes in the structure which cause the relative distribution of income to change, as suggested in connection with the example above. Otherwise the most pressing problem in this field is to have a set of institutional relationships which is general enough and complete enough to have a well-defined place for every instrument that might conceivably come into use.

Demographic, biological and ecological relationships are partly similar to technical relationships from the present point of view. Some of the demographic relationships may border on or overlap with the class of behavioural relationships.

As to the forecasts of *non-controlled exogenous variables* one may perhaps also raise a question about autonomy. Some variables are of course always non-controlled and exogenous in the most absolute sense, but for other variables treated as z-variables in our scheme changes elsewhere in the system may call for a change in the treatment of these variables. For instance, labour supply may sometimes be treated as exogenous and non-controlled, but certain changes in taxation or social policy may change the basis for this assumption.

For the preference relationships the situation is in principle rather simple, since we consider the preference relationships as representing the preferences of a well-defined central authority. It is mainly a question of completeness. If the planning agency maximizes a preference function subject to the constraints of the model including perhaps also preference constraints, and the Central Authority after having seen the results of this operation decides to change the preferences because of what is revealed by the elaboration of the plan, then the preferences have not been correctly or completely formulated in the first instance. The fact that preferences may shift over time for other reasons is a different matter. One should however be aware of the consequences for the formulation of the preference relationships of the fact that planning models in practice are more or less incomplete, see the discussion towards the end of Section 4.5. This could perhaps be expressed by saying that the preference relationships are not autonomous vis-à-vis certain changes in the formulation of other parts of the model.

If we should do our utmost to secure a high degree of autonomy for the various relationships included in a planning model, then I think the relationships must often be given functional forms which are not standard in economic theory. Often supplementary "if-statements" would probably be necessary. A typical example might be a behavioural relationship for private investment. Under certain conditions investment would probably be determined by profitability calculations on the side of the investor, and we would have a type of relationship which is common in investment theory. Under other conditions the availability of sources of finance would be the limiting factor (perhaps under a system of direct regulation of the rate of interest), and in other situations again the availability of materials or labour or the capacities in the investment goods sectors might be the limiting factors. One might also switch between cases in which the producer and investor behaves as a quantity adapter under given prices and situations in which he produces according to the stock and flow of orders. (For a theory which includes such a switch between different "strategies", see for instance *T. Haavelmo, A Study in the*

Theory of Investment.) Sometimes such more complicated and autonomous relationships based on "if-statements" could be combined into relationships which say for instance that private investment is equal to the minimal element in a set of variables, this set containing variables which express the desire of the investor, the availability of sources of finance, the availability of labour and manpower, etc. Such relationships may be hard to estimate by traditional econometric methods, but if they can be established, then it would often not be too difficult to handle them computationally by means of modern computational equipment.

From the discussion given above it may appear as if the process of constructing models consisting of autonomous relationships is fraught with difficulties in almost every direction. This is indeed true – to establish a model consisting only of absolutely autonomous relationships is an unattainable ideal. In practice the question of autonomy of relationships is a matter of degree. The purpose of the discussion above is therefore only to sharpen the awareness about the problem and stimulate efforts to achieve a relatively high degree of autonomy of the relationships used. It is not to describe the problem as being so overwhelmingly difficult that one might just as well give up using formalized models altogether. After all, if one gives up using formalized models in planning, then planning will proceed on the basis of some sort of implicit model as pointed out in Section 4.2, and there is no reason to believe that this implicit model would consist of more autonomous relationships than the best formalized model we might be able to establish.

References for Section 4.6

C.F. Christ, *Econometric models and methods* (Wiley, New York and London, 1966). Especially p. 20.

T. Haavelmo, *The probability approach in econometrics* – See reference under Section 4.2. Section 8.

T. Haavelmo, *A study in the theory of investment* (University of Chicago Press, Chicago, 1960). Especially Section 33, II.

J. Kornai, *Anti-equilibrium* – See reference under Section 3.12.

J. Marschak, "Economic measurements for policy and prediction" – See reference under Section 3.2.

4.7. Econometric Methodology and Planning Models

The title of this section may be described as a headline in search of a text. The purpose is to draw attention to problems which are important, but which have not been very extensively treated in the literature.

In establishing formalized models for planning purposes we need a methodology for giving quantitative specification to the models, i.e., we need econometrics. The most common, and in many respects very sophisticated econometric methodology may however not be quite appropriate in a planning context. This refers mainly to econometric methods designed for estimation of the coefficients of quantitative models on the basis of time series data.

The usual framework for this purpose involves the distinction between endogenous variables and exogenous variables. Exogenous variables in the context of econometric methodology include both instrument variables (a) and non-controlled exogenous variables (z) in our terminology. These are treated as either non-stochastic or stochastic, but in the latter case they are assumed to be distributed independently of error terms in the equations of the model. The "independent" variations in instrument variables and non-controlled exogenous variables generate the variations which can be taken advantage of for estimating the coefficients in the model. As is well-known there may be identification problems involved, but the more there are of instruments and non-controlled exogenous variables which have varied in the observation period, the better are the chances that we will be able to estimate the coefficients of the model.

On the assumptions made in common econometric methodology we could always estimate the coefficients of the reduced form equations, i.e., estimate the model in the form $x = f(a, z)$. For some *forecasting* purposes this may be all we need. However, these relationships are highly confluent in the terminology of the preceding section, and for planning purposes we need relationships with as high a degree of autonomy as we can achieve. For a historical period for which data are available a certain structure represented by $x = f^{\dagger}(a^{\dagger}, z)$ has been in operation. Here $a^\dagger$ is the vector of instruments which have been used, and $f^\dagger$ is the appropriate form of the structural model. For the future for which we intend to plan, another instrument vector a may be relevant; this may include many of the same instruments as $a^\dagger$, but in addition there may be some new instruments. (We might of course also have reasons to expect another vector of non-controlled exogenous elements, in the planning period than in the observation period, but this is more of a common problem for planning and other uses of models.) With new instruments included the form of the structural model must also undergo some changes, i.e., f will not be identical to $f^\dagger$. Nevertheless there will of course usually be very much of information contained in $f^\dagger$ which is relevant also for establishing f. For establishing f it therefore ought to be possible to utilize information gained by estimating $f^\dagger$. There is however no way of going directly from $f^\dagger$ to f. The only reasonably safe way would be to estimate the "original form" of the equations from which $f^\dagger$ is derived and sort out the ones that have a sufficiently high degree of autonomy with respect to the changes in the structure which we intend to introduce by changing the list of instrument variables. The relationships thus selected may not be sufficient for establishing the complete model for the new situation. They must then be supplemented with information drawn from other sources than historical time series.

This suggests the following conclusion: *for planning purposes other sources of information than time series data may be relatively more important than in the case of economic forecasting.* These other sources may be cross-section data, technological and engineering information, interview data and institutional data permitting the elaboration of institutional relationships. In certain fields *experimentation* may also be feasible and provide useful information. (Some references to literature on experimentation in social sciences were given in Section 3.2.) Furthermore, systematic use of expert information along the lines suggested by the *Delphi Method* may add to the information basis for constructing planning models.

However, one should of course not abstain from using the information contained in historical time series data, and what has been said above does not invalidate the common econometric methodology in this context. There is however a deeper problem which refers to the correctness of the assumptions about the exogenous variables. For the truly non-controlled exogenous variables there are of course no problems. For variables which are in fact not non-controlled exogenous, but only treated as if they were (see Section 4.5), there are methodological problems, but these are not different from problems encountered also in connection with forecasting problems. The main problem refers to the instrument vector a. The usual methodology proceeds as if the values of the elements in a are chosen as independent variables. This might be all right if for instance government expenditures are decided *only* for "narrow" and specific purposes and not with a view to the influences on the general economic activity, if tax parameters are chosen only for budgetary reasons and not for the purpose of regulating total activity, if the discount rate is chosen by the Central Bank also on the basis of narrow monetary considerations, and so on. As soon as macroeconomic planning is consciously introduced, such assumptions are however no longer valid. Instruments are chosen for the purpose of influencing the elements of the vector of target variables x. In a dynamic context the instruments are set on the basis of information accumulated up to the point of decision and expected effects for the coming periods. Ideally they should be determined recurrently as part of a strategy, as suggested in Section 2.6. Then the traditional statistical assumptions about the instrument variables no longer hold. The active use of the instruments in response to observations generate correlations which violate the assumptions underlying the common econometric methodology. There may be lags involved in this process which help to avoid such a high degree of simultaneity that identifiability is lost, but one should clearly not apply the common methodology based on the assumption that the instrument variables are exogenous in the statistical or econometric sense.

These problems have to some extent been recognized in scattered papers in econometrics, particularly in connection with attempts to find out by means of statistical and econometric studies the relative strength of monetary policy and fiscal policy in regulating total economic activity. It has been shown that, when instruments are actually used for the purpose of regulating the activity, then simple regressions or correlations between the development of target variables and instrument variables may easily be completely misleading. The papers by *M.H. Peston* and *J.R. Crotty* referred to below discuss some aspects of this problem and also give further references to other relevant papers. *A.S. Blinder* and *R.M. Solow* have also commented on the problem and suggest that "treating the fiscal and monetary tools, which are exogenous in the economic sense (that is, determined outside of the economic system), as exogenous in the statistical sense (that is, independent of the error term) involves a specification error that all econometric models will continue to commit until they specify and estimate proper reaction functions for the authorities. We wonder (and now we are only speculating) if this observation does not go a long way toward explaining the poor policy predictions of some of these models despite impressive goodness-of-fit statistics." Papers by *W.D. Fisher* and by *C.J. Åberg* suggest some more general problems. Åberg's view is that "the really exogenous variables in such cases as these are in fact the policy goals and not the instruments and this ought to be taken into account in the estimation procedure." Fisher does not directly treat the problem caused by the fact that instruments are turned into endogenous variables in the econometric sense, but he develops estimation methods for the (linear) reduced form model from the viewpoint of decision-theory when it is known that the estimated reduced form equations are going to be used in connection with the maximization of a (quadratic) preference function. As suggested at the opening of this section there is need for further work on these problems. In the meantime one may perhaps seek some comfort in the fact that economic planning has perhaps not yet been sufficiently efficient to make these problems acute, and observed time series may be used somewhat more confidently than what would be appropriate if we had already had a long period with efficient planning. However, reasonable guidelines seem to be the following: *try to establish as much as possible of information from other sources in addition to historical time series, and to the extent that time series are used, employ estimation methods which are as robust as possible,* i.e., methods which are not sensitive to misspecification of the underlying assumptions. Several studies in econometric methodology have paid particular attention to the robustness of various methods, so there is some help to be found concerning this question.

References for Section 4.7

A.S. Blinder and R.M. Solow, "Analytical foundations of fiscal policy", in *The economics of public finance*, edited by A.S. Blinder et al. (The Brookings Institution, Washington, 1974).

J.R. Crotty, "Specification error in macro-econometric models: The influence of policy goals", *American Economic Review* (1973). See also discussion in the same journal (1976).

The Delphi method: Techniques and applications – See reference under Section 2.5.

W.D. Fisher, "Estimation in the linear decision model", *International Economic Review* (1962).

M.H. Peston, "The correlation between targets and instruments", *Economica* (1972).

C.J. Åberg, "Forecasts, uncertainty and decision-making", *The Swedish Journal of Economics* (1967).

4.8. The Model in Confrontation with Realities

As I have suggested on several occasions before, the construction of a planning model is not something which is done once and for all, but a process of modifications and extentions in response to new evidence and new problems. Since the construction of a model of the size now often used, with hundreds or thousands of variables, is quite a large investment, and since it will be so to speak embodied in data files, computational programmes, etc. and since the users of a model need training and experience in using it, it would not be correct to speak of a *continuous* process of modifications and extentions. Major revisions will have to take place only at some intervals. Re-estimations of the coefficients of a model may however take place as continuously as the flow of new data permits. In connection with many planning models this will almost be a matter of routine, computational programmes for such reestimations being parts of the full programme packet of the model.

Figure 20 suggests the loop of constructing and revising the model according to experience gained. "Theory" and "facts" and prior decisions about permissible instruments are combined to produce the model; the structural model is combined with preferences and expectations about non-controlled variables so as to derive a "calculated plan"; observed "events" of various sorts, which may not have a natural place in the model, and "supplementary considerations" of various sorts are used to modify the results of the calculations on the formalized model so as to arrive at an "adopted plan"; supplementary considerations and observed events may of course appear and have their impacts upon policy also after the plan has been adopted, so that "actual actions" may deviate more or less from what was intended in the adopted plan; these actions finally give rise to observations on the "actual development of the economy," the experiences from which again influence the starting point of the scheme. The "feed-backs" may be of a gradual and long-term nature and influence basic theory and preferences, or they may be of a more direct nature giving rise to the more routine adjustments of the model

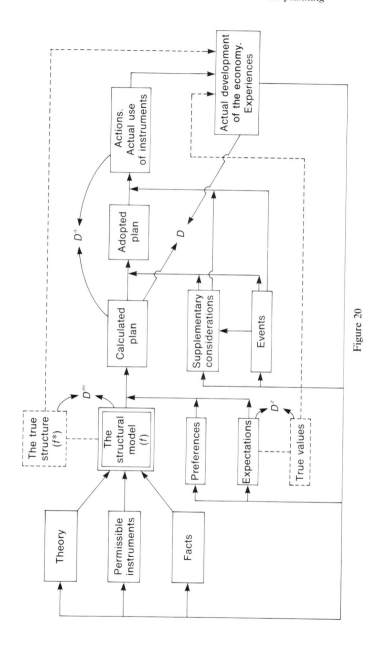

Figure 20

and expectations about non-controlled exogenous variables. They do also influence the way in which supplementary considerations and adjustments are brought to bear upon the calculated plan before a plan is officially adopted.

Part of the purpose of the process of revisions of the model and planning procedure would be to narrow down the revealed discrepancies between actual developments of the economy and the development envisaged in the adopted plan. In this process considerations which are previously brought in as "supplementary considerations" in the middle of the diagram would be moved to the left part of the diagram so as to be included in the formalized part, through the elaboration of the set of permissible instruments, the structural model and the formal representation of preferences. (The diagram used above is inspired by, but different from a diagram used by *R. Stone* for expository purposes. One of the differences is that Stone's diagram seems to imply a splitting of the planning process into a selection part and another part in which the use of the instruments is decided upon. Our diagram is nearer to the "ideal" planning procedure.)

In the figure we have also suggested the roles of the true structure and of the true values of the non-controlled exogenous variables. The model actually used and the expectations held about the exogenous variables influence decisions with regard to the instruments, but the actual development of the economy is of course determined by the *true* structure and the *true* values of the exogenous variables besides the values of the instruments.

In this process of confronting model calculations with actual experiences it may be of great value to try to separate the various causes of discrepancies. Let us therefore briefly discuss the possibilities of tracing components of the discrepancies back to the various possible causes. I shall conduct the discussion in terms of deterministic models, and only give some brief suggestions concerning the stochastic case at the end of the section.

We may as already suggested distinguish between two models: *the model actually used* in the computations for the plan, and the *"true model"*. We use the following notations:

(5)

Model actually used: $x = f(a, z)$,

True model: $x = f^*(a, z)$.

For target variables, instrument variables and non-controlled exogenous variables we now introduce a double notation, using the suffix "pl" for plan values and "obs" for observed values, i.e.:

(6)

Plan values: $x^{pl}, a^{pl}, z^{pl},$

Observed values: $x^{obs}, a^{obs}, z^{obs}.$

If there were no "events" and "supplementary considerations" as introduced in Figure 20, then the planned and the observed use of instruments would be the same, i.e., $a^{pl} = a^{obs}$. In general we shall not assume this to be the case.

For the non-controlled exogenous variables one might introduce a notation which indicates that this element is forecasted rather than planned. However, when we use the notation z^{pl} the idea is that this represents the values of the non-controlled exogenous variables which are used *in the context of the plan elaboration*. There remains the question as to whether we should use the "calculated" or the "adopted" plan values for x^{pl} and a^{pl}. When the purpose is to test the formalized part of the procedure, then the "calculated" values would seem to be most relevant.

Since the plan figures then satisfy the model actually used, and the observed values satisfy the true model, we have:

(7) $x^{pl} = f(a^{pl}, z^{pl}),$

(8) $x^{obs} = f^*(a^{obs}, z^{obs}).$

The total discrepancy between observed and planned figures for the target variables is given by:

(9) $D = x^{obs} - x^{pl}.$

The symbol D is here a *vector* of discrepancies, just as x^{obs} and x^{pl} are vectors.

We now want to decompose this vector of discrepancies into vectors which may be attributed to different causes of deviations. We may distinguish between discrepancies due to a wrong specification of the model, discrepancies due to deviations between planned and actually executed policies with regard to the instruments, and finally discrepancies due to errors in the forecasts of the non-controlled exogenous variables. We introduce the notations:

D^m = Vector of discrepancies due to wrong specification of the model;

(10) D^a = Vector of discrepancies due to deviations between planned and actually executed instrument values;

D^z = Vector of discrepancies due to deviations between forecasted and realized values of non-controlled exogenous variables.

In Figure 20 the total discrepancy D and the origins of its components D^m, D^a and D^z are suggested between arrows.

The decomposition into the terms defined by (10) should preferably be done in such a way that the components add up to the total discrepancy, i.e.:

(11) $D = D^m + D^a + D^z$.

One way to do this is to use the following definitions:

(12) $D^m = x^{obs} - f(a^{obs}, z^{obs})$,

(13) $D^a = f(a^{obs}, z^{obs}) - f(a^{pl}, z^{obs})$,

(14) $D^z = f(a^{pl}, z^{obs}) - f(a^{pl}, z^{pl})$.

The idea behind (12) is that if we insert the actually observed values of the instrument variables and the non-controlled exogenous variables into the model we used in the planning process, then the discrepancy between the results of this and the observed values of the target variables must be due to a wrong specification of the model. Formula (13) gives the partial effect of the deviation between observed and planned use of instruments, keeping the non-controlled exogenous variables at their observed levels. Formula (14) gives the partial effect of the deviations between observed and forecasted values of the non-controlled exogenous variables, keeping the instrument variables at their planned levels.

It is easy to see that these definitions satisfy the requirement (11). In connection with these formulas one may observe the following points.

It might be interesting to calculate the effects of deviations in a and z by using the true model rather than the model actually used, but the actually used model is the only one which is known; there is therefore hardly any alternative to using this model for the assessment of the effects of deviations in a and z.

There is some arbitrariness in (13) and (14) in that we might have kept the non-controlled variables at their planned rather than at their observed values in (13) and the instrument variables at their observed rather than planned levels in (14). We would then also arrive at a decomposition which satisfies (11). It would also be possible to keep both z in (13) and a in (14) at their planned (or both at the observed) values; for obtaining a complete decomposition it would then be necessary to introduce an "interaction term" which would give an effect of the joint discrepancies in addition to the partial effects.

The problem pointed out here will appear only in a non-linear model. In a linear model the partial effects on x of discrepancies in a and z would be independent of the starting point so that one would not need to specify in (13) and (14) at which levels the "constant variables" are held, and there would be no difficulty in having the requirement (11) fulfilled without introducing any interaction term.

Above we have decomposed the total deviation in x into three components as defined by (10). In many cases it would of course also be interesting to carry out a more detailed decomposition. One might for instance subdivide the instrument vector a into subvectors corresponding to groups of instruments, for instance fiscal policy instruments, monetary policy instruments, etc., and calculate the consequences of discrepancies corresponding to each of these subvectors separately. The same can of course be done for the non-controlled exogenous variables z. The most detailed examination would be to explore the consequences of discrepancies in each component of a and each component of z separately, but this would in practice, in a large planning model, often give too many details to be manageable and useful.

The component in the decomposition (11) which is due to wrong specification of the model, i.e., D''', may be subjected to further studies. As it stands, calculated on the basis of formula (12), it gives the errors in each of the reduced form equations. On this basis it is not easy to trace the causes of the errors back to the original formulation of the model. Each of the equations in the reduced form will in general depend upon the whole structure of the model in the original form, i.e., on the formulation of all the equations in the original form. In practice there will in many models be a certain degree of recursiveness so that each equation in the reduced form may depend upon a subset rather than the full set of the equations in the original formulation, but the problem mentioned still remains, although to a somewhat lesser degree.

Let us assume that the model in the original form is

$$(15) \qquad \phi(x, a, z) = 0 \quad \text{or} \quad
\begin{cases}
\phi_1(x, a, z) = 0, \\[2mm]
\phi_2(x, a, z) = 0, \\[2mm]
\quad \cdot \qquad \cdot \\
\quad \cdot \qquad \cdot \\
\quad \cdot \qquad \cdot \\
\phi_n(x, a, z) = 0,
\end{cases}$$

where ϕ is a vector function so that $\phi(x, a, z) = 0$ represents n equations as indicated to the right in (15) if there are n variables in the vector x. [If not all endogenous variables are "target variables", then it would be correct to introduce an additional vector of variables – endogenous variables which are not target variables – in (15), and we would need as many equations in ϕ as the total number of endogenous variables. For convenience we omit this symbolism from our formulation.]

In the formulation (15) the equations are intended to have as high a degree of autonomy as possible. It should then be possible to discuss the error or possibly wrong specification of each particular equation in (15), and correspondingly try to improve the formulation at this specific point, without this having consequences for the other equations in the full system. This again illustrates the importance of the concept of autonomy of relationships. If the relationships were not autonomous, it would be meaningless to discuss the specification of a particular equation without at the same time raising questions about other equations in the system.

On the other hand, changes in the formulation of one equation in (15) will in general entail changes in all or many of the equations in the reduced form $x = f(a, z)$.

If we now insert observed values into (15), then we obtain a vector ϵ of errors:

$$(16) \qquad \phi(x^{obs}, a^{obs}, z^{obs}) = \epsilon.$$

A component of ϵ would indicate the error in the corresponding equation. For the definitional or balance equations in (16) there should be no errors. For the institutional equations there should also in principle be no errors if all details are spelt out in the equations, but as mentioned before some simplifications are necessary for practical purposes and then some errors may enter also in these equations. But the more vulnerable equations would be technical and behavioural relations (and perhaps demographic, biological and ecological relationships with which there is as yet less of experience in economic modeling).

By the insertion suggested by (16) we may detect the equations in which there are the most serious errors. We could not simply look at the numerical values of the various components of ϵ since there is some degree of arbitrariness in the formulations related to units of measurements of variables involved. Each equation in (15) would of course also remain the same if multiplied by a constant factor, but this would magnify the error component in (16) correspondingly. However, on the basis of the economic meaning of the various relations there will usually be a natural normalization; for instance, a consumption function will have a coefficient equal to one in front of the variable representing total consumption. One might then perhaps consider the component of ϵ in proportion to some average value of the variable which the equation "explains", or in proportion to some range of normal variations for the variable in question.

However, this confrontation only serves to detect which equations are most seriously inflicted with errors. It does not say *what* is wrong with the equation. This can only be found by further studies, either by bringing in more information from other sources, or by studying the same kind of test for a sequence of years by statistical or econometric methods. Interesting possibilities may arise for more systematic efforts to find out *what* is wrong with the various equations if there is for instance a sectoral break-down in the model so that there are, in the model, several equations of the same type. If one suspects that there is a special factor which causes trouble for the equations, one might try to establish comparable indicators for this factor in the various sectors and see if the observed errors are correlated with the indicator. For instance, if the standard form of some equation is based on an assumption about competitive behaviour, then one might try to relate observed discrepancies to some indicators of concentration, types of management, etc. Significant correlations might suggest the necessity of replacing the assumption of competitive behaviour by assumptions which take market power into account. An interesting attempt along these lines has been made by *J.B. Nugent* in the context of a planning model for Greece.

Apart from the last remark, the discussion above refers to the confrontation between model and realities for one year, or for some planning period if x, a, z, include variables referring to all years in a planning period. If we admit that there are stochastic errors in the equations of a model, then discrepancies for one single year, or a few years covered by a planning period, cannot be decisive. Even very unlikely things happen now and then, so a perfectly good equation in a statistical or econometric sense may turn out to be grossly wrong judged by the observations for one single year. A confrontation for one year can then be suggestive, but the final judgement must lie in a confrontation by means of statistical and econometric methods for a longer period.

A difficulty which one will encounter in practice in such confrontations between models and observations, is that the "observations" are themselves often not a true representation of realities. There are always errors of measurement involved in national accounting and related statistics. This is witnessed by the series of revisions to which national accounting figures are usually subjected during the first couple of years from the publication of the first provisional figures. These revisions are often of a considerable magnitude measured as proportions of the changes from one year to another, and one does of course not know that the figures are really true even when the revisions have ceased and the figures are presented as "final".

In the literature on planning models there is unfortunately far too little of systematic studies of the type suggested in this section. In the planning process it is always a more pressing task to work out the model and the plans for the future than to scrutinize carefully and in detail the experiences and errors from the past. However, there is much of interest in this connection to be found in a special chapter in *P.J. Bjerve's* book on *Planning in Norway* devoted to the "inter-

pretation of deviations between national budgets and accounts,"
although the model confronted with reality in this chapter is the
"implicit national budgeting model" rather than a model actually used
(see Section 4.2). In the *Central Planning Bureau* in the Netherlands
more has probably been done than anywhere else to compare
forecasts based on models with observed facts and to decompose
the errors according to origin. Some references are given in the list
below. Furthermore, very much of methodological interest in connection with the problems raised in this section is found in works by
H. Theil also referred to below. In recent years systematic studies of
the forecasting abilities of large American econometric models with
some attempts to decompose errors according to their sources have
also appeared.

Having made these references I consider it important to draw
attention to the limited value of conclusions which, in a planning
context, can be drawn from studies that are based entirely on a
forecasting viewpoint as is the case in most of the literature. It is
customary for instance to introduce a sort of measure of the degree
of difficulty of forecasting a variable, and then measure the forecasting errors in proposition to this degree of difficulty. As such an
indicator of difficulty is often used the average of the squared annual
changes over a period, perhaps corrected for a trend. This may be
very misleading for judging about *planning* performance. Consider
two countries, A and B. In country A there is a very inefficient
planning of the economy and the time series of the main economic
variables are characterized by violent and irregular cycles. Accordingly we have a high degree of difficulty of forecasting. Even
forecasts which are rather bad in absolute terms may appear quite
good when forecasting errors are measured in proportion to the
indicator of the degree of difficulty of forecasting. In country B there
is a much more efficient planning and the economy moves smoothly
along a desirable path. The various variables appear to be easy to
forecast. Even very small errors in absolute terms may then lead to
bad marks for the forecasters of the country. The model and methods
of country B may appear to be worse than those of country A. This is
a misleading conclusion in a planning context. The same is true also
for the popular method of comparing forecasts from some government agency with so-called "naïve forecasts", which would usually
consist in simple trend extrapolations or forecasting the same changes
for the coming year as observed in the current year. If planning and

steering of the economy are very efficient in keeping the economy on a smooth growth path, then it would appear as if naïve methods of forecasting were very efficient, and perhaps more so than model calculations. This would however be a false impression for judging about methodology in a planning context since it may be precisely because the sophisticated methods work well in guiding the decisions that the "naïve methods" are able to trace the development so well.

On this background I think several analyses and comparisons of forecasting ability, as between different countries, should be considered with great caution. The forecasting viewpoint is too narrow when there is in fact some planning and conscious economic policy taking place. The planning models can only be judged and compared in a broader context, according to the contributions they make to good planning and policy. In such a context the ability of a model to span a large set of alternatives as a basis for choice is of great importance. No "naïve method" can compete with mathematical models in this respect, and no comparison between planned and realized figures as if we were only concerned with forecasting can provide a basis for judging about the performance of a model in this crucial function.

From a certain point of view the analysis of the forecasting ability of mathematical or econometric models leads to conclusions which are too pessimistic as indicators of their usefulness for planning and policy purposes. It may in fact be said that the large econometric models have not yet proven their superiority in forecasting for instance for the US economy. *P.A. Samuelson* recently summarized available evidence in the following way: "The act of macromodelling has, I think, made steady progress. But I suspect it is yet the case that the best judgemental forecasts are still about as good or as bad as the best computer forecasts." A severe test for the models in the USA was the 1974 crisis. The models did not fare well. In the words of *O. Eckstein*: "In the 1974 crisis, the forecasts – and business, partly because it believed in them – made the most colossal forecasting errors since 1945, when forecasts had looked for a relapse to depression, instead of which a boom occurred. The 1974 forecasts said that the economy would probably begin to recover in early 1975, though we did warn of the risk of the 'deepest and most prolonged recession of the postwar period' and showed such an alternative simulation. The economy, in fact, entered the worst crisis since World War II." Now the interesting thing in our context is *why* the model forecasts failed. Again to quote O. Eckstein: "The models failed because they did not properly allow for the full impact of the food and energy situations and the end of price controls. Nor could we believe that the Federal Reserve would press the economy steadily downward while it was sinking on its own." This is not the complete explanation of the failure of the model forecasts, but the noteworthy thing is that a considerable part of the failure is ascribed to policy deviating from the expectations of the forecasters. This suggests that the models might do a better job in the service of economic planning and policy formation in which forecasting of important policy decisions from an outsider position is not a part of the job. The same conclusion is suggested by experiences from earlier periods in which the models seem to have performed better in simulating the consequences of changes in economic policy than in the elaboration of unconditional forecasts.

It might be added that O. Eckstein, writing in 1976, makes the following forecast about the use of the large econometric models in the USA: "The next administration of whatever party, will very likely reorganize the principal agencies responsible for economic policy in ways that permit the quantitative analyses to play a larger role and to adopt both a sophisticated cyclical and longer-range perspective for decisions."

If the prophesy just quoted should come true, then one would face the problem of whether one should use some of the already existing and more or less competing models or start constructing entirely new models. This problem is most acute in the USA where there is a proliferation of large-scale macroeconomic models, but the problem of which model or models to rely on comes up also in some other countries. In the literature there are now some attempts at designing criteria and methods for the choice between competing models. A broad discussion referring to many aspects is given by *O.P. Hall*. Most of the more specific literature is however concerned with models for forecasting rather than planning purposes. (See e.g., *P.J. Dhrymes* et al.) There is also the possibility of an eclectic approach by trying to combine the use of different models. *J.P. Cooper* and *C.R. Nelson* have performed an experiment in which they combined forecasts from different models into linear composites by choosing weights so as to optimize the accuracy of the forecasts. The result was that no model was the absolutely superior one; each one had something to contribute towards making the composite forecasts more accurate. Although Cooper and Nelson are mainly concerned with forecasting, they also go some steps towards a planning and policy use of the models by raising the question of how to determine instrument values for achieving certain targets when alternative models are at hand. Their proposal is that "the policy instrument be set so as to equate the linear composite prediction with the target, thereby minimizing expected squared error loss."

The composite obtained in this way could of course be interpreted as stemming from one new model which combines traits from previously existing alternative models. The approach does have some attractiveness up to a certain point. Pushed too far it will however yield a model which has lost too much of transparency and internal logical connectedness, and the total structure will make it difficult to identify autonomous relationships which, as explained in previous sections, are desirable in the context of planning. The eclectic approach mentioned above should therefore be considered as a strategy for a temporary and transitory stage when there are alternative models at hand, rather than as a substitute for an effort to construct models which utilize all available insight, information and experience from previous models in one unified framework.

References for Section 4.8

R. Agarwala, "Tests and uses of macro-econometric models: A critical survey", *Economics of Planning* 1969.

C.A. van den Beld, "Short-term planning experiences in the Netherlands", in *Quantitative planning of economic policy* – See reference under Section 4.1.

P.J. Bjerve, *Planning in Norway 1947–56* – See reference under Section 1.1.

Central Planning Bureau Monograph No. 10, *Forecasts and realization* (The Hague, 1965).

J.P. Cooper and C.R. Nelson, "The ex ante prediction performance of the St. Louis and FRB–MIT–PENN econometric models and some results of composite predictors", *Journal of Money, Credit and Banking* (1975).

P.J. Dhrymes et al., "Criteria for evaluation of econometric models", in *The Brookings model: Perspective and recent developments*, edited by G. Fromm and L.R. Klein (North-Holland, Amsterdam, 1975).

O. Eckstein, "Econometric models and the formation of business expectations", *Challenge Magazine* (March/April 1976).

G. Fromm and L.R. Klein, "The NBER/NSF model comparison seminar: An analysis of results", *Annals of Economic and Social Measurement* (1976).

Y. Haitowsky et al., *Forecasting with quarterly macroeconomic models* (National Bureau of Economic Research, Columbia University Press, New York, 1974).

O.P. Hall, "A policy model appraisal paradigm" – See reference under Section 4.2.

J.B. Nugent, "Linear programming models for national planning: Demonstration of a testing procedure", *Econometrica* (1970).

R.G. Ridker, "An evaluation of the forecasting ability of the Norwegian national budgetting system", *Review of Economics and Statistics* (1963).

P.A. Samuelson, "The art and science of macromodels over 50 years", in *The Brookings model: Perspective and recent developments*, edited by G. Fromm and L.R. Klein (North-Holland, Amsterdam, 1975).

C.A. Sims, "Evaluating short-term macro-economic forecasts: The Dutch performance", *The Review of Economics and Statistics* (1967). Contains also comparisons with Norway.

R. Stone, *A programme for growth, 5. The model in its environment* – See reference under Section 1.2.

H. Theil, "Who forecasts best?", *International Economic Papers*, No. 5 (MacMillan, London, 1955). Translation from Dutch.

H. Theil, *Economic forecasts and policy* (North-Holland, Amsterdam, 1965).

H. Theil, "Applied economic forecasting" – See reference under Section 2.7.

P. de Wolff, "Macro-economic forecasting", in *Forecasting on a scientific basis* (Instituto Gulbenkian de Sciencia, Centro de Economia e Financas, Lisboa, 1967).

AUTHOR INDEX

SUBJECT INDEX

DATE DUE FOR RETURN

21. APR 86.